Preface Books

A series of scholarly and critical studies of major writers intended for those needing modern and authoritative guidance through the characteristic difficulties of their work to reach an intelligent understanding and enjoyment of it.

General Editor: JOHN PURKIS

A Preface to Wordsworth (*Revised edn*)	JOHN PURKIS
A Preface to Donne (*Revised edn*)	JAMES WINNY
A Preface to Jane Austen (*Revised edn*)	CHRISTOPHER GILLIE
A Preface to Lawrence	GAMINI SALGADO
A Preface to Forster	CHRISTOPHER GILLIE
A Preface to Dickens	ALLAN GRANT
A Preface to Shelley	PATRICIA HODGART
A Preface to Keats	CEDRIC WATTS
A Preface to Orwell	DAVID WYKES
A Preface to Milton (*Revised edn*)	LOIS POTTER
A Preface to the Brontës	FELICIA GORDON
A Preface to T S Eliot	RON TAMPLIN
A Preface to Shakespeare's Tragedies	MICHAEL MANGAN
A Preface to Hopkins (*Second edn*)	GRAHAM STOREY
A Preface to James Joyce (*Second edn*)	SYDNEY BOLT
A Preface to Hardy (*Second edn*)	MERRYN WILLIAMS
A Preface to Conrad (*Second edn*)	CEDRIC WATTS
A Preface to Samuel Johnson	THOMAS WOODMAN
A Preface to Pope (*Second edn*)	I. R. F. GORDON
A Preface to Yeats (*Second edn*)	EDWARD MALINS with JOHN PURKIS
A Preface to Shakespeare's Comedies: 1594–1603	MICHAEL MANGAN

The founding editor of the Preface Books series, Maurice Hussey, died suddenly in June 1991. The publishers and author would like to pay tribute to his wisdom, inspiration and friendship as editor of the series.

A Preface to Shakespeare's Comedies: 1594–1603

Michael Mangan

Longman, London and New York

Longman Group Limited
Longman House, Burnt Mill,
Harlow, Essex CM20 2JE, England
and associated companies throughout the world.

Published in the United States of America
by Longman Publishing, New York.

First published 1996
ISBN 0 582 09499.2 CSD
ISBN 0 582 09590.5 PPR

British Library Cataloguing-in-Publication Data

A catalogue record of this book is
available from the British Library

Library of Congress Cataloging-in-Publication Data

Also available

Set in Linotron 300 10/11 Baskerville by 20

Produced by Longman Singapore Publishers (Pte) Ltd.
Printed in Singapore

Contents

For Zara

Prologue: Shakespeare's England – an overview

This volume is a sequel to another in the same series, *A Preface to Shakespeare's Tragedies* (London: Longman, 1991). As such it suffers from a common dilemma of sequels: how much to repeat from the previous book?

I have tried to repeat as little as possible, but inevitably there is some overlap – largely concerning factual information. The reference section at the end of the book has been revised, brought up-to-date, and re-focused so as to concentrate on matters more directly concerned with the comedies; nonetheless some of the bibliographical information, and the information about theatres and contemporaries, appeared first in the earlier volume, as did one or two of the details about theatre audiences in Chapter 3. Apart from this, I have tended to avoid any direct repetition of material which I have already covered in the *Tragedies* book. This means, inevitably, that some potentially relevant material has been excluded from this volume. Chapters which dealt broadly with religious and philosophical developments, Elizabethan and Jacobean society, the development of the language, the printing of the plays, and playhouse practice have as much to do with comedy as they do with tragedy, and part of the brief of the *Preface* series has been to look at texts within their historical contexts. What now follows in the rest of this prologue, therefore, is a summary of many of the main ideas which are discussed at greater length in the early chapters of the *Tragedies* book. I include it because many of the arguments which were elaborated in that volume are implicit in this. In particular this book, like its predecessor, takes the view that Shakespeare wrote about a society quite different from our own, that we cannot always assume a continuity of meanings between his world and ours, and that apparent similarities often mask a gulf between the lived experience of these worlds. It also assumes that we cannot – and should not – ignore the cultural factors which condition our own responses to these texts. To read, see, stage or perform a Shakespeare play is thus to engage in a confrontation between past and present meanings, between the historical moment in which the text is produced and that in which it is received.

Elizabethan society, Elizabethan English

That first historical moment, the moment of production, came at a time of social and philosophical turmoil. Between the time of the English Reformation in 1534 and the death of Elizabeth I in 1603, social and political patterns were changing rapidly, and the ways in which people made sense of their existence were changing accordingly. In the complex of religious and political developments which followed the Reformation, questions of religious dogma became intertwined with questions of national sovereignty and independence from European domination which have an uncanny air of familiarity about them today. England was rethinking its own national identity, having broken away from Rome, one of the traditional sources of authority. As a result, questions of the relationship between the individual subject and state authority were of prime importance in the sphere of political and social theory.

Correspondingly, in the field of scientific inquiry, a new way of thinking was developing. It was a way which owed much to the predominantly sceptical strain of Protestant thought, and it encouraged the scientist to start from his or her own observation of empirical data rather than from the axioms of traditional authority. It is what we now think of as 'the scientific method': truth is discovered by starting from observable facts, and progressing from them towards more general principles which try to account for these facts. It is a habit of thought which is now deeply ingrained in European thinking, so deeply that we may think of it as 'natural'. And yet, as late as 1620, the philosopher Francis Bacon was complaining that such an 'inductive' way of thinking had hardly even been tried, and that philosophers, scientists and others still clung to the converse habit: of starting with general assumptions about the universe, and then trying to trim all available facts to fit those assumptions. Bacon believed that the shift from that old way of thinking to the new would prove revolutionary – and he was right. The new philosophy would throw many things in doubt during the course of the late sixteenth and early seventeenth centuries: the fields of theology and politics would be affected just as much as that of scientific enquiry.

Many of those changes would have seemed unimaginable when Queen Elizabeth I came to the throne in 1558. The task which faced her then, and which continued to face her for most of the second half of the sixteenth century, was that of ensuring the survival of an infant state which seemed ready to collapse at any moment into political and economic chaos. By the end of her reign she had, in many ways, succeeded in this task and had presided over England's development into a strong nation state, one of the Old World's foremost mercantile and military powers. Domestically there were still many social and political problems: inflation, homelessness, poverty and constitutional crises continued to ensure that the ship of state ploughed through choppy waters. Nonetheless, Elizabeth – partly by ruthless exploitation of her own image as a figurehead – had effectively done the job she set out to do. Although the 1590s saw a growing sense of staleness and desire for change, Elizabeth's reign had substantially changed England's sense of its own national identity, and in doing so had also changed the political map of Europe.

The changes which occurred on the national and international level had their effects on a more local scale. Tudor theories of society had always depended on a strong sense of rank, order and degree: most of the images which preachers, social and political pamphleteers, and lawmakers put forward to describe the workings of society were hierarchical, and much energy went into suggesting that this hierarchical picture of society – what some commentators have called the 'great chain of being' – was the natural order of things, divinely ordained, and part of the structure of Nature itself. Yet this hierarchical model was under stress. In the early years of the seventeenth century the new King James I began to push the model to its limits, speaking often and eloquently about the divine sanction of his monarchy. Yet the vehemence with which he had to argue with his ministers and Parliament to get them to accept this idea shows how far the notion of the 'divine right of kings' was from being universally or uncritically accepted. Similarly, the theoretical image of an unchanged and unchanging order based on essentially feudal notions of degree had to contend with a new geographical and social mobility which went hand in hand with an emerging capitalist economy. Shakespeare's own attitudes towards these changes are far from clear – or even consistent. Sometimes he seems in sympathy with an old, pre-capitalist sense of how society should be organized; at others he aligns himself with a new order which is sharply anti-feudal. He himself, certainly, was a beneficiary of the new trends in society. The London stage was an epitome of Elizabethan commercialism: it was an aggressive and competitive venture, and through this venture Shakespeare became socially upwardly mobile, rising in both wealth and social status.

The period's change went deep – as deep as the language itself. For centuries it had been assumed that Latin was the only possible language for the communication of serious matters. While an established tradition of popular literature was growing up in English during the sixteenth century, it was not easy to dislodge the ancient languages, and especially Latin, from their positions as the languages of power. Access to the discourses of philosophy, theology, medicine and the law was limited to those who were sufficiently privileged to have been able to afford a classical education. Not surprisingly, there was a strong body of opinion amongst philosophers, lawyers and medical practitioners which insisted that English was not a proper language for these disciplines. Apart from the poverty and the immaturity of English, it was urged that Latin – which was still regarded as a living language – was a common European tongue which enabled scholars of different nations to converse with each other, that the study of classical languages would decay if English became too important, and (finally) that it was necessary to prevent the uncultivated from dabbling in matters of philosophy, law and medicine. The academic and professional classes of Elizabeth's reign understood very well the extent to which their knowledge of Latin and Greek confirmed them in their own positions of influence.

But now, as a counter-current to this, there was a new interest in the English language, an interest which sprang in part from England's changing rôle in international affairs. As England grew in importance as a mercantile power, so new linguistic opportunities and needs arose also; and as the nation came to view itself as a major player in European politics, and became increasingly concerned to establish its own autonomous identity, so the status of the English language as a respectable medium of intellectual thought gradually became accepted. This issue took on a particular urgency in the light of the intellectual changes which had followed the English Reformation earlier in the century. Since the Protestant tradition emphasized a personal relationship with God, unmediated by the hierarchical structures of priesthood, the new generation of English Protestants which emerged in the mid-sixteenth century found themselves with a growing need of literacy. Their new faith taught that salvation is to be found by reading and understanding the Bible. The existing Latin Bibles of the Catholic Church would no longer do: in order to liberate the text of God's word from the control of established authority, the first, and vital stage, was that the Bible itself be translated into the vernacular, into English. The second was that ordinary men and women should be able to read it. Hence the sudden rise in the literacy rate in mid- and late-sixteenth-century England: the village schools and grammar schools which sprang up around the country were one of the legacies of the Reformation. An intensified interest in the word went hand in hand with new forms of Christian belief.

It was a result, too, of more practical developments. If any single invention marked the end of the medieval period in Europe and the beginning of the Renaissance, it was that of the printing press. William Caxton's introduction of this into England in 1476 (less than a century before Shakespeare's birth) marked the advent of an access to information which was newly secularized. It meant that the monopoly on knowledge was no longer held by a small number of learned clerks. Books no longer belonged solely in the cloister and abbey: they could now be found too in the houses of lay people. The manuscript book was superseded by the printed volume, which brought with it a democratic access to ideas and information which was formerly inconceivable.

Thus, during the sixteenth century, English culture became increasingly literary rather than oral in nature. By the time Shakespeare was born the change was well under way, although it was by no means fully completed. The printed word was widely available by 1600, but it was to take many more generations before the habits and assumptions of an oral culture died away completely. Moreover, not everyone was able to benefit from the new upsurge of interest in education which the sixteenth century saw; and while the literacy rate underwent a dramatic increase during the period before 1600, and the provision of educational facilities blossomed, these developments were uneven and access to them was limited. Not everyone could afford tuition fees, nor (in what was still a predominantly agricultural society) the loss of their children's labour, especially in the fields at crucial times of the year. On the whole, the main beneficiaries of the educational expansion were males from the middling and upper ranks of the social scale, and especially those who were entering the growing ranks of the merchant classes. London, the nation's capital, the richest city in the country and the centre for trade, industry and arts, had a substantially higher literacy rate than the rest of the kingdom; even so, recent scholarship estimates that not many more than a third of the adult males in Shakespeare's London could read or write. Nevertheless, this represents a substantial increase in the literacy rate over previous years, and the age of the printed book had well and truly begun.

The increase in literacy, and the rise of a reading public, brought with it changes to the language itself. As printed communication became more widespread, so the need developed for more widespread agreements about how the language should be used. Thus grammatical rules began to be formalized, prescribing the ways in which different elements of a sentence are related to each other. It is possible to discern in the sixteenth century the beginnings of the standardization of modern English grammar.

Once again, changes happened slowly and unevenly. The grammar of Shakespeare's day was still an unsettled thing, with many alternative forms and a great variety of usages. And Shakespeare and his contemporaries benefited from the fact of this unsettledness. If one of Shakespeare's great strengths as a poetic writer is the flexibility with which he moulds his language to his own use, it is precisely because the language which he and the writers of his generation inherited was itself extremely flexible, and without some of the logical rigidity which was imposed by later grammatical developments. The structures of Elizabethan English are based on a grammar which is in many ways different from our own: it has its own rules and conventions, but – equally importantly – it is also less insistent on the following of such rules.

While the grammar of the language tended towards greater uniformity during this period, the vocabulary tended towards greater diversity. There was a growing demand for a richer and more precise vocabulary to cope with the rapid changes taking place in crafts and sciences, in the world of technical skills and intellectual pursuits, and also in everyday life. Trading with other nations (and coming into contact with other parts of England itself), exchanging not only goods but also ideas – all this required increasingly sophisticated communications systems. London, in particular, experienced an influx of people from all over the country, and from all over the known world. Through these contacts the common speech was enriched by words and phrases borrowed from the French, Italian and Spanish, and also by English local dialect vocabulary. Thus, during the late sixteenth and early seventeenth centuries the English language developed rapidly. It absorbed and naturalized influences from contemporary Europe; it also raided the classics and coined new English words based on Latin roots. It has been estimated that between 1500 and 1650, over ten thousand new words entered the language, and while many of these eventually fell by the wayside, many others remain in our vocabulary today. Thus the English language developed a sufficiently complex vocabulary to cope with the new conditions of a rapidly changing world; this was one of the culture's major achievements of the late sixteenth century. Not that this expansion of the vocabulary met with universal approval: on the contrary, it caused concern to many traditionalists and purists, who roundly condemned the introduction of these 'inkhorn terms' into the language. In *The Art of Rhetoric*, for example, Thomas Wilson asserted that 'Among all other lessons this should first be learned, that we never affect any strange inkhorn terms, but to speak as is commonly received: neither seeking to be over-fine, nor yet living over-careless, using our speech as most men do'. But while writers such as Wilson found it easy to mock those who used 'inkhorn' terminology, it should be remembered that the influx of new words into the language during this period was a response to a serious problem: the widely held doubt as to whether the vernacular language would really prove to be resourceful, sophisticated and flexible enough to act as a serious instrument of thought.

Shakespeare himself has been credited with introducing a good many words into common currency; on the other hand, he was not above the occasional conservative jibe at the linguistic excesses of the age. In *Love's Labour's Lost*, the schoolmaster Holofernes speaks a language stuffed full of inkhorn terms, as well as Latin tags, Italian references and incomprehensible constructions: on intercepting a letter, for example, he announces 'I will overglance the superscript . . . I will look again on the intellect of the letter for the nomination of the party writing to the person written unto' (*Love's Labour's Lost*, IV, ii, 130, 132–4). And Feste in *Twelfth Night* picks up on Sebastian's self-conscious use of the phrase 'vent thy folly':

> Vent my folly! He has heard that word of some great man and now applies it to a fool. Vent my folly – I am afraid this great lubber the world will prove a cockney. I prithee now, ungird thy strangeness and tell me what I shall 'vent' to my lady? Shall I 'vent' to her that thou art coming?
>
> (*Twelfth Night*, IV, i, ll. 11–16)

The English language's battle for recognition continued throughout Shakespeare's lifetime, and during this period a strong body of opinion continued to maintain that it was unworthy of serious consideration. But national self-assertiveness, theological and political considerations, and a popular demand for access to knowledge, all added impetus to the growth in importance of the English language. So did the commercial spirit. Books in English sold better than books in Latin. Booksellers and printers were not likely to object to the popular market which now existed for books of all kinds in English. For by the end of the sixteenth century, language had become a prime item in the commodities market.

Shakespeare, then, was lucky: he lived through a period in his country's history when the language was fertile in vocabulary and flexible in its structures, and (equally importantly) when the culture was intensely interested in questions about language. Language for Shakespeare and his contemporaries was an issue, even a problem, and his plays dramatize this. Frequently the plots themselves hang upon issues of language: promises made or broken, oracles delivered, messages misunderstood. The most obvious example of this is, perhaps, *The Merchant of Venice*, whose happy ending depends upon a detail of linguistic interpretation: Shylock shall have his pound of flesh – but not a drop of blood. Characters in Shakespeare's plays frequently talk about words and language: about the ways in which people use words, and about the limits of language. They question the extent to which words are adequate to 'capture reality', and they remark on the ways in which meaning continually slips away: 'words', as Feste says, 'are very rascals . . . words are grown so false I am loath to prove reason with them' (*Twelfth Night*, III, i, 20, 23–4). In both the comedies and the tragedies there are moments when a character is faced with the breakdown of language and a kind of semantic chaos looms before them. In the following incident from *A Midsummer Night's Dream*, Bottom the Weaver has just been released from a spell which gave him an ass's head and forced the Queen of the Fairies to fall in love with him. Not unnaturally, he believes the whole thing to have been a dream.

> I have had a most rare vision. I have had a dream, past the wit of man to say what dream it was. Man is but an ass if he go about to expound this dream. Methought I was – there is no man can tell what. Methought I was, and methought I had, but man is but a patch'd fool, if he will offer to say what methought I had. The eye of man hath not heard, the ear of man hath not seen, man's hand is not able to taste, his tongue to conceive, nor his heart to report, what my dream was. I will get Peter Quince to write a ballad of this dream. It shall be called 'Bottom's Dream', because it hath no bottom; and I will sing it in the latter end of the play, before the Duke.
>
> (*A Midsummer Night's Dream*, IV, i, ll. 202–20)

Bottom's language repeatedly breaks down as he tries to explain his experience. It is, he concludes, 'past the wit of man to say what the dream was'. Significantly, his response to this is to 'get Peter Quince to write a ballad of this dream'. He looks to art for a form which will begin to deal with the difficulty of saying exactly what he means. For Shakespeare too, art, story-telling, playwriting represented a possible way of coming to terms with, and perhaps overcoming, some of the limitations of language.

Plays and playhouses

The sale of playtexts was one of the results of the expanding commercial market for books, and Shakespeare's plays were sold both as comparatively cheap individual quarto editions and also, later, in the collected Folio edition. The printed playtext exists, though, at the point of a conflict of interest between the theatre company (which is the legal owner of a performed play, having bought it from the author) and a printer and bookseller. The latter, of course, will want to print and sell copies of any play which looks as though it might turn a decent profit. The theatre company, on the whole, may want to keep its monopoly on the play in order to make money from future performances: notions of copyright were in their infancy, and a printed play became available to anyone. As a result, some plays were printed officially, with the company and perhaps the writer being paid some kind of emolument by the printer and/or bookseller; many others, however, were pirated.

The importance of the publication of Shakespeare's plays in the First Folio of 1623 can hardly be overstated: John Heminges and Henry Condell attempted, carefully and patiently, to establish an authoritative text of Shakespeare's complete works as a tribute to their late friend and colleague. It was this volume which assured Shakespeare his unique place in literary history. It contained eighteen of Shakespeare's plays which had been staged, but which had never before appeared in print; along with eighteen more which had already been printed in quartos of varying reliability. Of the accepted dramatic canon, only *Pericles* was omitted.

Even so, the Folio raises as many textual questions as it solves. There are many discrepancies between these early editions of Shakespeare's plays in Folio and Quartos; and since the one thing we know for sure is that Shakespeare did not himself oversee the preparation of the Folio text, this leaves plenty of room for uncertainty. Subsequent generations of editors have traditionally laboured to separate the sheep of the 'true' Shakespearean text from the goats of pirated texts, foul papers and printers' errors. However, that seemingly straightforward aim, of discovering what Shakespeare really intended to say, is actually quite complicated. For playscripts differ in kind from the texts of novels and poems in that they are written to be performed. Thus they are both part of a collaborative project, and are also continually open to revision. Even if we had access to the actual manuscript papers of Shakespeare's plays, the problem of what the author 'really' wrote would remain.

The following sequence of events, for example, is by no means improbable. An Elizabethan playwright (let us say Shakespeare) writes a comic scene. He directs a rehearsal of it, in the course of which – perhaps because of suggestions from the actors or perhaps because he now sees something he missed while writing it – some of the lines are rewritten. When he sees the scene in performance he realizes that it is a bit too long; the audience is getting restive towards the end. So for the next performance he cuts out a couple of minutes of unnecessary action. At the same time, an improvised gag which one of the actors put in on the spur of the moment worked well: he instructs them to keep that in. He also adds a new joke of his own, based on some recent events in the news. When they perform the play in front of the Queen at Whitehall later in the month, this latest addition is deemed a little too topical: they leave it out. A few months later the play is taken on tour to the provinces: again the scene is revised, this time because the touring company has fewer actors than the London-based company, and cannot carry with it some of the larger stage properties. Then, when the company gets back to London and revives the play for the next season, one of the parts in the scene is now being played by an actor who is new to the company and who has particular skills: singing, perhaps, or physical comedy. The scene is changed once again to make use of his talents.

Where, in all this, is the 'original' text? We have a choice. On the one hand we may decide that a particular stage in the process constitutes the true original: the very first draft which was initially presented to the actors, perhaps, or else the very final draft after all the changes had been made. On the other hand we may decide that since a playscript written for performances may be subject to various rewritings at different times in its life, the search for the single original text may be illusory, and that there may be many 'original' versions of a play. It is this latter approach which I prefer.

Before the publication of the Shakespeare Folio, playscripts were rarely regarded as 'literature'. Plays belonged more to the low-life world of popular entertainment than they did to the rarefied world of high art; and like the actors who played in them, they were rarely seen as intellectually or socially respectable. In fact, the position in society of an Elizabethan actor was a paradoxical one. In 1572, an Act of Parliament 'For the Punishment of Vagabonds' had declared that all unaffiliated actors should be classed with rogues, vagabonds and other 'masterless men'. This meant that unless an actor was attached to a theatre company which enjoyed the patronage of one 'Baron of this realm or . . . honorable personage of greater degree' he was deemed to be a potential criminal. Until 1598 there was a clause which also allowed Justices of the Peace to license actors, but this was eventually rescinded. The Act for the Punishment of Vagabonds effectually ensured that the number of acting companies in the kingdom would be very limited, and that they would depend upon the tolerance of nobility and royalty. Thus actors, writers and company managers needed to tread carefully, and ensure that they kept on the right side of their patrons. Apart from the personal interest of their own individual patron, they had also to ensure that their plays did not offend the Master of the Revels, whose office was responsible for stage censorship during the period. Playwrights and actors alike could end up in prison for their involvement in plays which overstepped the invisible mark of acceptability as regards political criticism.

The emerging professional theatre was based exclusively in London. As a result, it was also frequently under attack from London's Puritan-influenced Guildhall, the seat of local government. To escape this hostility, nearly all the London theatres of the time were situated just outside the city walls, placing them beyond the legal jurisdiction of the Guildhall. Even so, caught between the demands of often-conflicting power-blocs within the city and at court, the theatre of Shakespeare's day often ended up as a pawn in political games of power. The legislation of 1598, for example, which deprived players of the protection of licensing magistrates was passed by Elizabeth's Parliament as a concession to the Guildhall's continual pressure for the total abolition of theatre.

Yet the theatre survived and caught the imagination of the paying public. From contemporary sources it is possible to reconstruct some of the material details of Elizabethan performances. We know, for example, that performances usually started at about two o'clock in the afternoon; they took place during the hours of daylight, since the outdoor theatres had no artificial lighting. There were several licensed companies playing in London at any one time, and competition between them was always fierce. The theatrical season began in September, playing through to the beginning of Lent, then resuming after Easter and continuing until early summer. London theatres then closed down for the summer months, since the hotter weather led to an increased risk of plague in the capital. Theatre companies might take on a provincial tour during the summer in order to supplement their income, playing in halls and inns and marketplaces like their medieval predecessors.

There has been much debate about the physical details of the sixteenth-century London theatres, and various attempts have been made to reconstruct the auditorium of the typical Elizabethan playhouse. These playhouses have traditionally been divided into two kinds: the 'public' (or 'amphitheatre', or 'outdoor') theatres such as the Rose, the Globe and the Swan, which were the main adult professional venues until 1609; and the 'private' (or 'hall', or 'indoor') theatres such as the Blackfriars Theatre, which before 1609 were used almost exclusively by companies of child actors. Archaeological discoveries of the remains of the Rose playhouse, where some of Shakespeare's earlier plays were probably first staged, have added new details to our picture of the Elizabethan outdoor theatres. Excavations uncovered the foundations of a theatre with a shallow thrust stage, which was thirty-seven feet wide at its widest point at the back, and which narrowed to twenty-five feet at the front. The yard in which the lowest-paying members of the audience stood, was raked to give a better view to those at the back. What is most striking about the Rose, however, is its intimacy. Its overall diameter was only approximately seventy feet, and the front of the stage was only thirty-six feet from the gallery at the back of the auditorium, where more privileged patrons could pay for a seat and some cover from bad weather. And yet this small theatre was, according to recent estimates, able to hold about two thousand spectators! I shall be looking in more detail at the experience of Elizabethan play-going from an audience's perspective in Chapter 3; but one preliminary observation which can be made is that the play-goers of Shakespeare's London seem to have been perfectly prepared to be packed tightly into a small space in order to see a good play.

It is difficult to estimate how typical the Rose Theatre's details were of Elizabethan theatres in general. Other outdoor playhouses may have been differently configured. The Globe, for example, where Shakespeare's company was based for the second half of his career, was probably larger than the Rose. In fact, about Shakespeare's Globe itself there is frustratingly little documentary evidence. We know that it stood on Maiden Lane (now Park Street) in the Bankside area on the south bank of the Thames. Surviving engravings of London panoramas show the Globe to be a round or polygonal building with a thatched roof, and we know that the timbers of the Burbages' original Theatre in Holywell Lane were used in its construction. Apart from this we have very little first-hand information, although scholars have built up a detailed conjectural picture of the theatre by drawing on known facts about other Elizabethan playhouses, and by making deductions based on the stage directions from plays which were performed at the Globe. There are various general features which the Globe probably shared with most other outdoor theatres: actors' entrances and exits would have been made by way of doors in the upstage walls; the use of trapdoors and pulleys may have allowed for one or two special effects, but scenery was kept to a minimum. A company's scenic stock would probably have been composed of various pieces of stage furniture, to be carried on and off between scenes, or occasionally lowered from a flying-space above the stage. As for publicity, the audience would have been alerted to what was currently playing at the theatre by means of hand-written playbills posted around the town. The cost of admission was not exorbitant: one penny remained the basic standing-room admission price to most outdoor theatres between 1576 and 1642 (although this fluctuated a great deal in real value during this time).

The indoor theatres were more expensive. These all-seater houses charged a minimum of sixpence, while the very best seats could cost two shillings and sixpence. Although sometimes called 'private' theatres, they were actually no more 'private' than the outdoor ones – apart, that is, from the degree of exclusivity which the higher admission charges conferred upon them. They were owned and managed in exactly the same way as the outdoor theatres, and often by the same people (Burbage, for example, managed both the Globe and Blackfriars). But, inevitably, the indoor theatres attracted a more privileged clientèle. Partly because of this, but also because of the different physical attributes of these spaces, a different kind of drama began to emerge in the early seventeenth century. This was a drama which was more appropriate to the smaller enclosed space, one in which the stage was illuminated by artificial lighting, in which stage effects became more ambitious, and in which the use of music before, during and after the play became increasingly elaborate. Shakespeare's company, the King's Men, opened the first of the adult indoor theatres in 1609 when they moved into the Blackfriars premises. They ran this indoor theatre in tandem with their outdoor one until 1613, when the Globe was destroyed by fire during a performance of Shakespeare and Fletcher's *Henry VIII*.

Many of the actors who played at the Globe and at Blackfriars had a financial stake in the company for which they performed. The Lord Chamberlain's Men had been formed in 1594, and the company flourished under that name until 1603, when the newly crowned James I claimed the company as his own and allowed them to call themselves the King's Men. The Lord Chamberlain's/King's company was run by a group of shareholders, who were known as 'the housekeepers', and who held the Globe Theatre in joint-tenancy. These housekeepers were headed by Richard Burbage and his brother Cuthbert, who were the principal shareholders, owing 50 per cent of the company. The remaining 50 per cent was divided between sharers; the exact number varied over the years, but most of them were actors. Among them was William Shakespeare, who had bought into the company in the year it was formed, and who was a large shareholder, owning about an eighth of the company. It was this investment which provided him with a secure income while other equally prolific (and, in their day, equally successful) writers struggled to make a living from their words.

In addition to the sharers, the company regularly employed other actors, hired on a daily or weekly basis. In good times their daily pay might be as high as one to two shillings; in bad times they might not get paid at all. Musicians had to be licensed separately by the Revels Office, and were paid at a higher rate than the hired actors. Theatre companies tended to use smaller casts than we might imagine (primarily for financial reasons) and there was much doubling and trebling of parts. The majority of the stage crew were also hired men and were paid about the same as hired actors. The most important member of the backstage staff, especially when the company was staging a new play, was the 'book-keeper', or 'book-holder'. It was his responsibility to deal with matters relating to the manuscript of the play from which the actors would be working. The book-keeper was in charge of ensuring the text was approved by the Revels Office, of preparing a production script, and of distributing the parts amongst the actors. He also oversaw the running of the performance. One of the book-keeper's responsibilities was to write out a synopsis of the play's episodes, its characters, and which actor was playing which part. This would be displayed prominently somewhere backstage, simply in order to ensure that actors knew where they were in the play! With a different play being performed nearly every day of the week, this is not as ludicrous as it may seem. Moreover, the plays received comparatively little rehearsal time, and players relied a good deal on their ability to improvise moves on stage within a series of traditional guidelines, and on their rapport with each other and with the audience. The demands made on the actors' time, energy and attention were enormous, and they needed all the help they could get. Thus the book-keeper combined many of the functions of a modern-day prompter, stage-manager, director and producer, and was central to the somewhat makeshift yet increasingly professionalized business of putting on a play in the Elizabethan and Jacobean theatre.

The English professional theatre underwent an extraordinarily rapid process of growth and development between its beginnings in 1576 and the time of Shakespeare's death in 1616. In many ways these developments mirrored those of the society to which that theatre belonged. All historical periods could lay claim to being a time of change, in which dominant patterns of thought and social being are simultaneously imbued with echoes of the past, and with emerging forms which have yet to find their final shape; and for each era these tensions between the fading, the dominant and the emergent cultures configure themselves slightly differently. The England of the 1590s, when Shakespeare wrote most of his comedies, contains much that belongs to a vanishing feudal and pre-Reformation society; much, too, that reminds us that this society is little more than a generation away from the English Civil War. These cross-currents swirl through the social life of the period, and through the writings and performances which dramatized that life.

In this volume I have attempted to supplement the rather general and panoramic view of theatre in society which I have just summarized, with something which has a rather tighter focus. My starting-point is an attempt to find an overlap between the social, historical and theatrical contexts of Shakespeare's comedies. Consequently I begin by looking at a single phenomenon which, I would suggest, brings these various contexts together: the phenomenon of laughter. Thus the early chapters of this book ask questions about the function of laughter in Elizabethan and Jacobean society; the network of social practices particularly relevant to various kinds of laughter; the theatricalization of laughter; the professional laughter-makers, fools and clowns; and the expectations and experience of Elizabethan audiences regarding comedy and theatre-going. The first part concludes by discussing some of the main critical issues which have been raised by the comedies. I shall then go on in the second part of the book to look at a series of plays by Shakespeare which – despite many arguments to the contrary – I still believe to have a great deal to do with laughter.

Part One

Contexts of Comedy

1 Laughter and Elizabethan society

Cultural distance and the study of comedy

Twelfth Night. Feste, the clown, licensed fool, enters to his drinking-companions, Sir Toby Belch and Sir Andrew Aguecheek. The latter, delighted to see him, greets him with the following reminiscence.

> *Sir Andrew* . . . In sooth, thou wast in very gracious fooling last night, when thou spok'st of Pigrogromitus, of the Vapians passing the equinoctial of Queubus: 'twas very good, i' faith: I sent thee sixpence for thy leman: had'st it?
> *Clown* I did impeticos thy gratillity: for Malvolio's nose is no whipstock, my lady has a white hand, and the Myrmidons are no bottle-ale houses.
>
> (II, iii, ll. 22–9)

For years, actors and editors alike have been struggling valiantly to find in this kind of Shakespearean comic line some vestige of meaning which might be communicable to audiences and readers. In 1778, already nearly two centuries distant from Shakespeare's wordplays, Samuel Johnson conjectured that some sense might be made of the phrase 'impeticos thy gratillity' were it to read 'impeticoat thy gratillity' – meaning to put a gratuity into the pocket of a petticoat – and he changed the Folio text accordingly. Clutching gratefully at this straw, the Arden editors J. M. Lothian and T. W. Craik suggest the following gloss of Feste's lines:

> This speech begins as a kind of sense, and then sinks, or rises, into 'the best fooling'. The Clown acknowledges Sir Andrew's present ('gratillity' = gratuity; 'impeticos' = pocket in my long coat, the usual wear of fools, cf. Hotson, *Shakespeare's Motley*, frontispiece); then, with a pseudo-logical 'for' (which should have discouraged further explication), he utters a trio of related remarks. 'My lady' is obviously Olivia rather than his 'leman', since it follows upon mention of Malvolio's nose; the Myrmidons are the followers of Achilles, cf. *Troil.*, V. iii. 33. There is no evidence whatever for a London tavern called the Myrmidons (nor, if there had been such a tavern, would it be referred to with a plural verb and noun). The explanations offered by Steevens and Hutson (given by Furness) have been

extended by Wilson, Ribner and Charney; other explanations, relating to contemporary persons (Knollys, Queen Elizabeth, the Yeoman of the Guard), are proposed by Hotson (p. 50). All one can usefully say is that the reference to Malvolio is derogatory, the reference to Olivia is complimentary, and the reference to the Myrmidons is pure nonsense.[1]

These are some of the things we can do, then, with such lines: we can seek to amend them and change them for words which make more sense to us. We can analyse their structure and show that a pseudo-logical connective is followed by a trio of related remarks. We can search the writings of previous generations of readers and scholars. We can attempt an archaeological dig for some forgotten contemporary reference such as a London tavern called 'The Myrmidons' or an allusion to the Yeomen of the Guard. And in the end perhaps we can say something noncomittal about tone: 'derogatory . . . complimentary . . . pure nonsense'.

One thing we cannot do with them (or not easily) is laugh at them. Laughter involves understanding; it implies collusion. Who today can collude in this laughter? Sir Andrew Aguecheek, it seems, finds heartily funny a series of gags which Feste told the previous night concerning Pigrogromitus and the Vapians passing the equinoctial of Queubus. Is this, too, 'pure nonsense' or is there some lost reference here which makes Sir Andrew's amusement pertinent? Or are we being asked to laugh at a knight so easily amused that he will laugh at pure nonsense? Is the gag, in fact, that there is no gag, that Feste's babblings are pure sound, signifiers without signifieds? Or are we missing some joke so obvious – in Elizabethan terms at least – that even the dim-witted Sir Andrew can get it?

There are few things in Shakespeare's plays which make it so clear that he is *not* our contemporary as these verbal witticisms. They stand like signposts written in an alien alphabet, simultaneously promising and denying enlightenment. The very act of attempting to understand them reinforces the truth that laughter is culturally specific. The raising of a laugh in the theatre – or even a decent smile – depends on mobilizing a set of shared points of reference. Shakespeare's own audience, confronted with Pigrogromitus and the Myrmidons would (presumably) know *either* that this is all pure nonsense and that Sir Andrew is being sent up *or* that some comprehensible remark is being made about some current phenomenon. Not all of them would know this, perhaps, for audiences are strange creations, being both wave and particle, individual intelligences and the collective mind. Even so, enough of them would know enough about what is happening in those lines to provide the critical mass which creates the laughter. The quality of the laughter varies according to which interpretation is appropriate.

We are cut off from sharing in this response; our awareness that we do not *know* makes any laughter we are capable of different in kind from that which Shakespeare's text first generated. We may sometimes manage to decode these verbal conundrums, to translate them or interpret them – but that is not the same as being able to 'get' them. To get the joke is to affirm oneself as a member of a community, and we are separated from that interpretative community by four hundred years.

Not that we never laugh: a good comic actor can make the most meaningless of lines funny and a twentieth-century audience can be entertained by seventeenth-century gags whose very impenetrability is a source of amusement. But this is a different joke. We laugh sometimes with relief: with self-congratulation that we have 'understood' the joke, that we are not excluded from the circle of the knowing. Or else the joke is at our own expense, and we laugh self-mockingly at ourselves, at our folly in sitting in our theatre, paying for our tickets, in order to be entertained by lines which neither we nor the actor on the stage can ever fully understand.

In later chapters I will be looking at the connections which exist between theatrical comedy and laughter. The links between the two may seem self-evident at first – yet if, as I suggest above, we lack any immediate access to much of the laughter of the plays, it is hardly surprising that most academic theories about Shakespearean comedy emphasize that laughter is not the point. Is this a typical classroom exchange?

Student Why is this called comedy? (*Defiantly*) I don't think it's very funny.

Teacher Ah, but in the literary sense, comedy is not about laughter. It is not like stand-up comedy or situation comedy. It is about a certain pattern of action, about the movement from chaos to order, from discord to concord; it is about the integration of the individual and society, the resolution of conflict, the restoration of the moral order. It is the *mythos* of spring – the celebration of life.

Student Oh. Right.

Much of what this fictional teacher says is true. Some of it will be repeated and expanded in later chapters. We will see that some Elizabethan literary theorists and playwrights make the same point, and that some more modern critics have taken the idea to an extreme. For example, L. C. Knights – an eminent commentator on Renaissance comedies – asserted that 'once an invariable connection between comedy and laughter is assumed, we are not likely to make any observation that will be useful as criticism'.[2]

Yet this book starts from the premise that laughter *is* relevant to a study of comedy; and while we may recognize the cultural distance which separates our laughter from the laughter of Shakespeare's first audiences, we need not be completely discouraged by it. Certainly there are plenty of Shakespearean jokes that we don't get, but there are also many that we do. Shakespeare's comedies still make theatre audiences laugh: it seems a perverse kind of academicism to declare that this laughter somehow does not matter. Among the contentions of this book will be (1) that Shakespeare's comedies utilize various strategies of laughter for various ends; (2) that this involves different 'kinds' of laughter; (3) that these kinds of theatrical laughter have their analogies in the wider social functions of laughter in Elizabethan England.

It may seem strange to talk about the social functions of laughter. Laughter, after all, is something which we tend to take for granted. It is easy to assume that it is simply a natural attribute of being human – indeed it is often said that laughter is one of the distinguishing marks of being human. It is one of the (comparatively few) things that we do that other mammals do not. If laughter has a social function, it may be thought, it is this: to mark us off from the rest of the animal kingdom. But this is not taking the question far enough. Many of what we take to be 'simply natural human attributes' are actually dependent in various ways upon cultural conditioning. From family structures to gender identity, those things which everyday consensus belief sees as natural are actually socially constructed; they are in part at least determined by a range of social pressures, which shape them even if they do not always cause them.

And so it is with laughter. We laugh 'naturally' in part because we have learned from our culture that it is 'natural' to laugh; we have also learned what it is natural to laugh at. Laughter is not a constant, timeless, unchanging phenomenon but the product of specific human relationships. A detailed history of laughter (which this is not intended to be) would have to start with the fact that different ages have placed different values on laughter: not only do different periods find different things funny, but the very act of laughing – this 'natural' activity – is accorded different values in different historical periods. Polite society in the eighteenth century, for example, tended to disapprove of audible laughter altogether. It showed, they believed, a lack of dignity and of bodily control which was unbecoming in a lady or gentleman.

Whereas the twentieth-century cliché holds that laughter delineates humans from animals, the eighteenth-century commonplace was just the opposite – that laughter debased men and women, making them more and more like animals. 'There is nothing so illiberal and so illbred as audible laughter,' Lord Chesterfield advised his son in 1748, '. . . not to mention the disagreeable noise that it makes and the shocking distortion of the face that it occasions.'[3] In different historical periods, then, laughter may be accorded different kinds of status, and may serve different purposes. In this chapter we shall examine some of the purposes it fulfilled in the culture which also produced the comedies of Shakespeare.

While the status and function of laughter differs from one age and culture to another, a repeated function which it can be found to serve is that of providing a way of coping with issues which individuals and societies find threatening, embarrassing, or disturbing. We are all familiar with the phenomenon of nervous laughter: that laughter which occurs at seemingly inappropriate times, at moments of anxiety or self-consciousness. It may well be that this 'nervous laughter' is not an odd and unusual aberration from 'normal laughter', but an essential dimension of laughter itself. Thus, in very much the same way that an individual may laugh when nervous or embarrassed, so a whole society or social grouping may develop a culture of laughter around those issues which embarrass or threaten it. To put it at its most obvious, this means that racist jokes become popular at times and in places where racial issues are a source of anxiety or embarrassment; sexist jokes are told amongst social groupings for whom sexual identity is a source of anxiety or embarrassment, and so on. We laugh most loudly at those things which most concern or disturb us. At the same time, and in reaction to this, certain codes spring up amongst sub-groups within a society concerning what is or is not a permissible subject for laughter. This is easy enough to see in our own society. We may or may not think it acceptable to laugh at jokes about race, colour, gender, disability, religion etc. In making decisions about this, one way or the other, we also make decisions about our own relationship to and alignment with different cultural groups and belief-systems.

Thus in exploring the social function of laughter we will also find ourselves examining the anxieties and points of tension within a society. The character of a social grouping may be in part defined by the things it laughs at, and if we knew more about the laughter to be found in Elizabethan society we would know significantly more about that society as a whole. Yet the way in which this happens need not be as clear-cut as this makes it seem. On the one hand, not every joke about racial issues is a racist joke, nor every joke about sexuality sexist. Humour need not reinforce existing prejudices: it can also allow us to re-examine them. The line between these two functions is not always easy to discern; often it depends less upon the joke itself than upon the context and the spirit in which it is told and heard. And on the other hand, whatever our consciously-held beliefs about what is or is not a suitable subject for laughter, our internal moral censors may always be bypassed, with the result that we find ourselves laughing at jokes of which another part of our minds disapproves. Jokes, as Freud discovered, do not operate only on a conscious level; and the skill of a good comedian involves the crafting of humour so that it makes contact, too, with the listener's or reader's subconscious.

To examine the laughter of any society is, however, a forbidding task of cultural archaeology: all we can do is sift through the remaining fragments and try to reconstruct something from them. We do not have the luxury of observing at first hand who laughed – or refrained from laughing – at what, and in what context. Yet there are places in which we can look for records of what Elizabethan society did laugh at. Literary texts are one such place, of course. Jest-books were written and published with the express aim of making the reader laugh; satires and pamphlets aimed at manipulating that laughter for didactic, moral and political ends. We find records of laughter, too, in documentations of social activity. Sermons, surveys, tracts, travel books, letters, diaries, civic and parish records, all contain accounts of social situations in which merriment and laughter feature. From these we can build up a picture of the place of laughter in Elizabethan and Jacobean society. For convenience, I shall look at it under three separate (though sometimes interacting) headings: everyday laughter; the laughter of inversion, carnival and misrule; and the laughter of ridicule.

'Replete with mirthful laughter': everyday laughter

We do not have, of course, any direct access at all to the everyday laughter of Elizabethan times. We cannot observe it in its entirety with all its complexities and contradictions. Perhaps worse, because sentimentalized images of an Elizabethan 'Merry England' were once in vogue amongst popular historians, and are now distinctly out of favour, the very notion of the everyday laughter of the men and women of the period may now seem to incur the risks of the same kind of naïveté. Yet people did laugh in sixteenth-century England, and occasionally in the documents of the time we find reference to this. For example, the conduct books of the period set out rules for social behaviour among the aspiring merchant classes. The following advice is from an early Tudor conduct book addressed specifically to women (and which, of course, was almost certainly written by a man!). It stresses that a woman should laugh quietly and decorously:

> Woman's beauty that purchase will praising,
> Would that the woman set her busy cure
> To maintain in herself a low laughing
> To laugh over high beseemeth no creature.[4]

Although the author is particularly concerned with women's laughter, it should be noted that it is not only women who are recommended to keep their laughter discreet: loud laughing 'beseemeth no creature'.

Conduct books and manuals of advice are useful indicators of how society (or some sections of it) thought people should behave. They are less reliable as guides to what actually happened in people's lives. In any case, they focus on behaviours rather than causes of behaviours; they give comparatively little insight into what people in sixteenth-century England found funny. More can be learned about the Tudor and Stuart sense of humour from the printed collections of jokes and tales which comprised the jest-books of the sixteenth and seventeenth centuries. Jest-books had been popular since the Middle Ages, when they first appeared in Latin. The first of the English jest-books, *A Hundred Merry Tales,* appeared in 1526, but the late sixteenth and early seventeenth centuries saw a great increase in their production, as well as a change in their style. Jest-books of the earlier period were frequently anonymous, although often the tales were attributed to a single real-life or mythical comedian such as John Skelton, John Scogin or Richard Tarlton, and they had tended to reprint the same jokes over and over, perhaps changing names and places.[5] The new generation of jest-book writers included the playwright Thomas Dekker; the comic actor of the Lord Chamberlain's Men, Robert Armin; and King James I's court jester, Archy Armstrong. As well as containing original stories, examples of popular folk-humour and anecdotes of contemporary life, their best-selling volumes included anglicized and condensed versions of French, Spanish and Italian *fabliaux,* sermon-like exemplary tales, and even translations of classical tales.

Many of the jest-book stories combine the strong narrative element which had been characteristic of the medieval style of jest-book, with a new emphasis on verbal wit, repartee and punning; the Elizabethan and Jacobean taste for jests involved both wordplay and story-telling. The narratives encompass a relatively narrow range of subject matter, and the tensions and confrontations which they depict are fairly predictable. They are those between country-folk and townsfolk; between English people and foreigners; between ordinary honest folk and the learned scholar or clergyman; between men and women. The following example from *Jests to Make You Merry* by Thomas Dekker and George Wilkins is not untypical:

> A young bride that had married a stale old bachelor sat at the wedding dinner with a very sad and discontented look, to think what a bad market she had been at. But an ancient, merry Gentlewoman sitting next to her cheered her up in her ear thus: 'Daughter,' quoth she, 'never repent the bargain thou hast this day made, for an old horse will hold out a long journey as well as a nag of four years old.'
>
> 'It may be so,' quoth the bride, 'But as little skill as I have in riding, I doubt whether he can hold out in some highways that I could name.'[6]

The structure is that of repartee – a wittily-phrased retort to a seemingly innocent remark – and the humour turns on wordplay based on euphemism. But behind that lies the wider subject matter of the social and marital relationships between men and woman. In particular the joke's situation refers to the strained marital situation between two unevenly-matched spouses, uneven in this case because of their disparity in age. This, of course, is a traditional source of humour in medieval literature, in folk-tales, and in comic traditions such as that of the *commedia dell'arte.* It in turn depends upon a set of traditional social practices and expectations concerning family formation in which marriages may be arranged as liaisons between families rather than as love-matches between individuals, and in which the wife's status is more nearly that of possession than partner. This jest is, in part, a rueful reflection on the plight of the women in an unhappy marriage.

The joke does more, though, than just reflect the traditional situation. It marks a kind of change, too. During the late sixteenth and early seventeenth centuries economic, familial and material considerations were gradually becoming less important as factors in the choice of marriage partners, and the lower down the social scale one looks the more true this was. A repeated theme in Shakespeare's comedies is the conflict between young love and parental mandate, and in this conflict the choices of young love are invariably vindicated. In this jest-book tale something of the same societal changes can be seen. The young bride in the joke is no voiceless chattel, nor is she sexually ignorant. If the joke is 'about' her plight, it is also about a mismatch between the traditional rôle which she is expected to play and her own desire for an active sex life. Perhaps in the end, it is about a male anxiety that times are changing, and that young women are no longer the pure and innocent things they used to be in the old days.

Many of the 'jests' in the Elizabethan jest-books are presented, as this one is, as if they were real-life incidents. The famous clown Will Kempe, who preceded Armin as chief comic player with Shakespeare's company, the Lord Chamberlain's Men, published a book which actually was based on an actual event. *Kempe's Nine-Day's Wonder* was a description of his own marathon morris dance, a nine-day's dance from London to Norwich which he undertook in 1600. In this Kempe has a few things to say about laughter – usually in the form of boasts about his own ability as a comedian. The following anecdote, however, recounts an impromptu moment not of his own devising:

> In this town of Sudbury, there came a lusty tall fellow, a butcher by his profession, that would in a Morris keep me company to Bury: I being glad of his friendly offer, gave him thanks, and forward we did set: but ere ever we had measur'd half a mile of our way, he gave me over in the plain field, protesting, that if he might get a 100 pound, he would not hold out with me; for indeed my pace in dancing is not ordinary.
>
> As he and I were parting, a lusty Country lass being among the people, called him faint-hearted lout, saying, 'If I had begun to dance, I would have held out one mile though it had cost my life.' At which words many laughed. 'Nay', saith she, 'if the Dancer will lend me a leash of his bells, I'll venture to tread one mile with him myself.'[7]

Kempe continues the story in verse, recounting how she kept her word and danced the mile with him.

> A country lass, brown as a berry
> Blithe of blee in heart as merry,
> Cheeks well fed and sides well larded,
> Every bone with fat flesh guarded,
> Meeting merry Kempe by chance
> Was Marian in his Morris dance,
> Her stump legs with bells were garnished,
> Her brown brows with sweating varnished;
> Her brown hips when she was lag,
> To win her ground, went swig a swag,

Which to see all that came after,
Were replete with mirthful laughter.
Yet she thumped it on her way
With a sportly hey de gay,
At a mile her dance she ended,
Kindly paid and well commended.[8]

There are several kinds of laughter in this anecdote. The crowd in the prose section of the story first laughs at the 'country lass's' jibe. At whom is this laughter directed? At the butcher for his lack of manliness? Is the crowd supporting the girl for pointing it out? Or laughing at her for her claim to be able to do better? In the verse they are certainly laughing at her physical ungainliness, and Kempe himself makes much of her size. Yet the spirit of the anecdote does not suggest that it is merely about victimization or cruelty. Kempe stresses the 'merriness' of the girl and of himself, as well as that of the crowd; and the 'mirthful laughter' of the onlookers must make room for an element of the genuine respect which Kempe himself, the 'head-Master of Morris-dancers' shows for the country lass. The laughter in this tale has more than one dimension. It laughs *at*, but it also laughs *with*. It has no liberal qualms about making fun of one who is differently sized, yet it is in spirit inclusive rather than exclusive. It has in it both aggression and good-humour.

I want to stress the multi-faceted nature of this everyday laughter because it contrasts strongly with what many Elizabethan commentators themselves have to say about laughter. If we are to believe some of the cultural theorists of that time, laughter to the Elizabethans meant only something done in scorn or out of cruelty. Thomas Wilson put it baldly in his *Art of Rhetoric*, 'The occasion of laughter is the fondness, the filthiness, the deformity and all such evil behaviour as we see in others'.[9] Sir Philip Sidney's opinions about the causes of laughter in everyday life also contrast sharply with the evidence of Kempe's anecdote. He sees laughter as an expression of cruelty: something aimed at 'deformed creatures'[10] or at somebody else's misfortune; and Ben Jonson reiterates the Renaissance commonplace that laughter springs from 'meane affections'.[11]

It would be useful to see a Renaissance writer explore the causes and implications of laughter for its own sake in more detail than can be found in these passing remarks by Sidney, Jonson and Wilson. No full-length work of this kind exists in English, but there is one by the French writer, Laurent Joubert, whose *Treatise on Laughter* (*Traité du Ris*) was first published in 1579, although probably written rather earlier.[12] Joubert's lengthy exploration of the phenomenon of laughter – which he describes as 'one of the most astounding actions of man'[13] – looks at it from a variety of standpoints. He attempts to categorize various degrees and kinds of laughter; to examine the causes of laughter; and to explore some of its effects. While he, too, reflects some sense that laughter is an aggressive function, his treatment is much more far-reaching and sophisticated than that of most of his contemporaries. He looks at laughter as something which has a variety of causes, and which operates in a variety of different ways.

The three books of Joubert's treatise draw both on classical Aristotelean philosophy and sixteenth-century medical science. In Book I he undertakes a detailed physiological description of the bodily mechanics of laughter and relates that to the spiritual dimension. He goes on to list and examine some of the causes of laughter. Book II is devoted to a taxonomy of laughter itself (including various kinds of false laughter). In Book III questions are raised about the ultimately beneficial (or otherwise) effect of laughter.

Joubert divides and subdivides his categories. He distinguishes the 'laughable in deed' (comic events as witnessed directly) from the 'laughable in word' (those events, or similar, recounted in writing or speech). Verbal causes of laughter *(l'ouïë)* are contrasted with visual causes *(la vuë).* He spends a great deal of time categorizing different kinds of verbal humour. He contrasts the different ways in which words may be used to evoke laughter: on the one hand they may tell stories, representing events which 'are recounted as having been done and witnessed, and which during their narration seem to be before our eyes'[14] – and to this extent resemble and repeat some of the categories of the laughable in deed. On the other hand there are those humorous uses of language which draw attention to themselves – such as wordplay, which he again subdivides and categorizes.

More relevant to our immediate purposes, events witnessed directly are again subdivided into chance events, accidental happenings which give rise to mirth, and deliberate actions intended to cause laughter. Deliberate actions, once more, fall into two categories: practical jokes ('tricks we do to laugh, or to hurt another, but in unimportant things and in fun')[15] and 'imitation' – pretending to be something other than that which one really is. It is interesting to note how much of the action of Shakespeare's comedies might be subsumed under these two categories: his plots repeatedly involve both practical jokes and people pretending to something other than what they really are, through either disguise or other kinds of imposture.

Accidental happenings which Joubert thinks of as funny usually involve some kind of bodily ignominy. The subdivisions here comprise *les parties honteuses* (the shameful parts, or genitals); *le cu* (the buttocks and anus); *la cheute* (the comic fall); *la deception* (the error); *legers dommages* (inconsequential loss).

> If perchance one uncovers the shameful parts which by nature or public decency we are accustomed to keeping hidden, since this is ugly yet unworthy of pity, it moves the onlookers to laughter . . . It is equally unfitting to show one's arse, and when there is no harm forcing us to sympathize we are unable to contain our laughter.[16]

The all-purpose Joubertian gag, it seems, would involve somebody without any trousers on who falls down, lands on his backside and breaks a few objects in the process. Slapstick, it seems, has changed little in the last few hundred years.

But Joubert analyses his issues carefully. A recurring theme of his is the relationship between laughter and sympathy. These are responses which he sees as mutually exclusive: to evoke laughter, a situation must not be one in which we feel pity. However, unlike some Renaissance moralists (and some philosophers of later times) Joubert does not conclude from this that laughter is essentially cruel or dehumanizing; rather he insists that while to laugh at another's discomfort is common enough, that laughter has certain limitations. It is funny to see someone fall in the mud, and even funnier if that someone is a 'grand and notable personage'; the more dignified the victim the greater the joke. But if that person is a relative or good friend of ours, says Joubert, this would not be funny after all, 'for we should be ashamed or moved by it'.[17] Moreover, once the damage becomes too serious, pity steps in and precludes laughter. He makes this point again in a vivid postscript to the example quoted above, of the man unfittingly showing his backside:

> But if another suddenly puts a red-hot iron to him, laughter gives way to compassion, unless the harm done seems light and small, for that reinforces the laughter.[18]

Compare what Joubert says about laughter, seriousness and sympathy, to some of the effects in Shakespearean comedy. In *Twelfth Night*, for example, the punishment of Malvolio begins as a good laugh: the pompous steward's backside is, metaphorically, bared. Yet as the cruelty mounts to the point where even Malvolio's tormentors begin to get weary of it, the tone of the humour becomes more complex and self-questioning. It is as if Shakespeare is testing out the boundaries at which 'laughter gives way to compassion'.

In the end, Joubert's *Treatise on Laughter* has the same problems as any treatise on laughter: its rather earnest tone and its methodical attempts at a taxonomy of laughter make the examples of humour it gives seem distinctly unfunny. (Conversely, some of the examples of what is *not* funny merely challenge the imagination to disprove the author's judgements.) He makes it all sound rather mechanical – as if certain things *always* evoke laughter, or as if compassion *always* intervenes at a certain point. Humour is less predictable than that – indeed unpredictability is one of the things that can make otherwise serious events funny. It is impossible to draw a matrix which adequately categorizes laughter in the way Joubert tries to do. Nonetheless, we should be grateful to him for the attempt, since he gives a vivid insight into some of things which made people laugh in the sixteenth century.

'My Lord of Misrule': festival, carnival and inversionary laughter

Throughout the Middle Ages and continuing (despite attempts to suppress them) into the seventeenth century there existed, all over Europe, various folk-customs, traditions and rituals whose function was to parody the forms and emblems of authority. Often lumped together under the generic term of 'misrule' and, more recently, 'carnival', these traditions had the common aim of poking fun at the mighty, and of burlesquing the solemnities of ceremony.[19] By 'inversionary laughter' is meant the laughter associated with these practices, rituals and customs, whose function was temporarily to 'turn the world upside down'. As the historian Keith Thomas explains,

> [a] moral function underlay much of the inversionary laughter, the 'holiday humour' which accompanied those occasions of licensed burlesque and disorder which were an annual feature of most Tudor institutions and which, on holidays like Christmas or Shrove Tuesday, occurred throughout society at large. It was not only the court jester who was privileged to draw mocking attention to the delinquencies of his superiors. At colleges and inns of court there were Christmas princes and lieutenants elected from among the students; they burlesqued authority in the same way as did mock-mayors in many towns or lords of misrule in the countryside.[20]

Most of the contemporary accounts we have of these practices come from the writings of their many detractors. The English

Puritan polemicist Philip Stubbes, for example, writes disapprovingly of the way in which, in a country parish, the followers of the Lord of Misrule would interrupt the divine service:

> First, all the wild-heads of the parish, conventing together, choose them a Grand-Captain (of all mischief) whom they ennoble with the title of 'my Lord of Misrule', and him they crown with great solemnity, and adopt for their king . . . And in this sort they go to the church (though the minister be at prayer or preaching), dancing and swinging their handkerchiefs over their heads, like devils incarnate, with such a confused noise, that no man can hear his own voice. Then, the foolish people they look, they stare, they laugh, they fleer, and mount upon forms and pews to see these goodly pageants solemnized in this sort.[21]

Instead of attending to the solemnity of divine service the revellers invade the church with dancing and confused noise; their worship is directed not towards the Christian God or his supposed representatives on earth, but towards the Lord of Misrule – a principle of freedom, chaos and anarchy. Small wonder, it may seem, that the devout churchman would object to such sacrilege.

Yet these inversionary customs and festivals had long coexisted side by side with traditional religious practices. The medieval Christian calendar, both in England and in continental Europe, was dotted with special occasions when 'holiday licence' extended to the regular parodying of the usual structures of authority. Details varied from place to place, but key saints' days on which such inversionary customs took place included Saint Nicholas's Day (6 December), Saint Thomas's Day (21 December), Saint Catherine's Day (25 November) and the Feast of the Epiphany (6 January – also known by the name Shakespeare used for it: Twelfth Night).

In France, for example, the Feast of Fools flourished at Epiphany time in the cathedral towns; a subdeacon or other very minor clergyman would be elected 'bishop' or 'Pope' or 'King of Fools' for the time, and would usurp the place and powers of the actual ecclesiastical authorities. Under his 'law' there took place revels which would have made Philip Stubbes blench. The mass itself was parodied by those who, at other times, celebrated it solemnly; swinging sausages instead of censers the words and actions of the church's most holy ritual were burlesqued. On occasion, for example, an ass was substituted for the celebrant of the mass, whose brayings were answered by the brayed responses of the congregation.[22] In medieval England it would be a 'boy-bishop' rather than a subdeacon who presided over the travesties of liturgical services which similarly mocked ecclesiastical authority. Elected for a period which lasted until after Christmas itself, his reign ran parallel to, and interacted with, the traditional celebrations of the Christmas holy-day period. It was accompanied by revels, dancing, singing and fancy dress:

> . . . diverse and many superstitions and childish observations have been used, and yet to this day are observed and kept in many and sundry parts of this realm, as upon Saint Nicholas, Saint Catherine, Saint Clement, The Holy Innocents and such like; children be strangely decked and apparelled to counterfeit priests, bishops and women; and so led with songs and dances from house to house, blessing the people, and gathering of money . . . [23]

The Russian critic Mikhail Bakhtin uses the term 'carnival' to describe these inversionary rituals, and in a famous explanation of the meaning of carnival he draws out some of their implications. He sees the carnival tradition as being inseparable from the official pageants, processions and ceremonies which were so important to medieval and early modern Europe.

> . . . Carnival festivities and the comic spectacles and ritual connected with them had an important place in the life of medieval man. Besides carnivals proper, with their long and complex pageants and processions, there was the 'feast of fools' (*festa stultorum*) and the 'feast of the ass'; there was the special free 'Easter laughter' (*risus paschalis*), consecrated by tradition. Moreover, nearly every church feast had its comic folk aspect, which was also traditionally recognised. Such, for example, were the parish feasts, usually marked by fairs and varied open-air amusements, with the participation of giants, dwarfs, monsters and trained animals.[24]

In Bakhtin's view these rituals of inversion, in which the mighty were put down from their seats, and the humble and meek were exalted, had a genuinely subversive effect. He makes a distinction between the concept of carnival and those official rituals and ceremonies which were designed to 'sanction the existing pattern of things and support it'.[25] The carnival spirit is separate from and critical of the authorized celebrations, and it creates temporarily an oppositional subculture. It binds a community together, but they are thus bound in opposition to official culture.

> [Carnivals] were sharply distinct from the serious official, ecclesiastical, feudal and political cult forms and ceremonials.

> They offered a completely different, non-official, extra-ecclesiastical and extra-political aspect of the world, of man and of human relations; they build a second world and a second life outside officialdom: a world in which all medieval people participated more or less, in which they lived at a given time of the year. If we fail to take into consideration this two-world condition, neither medieval cultural consciousness nor the culture of the Renaissance can be understood.[26]

The battle between Carnival and Lent was a pervasive symbol in late medieval and early modern culture, represented by painters such as Pieter Bruegel. Bakhtin points to a symbolic vocabulary which Renaissance culture would itself have recognized; and although the meanings which he ascribes to it might not always have been those which official Renaissance culture would have accepted, that is the whole point: that there are meanings available over and beyond those sanctioned by official culture.

Laughter is central to this concept of carnival. The laughter of carnival, according to Bakhtin, has its own special properties: it is, he says, 'the laughter of all the people . . . universal in scope and directed at all and everyone, including the carnival's participants'.[27] The experience of carnival is participatory: it is not something to watch from the sidelines, but something with which to become involved, and the laugher is implicated in the laughter. It is also, he asserts, an ambivalent laughter, simultaneously celebrating and mocking, sympathizing and deriding. Carnival laughter, above all, is a laughter which works against the traditional hierarchies, ranks and norms of the everyday world.

> . . . all were considered equal during carnival. Here, in the town square, a special form of free and familiar contact reigned among people who were usually divided by the barriers of caste, property, profession and age. The divisions of medieval social order were exceptionally strong. Therefore such free, familiar contacts were deeply felt and formed an essential element of the carnival spirit. People were, so to speak, reborn for new, purely human, relations.[28]

This is, perhaps, a rather idealized version of community. Yet Bakhtin's concept of carnival has been an extremely influential one in recent criticism. Not only social hierarchies were to be subverted by the world of carnival, but concepts of decorum too. The laughter of carnival involves bathos, bringing things down to the materialistic and bodily levels. The imagery of carnival involves food and drink, and a revelling in bodily parts and functions: bowels, buttocks, genitalia, urinating, defecating and copulating. Carnival speech and language, too, escapes exuberantly from the confines of official decorum; it is abusive or irreverent, parodic and vulgar, and characterized by variety.

Bakhtin's concept of carnival has made a major contribution to critical discussions of comedy. The emphasis which Bakhtin places on laughter suggests for comedy a more central place in the literary hierarchy than traditional criticism has offered. More specifically, his analysis has raised the possibility that comedy as a dramatic genre has a function similar to that of the social rituals of carnival. Certainly, carnivalesque tendencies can be seen in many kinds of comedy: an irreverence for the solemnities of authority, verbal exuberance and wordplay, a delight in vulgarity, and a celebration of the pleasures of the body. Falstaff is a vivid embodiment of the carnival spirit; so are the Marx Brothers. Bakhtin's insistence on the social nature of the carnival event is especially relevant to the historian of theatrical forms. The participatory event of carnival and the staged event of the theatrical performance touch upon each other in many ways. The nature and purpose of theatre was the subject of vigorous debate in Elizabethan and Jacobean England, and the relationship of theatre to the cultural life of the community as a whole was hotly disputed. But one way in which that theatre sometimes functioned was to provide a space in which the energies of carnival could exist: an alternative place of opposition to official culture (or at least to some definitions of official culture), where a variety of speech could be heard, where clowns and fools could mock authority, and where traditional hierarchies could be turned temporarily upside down.

What Bakhtin calls 'this two-world condition'[29] – the condition of living for the most part in a world defined by official culture, yet also having occasional access to another, freer and more subversive world, the world of carnival – is a powerful image for what happens in so many of Shakespeare's plays. In histories and tragedies, as well as comedies, oppositional worlds are set up which frequently embody alternative values or challenge some implied official norms. Hal in *Henry IV Parts 1 and 2* lives in both the official world of his father's court and in the carnivalesque world of the Eastcheap taverns before finally having to choose in favour of the former. In *Antony and Cleopatra* Mark Antony is torn between the official culture of the Roman Empire and the 'holiday' culture of Egypt which represents, for him and his fellow-Romans, the bodily pleasures of carnival. In plays such as *A Midsummer Night's Dream* and *As You Like It*, locations like the Forest of Arden and the wood outside Athens clearly offer an alternative realm to the official culture of the plays' worlds, which are represented by Theseus and the 'sharp Athenian law', or by the tyranny of Duke Frederick. Thus they, too, have something of the carnivalesque about them. The most extreme of these oppositional worlds exists in *The Winter's Tale*: Leontes's court in Sicily is by turns oppressive and sorrowful, while the 'low-life' world of Bohemia is colourful, lively and celebratory. Significantly, most of the action in Bohemia is actually set at a time of rural carnival, as the shepherds celebrate after their sheep-shearing.

These are plays which have two very distinct and opposed locations: Bakhtin's 'two-world condition' is given a geographical materiality. But the effect of carnival is felt too in those plays where the two worlds exist in more or less the same location. In *Measure for Measure* the dynamic of the play is the conflict between the repressive officialdom of Lord Angelo's government and the carnivalesque underworld of Vienna's stews and brothels. Most clearly, though, there is *Twelfth Night*, a play which bears the name of a time of carnival. In Elizabethan times Twelfth Night, the last night of the Christmas festivities, was one of the high points on the calendar of holidays, and throughout this comedy the oppositions of carnival are played out in the relationship between the plot and the sub-plot, between the love affairs above and below stairs, between the champions of abstinence and those of revelry. *Twelfth Night* both stages and complicates the battle between Carnival and Lent, and its implied opposition between virtue on the one hand, and cakes and ale on the other.

Malvolio's real-life Elizabethan counterparts were those writers like Philip Stubbes, who inveighed against the customs of carnival and misrule. The very violence of their language suggests that Bakhtin might have been right in his emphasis on the subversive nature of carnival. To Stubbes and his fellows these customs of misrule were 'execrable pastimes [which] offer sacrifice to the devil and Sathanas'.[30] Nor was it only the extreme Puritan factions who objected: the authorities of established church and state frequently displayed a nervousness about the potential effect of inversionary rituals. Henry VIII attempted to suppress the elections of boy-bishops in 1541, as had both local and national governments in France and Germany during earlier centuries. These official interdicts, however, were only intermittently effective; despite repeated attempts to suppress them, the rituals of inversion continued to flourish. Many critics and social historians agree with Bakhtin in regarding them as popular institutions which opposed official culture, offering to 'the common people' ways of articulating resistance to that official culture, and alternative ways of seeing the world – ways over which that official culture had no control.[31] According to this view, the laughter of inversion and the rituals which accompanied it constitute a positive and liberating challenge to the oppressive established order.

An alternative view, however, suggests otherwise – that the established order was always perfectly able to cope with the laughter of inversion; that indeed it welcomed it as something which strengthened its own hand. This is what might be called the 'safety valve' theory of laughter and comedy. As one observer of the time put it, the feasts of fools and celebrations of misrule served the same function for a rigidly hierarchical society as the bung-holes did for a wine cask: these needed to be opened occasionally to release the pressure of the fermenting wine and to prevent the barrels from breaking altogether.[32] Similarly the inversionary rituals give an opportunity for social pressures to be 'released' – expressed, that is, in a predictable and comparatively harmless form. Certain tensions which might otherwise build up and lead to societal breakdown are therefore controlled. Thus even potentially subversive laughter becomes something which is socially cohesive: a safety valve which actually reinforces the structures of authority in society. This view stresses the temporary nature of holiday licence: the fact that the period of misrule comes to an end, sooner or later, and that life returns to normal, with nothing changed. It stresses, too, that inversionary laughter is, literally, licensed laughter – it is allowed. Yet this allowing, this licensing, is done *by* someone: the authorities permit the period of carnival, and thus also have it in their power to refuse such licence.

This reading of the relationship between inversionary laughter and the structures of authority in society doubtless has some truth to it. Taken to its logical extreme it implies a rather bleak and essentially totalitarian view of social processes. It suggests that the ruling classes, the authorities, the representatives of 'official culture' control things absolutely, and it leaves little room for resistance to that control, or for spontaneity on the part of those ruled, who are effectively merely cooperating in their own oppression.

Proponents of this view, too, can point to the ways in which the traditions of misrule, far from mounting any serious challenge to the thinking of the ruling classes, could easily be assimilated into the practices of those classes themselves. The anarchic rural Lord of Misrule who so infuriated Philip Stubbes may have interrupted the church services at village level, but at another level of society the Lord of Misrule was far from disruptive. Enid Welsford describes the Christmastide function of the Lord of Misrule in the households of sixteenth-century royalty and nobility:

> The English Lord of Misrule is . . . a temporary court official appointed to provide entertainment for the Christmas holidays . . . Stowe informs us that kings and noblemen had a 'Lord of Misrule' or 'Master of Merry Disports' to devise 'disguisings, masks and mummeries' during the Christmas season; Holinshed gives similar evidence and there are references to Lords of Misrule at the Scottish and English courts during the fifteenth and sixteenth centuries.[33]

This courtly Lord of Misrule made his last official appearance in England at the court of the young King Edward VI, where the post was filled by the learned and distinguished George Ferrers. Even in the Universities of Oxford and Cambridge, where the custom persisted considerably longer, the Christmas Lord of Misrule (known as Rex Regni Fabarum: Lord of the Bean-Kingdom) was kept busy enough presiding over festive entertainments, but ruled over 'a set of very well-behaved fools, who caper beneath the watchful eyes of dons and censors'.[34] The figure Welsford describes is no anarchic, Falstaffian figure – indeed the Shakespearean character he most resembles is the anaemic Aegeus, who offers Theseus a choice of entertainments at the beginning of Act V of *A Midsummer Night's Dream*. Paradoxically, when the disruptive energy of the folk-custom becomes assimilated into the court it is transformed into something very much like the formal post of 'Master of the Revels' – the figure who was also the court's chief literary and dramatic censor. This process certainly suggests the ways in which official power was able to contain seemingly subversive and inversionary elements.

Yet as the sixteenth century progressed, the calls for the suppression of the rituals of misrule increased in volume and frequency. The Lord of Misrule made no appearance at Elizabeth's court, and Puritans like Philip Stubbes demanded the end to such practices elsewhere. Perhaps what made them so unpalatable was not so much their inherent subversiveness as their ancient association with the now-hated Roman Catholic Church. Or perhaps the new structures of authority which developed in Elizabethan England were, being less well-entrenched, less confident of their own ability to assimilate and contain. At any rate it appears that the Protestant (and, increasingly, Puritan) temper of late-sixteenth- and early-seventeenth-century England seemed less able to countenance or contain the energies of inversionary laughter.

While the rituals of inversion were not suppressed by official decrees, they did, however, undergo changes of form. Some of these reflected the changes in society which were taking place in sixteenth- and seventeenth-century Europe, changes which perhaps made the original ecclesiastical high-jinks seem no longer entirely appropriate. What had started out as a parody of the rituals of medieval cathedral communities developed into a subculture of life in the early modern city. In the towns of continental Europe, 'fool societies' developed as the cathedral customs declined. These '*sociétés joyeuses*' flourished particularly in the sixteenth and seventeenth centuries in France and Germany; they were associations of young men dedicated to 'playing the fool', to representing, celebrating and critiquing the folly of society. While they had their origin in the practices of the Feast of Fools, they eventually detached themselves from any specific date: misrule was no longer tied to seasonal festivals.

In England these fool societies were never popular. The inversionary rituals of rural life maintained a closer connection with the traditional festival dates. Once more though, they became secularized. The customs of misrule which Philip Stubbes portrays have an aggressive anticlericalism about them: when these revellers engage with the church it is as an invading force. Here he describes the intrusive celebrations of the Lord of Misrule in greater detail:

> Then, every one of these his men, he investeth with his liveries of green, yellow or some other light wanton colour; and as though that were not (bawdy) gaudy enough, I should say, they bedeck themselves with scarfs, ribbons & laces hanged all over with golden rings, precious stones, & other jewels: this done, they tie about either leg twenty or forty bells, with rich handkerchiefs in their hands, and sometimes laid across over their shoulders and necks, borrowed for the most part of their pretty Mopsies & loving Besses, for bussing them in the dark . . . [35]

The rites of the Lord of Misrule which Stubbes describes here are a rural phenomenon, a folk-custom celebrated in the villages and small towns of the English countryside. As should be clear from his description of the revellers' costumes, these misrule festivities were linked with morris dancing – originally 'moorish dancing': another heathen connotation to trouble the pious! The earnest folksiness of much twentieth-century morris dancing is misleading: in Elizabethan culture it stood for something more vital, something which disturbed the souls of the spokesmen for official culture. A preacher at St Paul's Cathedral in 1578, John Stockwood, was one of many besides Stubbes who made the link between the traditions of misrule and the paganism of the morris dance; both, to his mind, were equally antagonistic to the true faith.

> There be not many places where the word is preached besides the Lords day . . . yet even that day the better part of it is horribly profaned by devilish inventions, as with Lords of Misrule, Morris dancers, Maygames, in somuch that in some places they shame not in the time of divine service, to come and dance about the Church, and without to have men naked dancing in nets, which is most filthy . . . [36]

Morris dancing itself forms a significant strand in the development of comedy: part entertainment and part ritual, it acts as a bridge between the general festivities of the country community and the performance in the London theatres. As the sixteenth century progressed, as London grew as a mercantile centre, as the dominant culture of England became more urban, less directly dependent upon the land and less in touch with the changing times of the year, so here too (as in continental Europe) the spirit of misrule grew away from its seasonal roots.

Thus, instead of a time of licence, a seasonal period of carnival or festival in which it is possible to turn the world upside down so that (in accordance with Scripture) the first becomes last and the last first, a new phenomenon grew up: a *place* of licence. The playhouses of Elizabethan London became places of licensed misrule, presenting their performances of plays which had also been licensed by the paradoxically-entitled Office of the Revels. This displacement involves both continuity and discontinuity. Here in the playhouse the world could be imagined in a multiplicity of alternative ways – a necessary development for a society which was in need of increasingly complex images of the world. The inversionary rituals of the Middle Ages had existed in reaction to a hierarchical vision of society in which everyone knew their place. Vestiges of such a vision, a world-view, were still available, and still addressed by the rural rites, but in the rapidly changing world of the city a more complex and less stable vision of society was emerging. The changing social structures of Tudor and Stuart England had outgrown the comparatively simple medieval division of society into 'nobility' and 'commons' and was now seeing the growth and complexity of the new middle classes: the 'middling sort'. It was predominantly for this middling sort that the London theatres catered, and they demanded a more sophisticated stimulus than the rituals of inversion could supply.

Nonetheless, the lurking presence of an inversionary laughter is an essential ingredient in the rise of English comic drama. Will Kempe, clown to the Lord Chamberlain's Men, is a usefully symbolic figure in this respect. He was the most renowned morris dancer of his day, whose most famous achievement was his 'Nine-day's Wonder' of a dance, which took him from London to Norwich. But Kempe's morrising also danced the spirit of carnival and misrule, from the countryside into the theatres of Elizabethan London – where it met every bit as much resistance from Stubbes and his Puritan allies as it had in its rural manifestations.

'Rough music': the laughter of ridicule

Words like 'carnival' and 'festive' have a rather positive tone to them: they suggest community, celebration and a sense of people being united. 'Ridicule', one might suppose, is the very opposite of this. With the laughter of ridicule we are dealing with a kind of laughter which is cruel and contemptuous; the kind of laughter Thomas Wilson and Ben Jonson wrote about, and which Sir Philip Sidney called a 'scornful tickling'.[37] In this section we will be looking at some punitive functions of laughter, and examining the ways in which sixteenth- and seventeenth-century communities used laughter and scorn as punishments – both official and unofficial – to uphold rules and affirm societal values and norms.

Just how closely this kind of laughter could be related to festival and inversionary laughter is shown by the following, not untypical, incident recounted by the social historian David Underdown.[38] A church ale was held in 1607 in Wells, Somerset in order to raise money for church repairs. The parish celebrated with feasting, processions, morris dancing and pageantry: there were portrayals of popular figures of folk-legend such as Robin Hood, Noah and his Ark, George and the Dragon. 'So far,' as Underdown says, 'it seems no more than a charming celebration of good neighbourhood in an unusually united community.'[39] The tone of the mirth began to change, however, when one of the figures in the procession, dressed as a satyr, was seen carrying a spotted calf: this was understood by all to be a pointed libel against an unpopular parishioner, one Mrs Yard, whom scandal linked with one of her neighbours, John Hole. As the procession continued, the victims were lampooned and ridiculed further – to the extent that the revellers were eventually taken to court.

The energy of carnival, as seen by Bakhtin, could become an expression of class solidarity: the affirmation of an alternative culture and a set of values which differed from official culture. That same energy could be directed, however, against individuals within a class or community for various purposes. A popular ritual may sometimes be an expression of rebellion against authority or oppression, but its laughter may also be self-regulatory, directed against an errant member of its own social group. The laughter of ridicule is essentially conservative, and its function is to punish the non-conformist, the deviant, the rebel or the rule-breaker. In the case of Mrs Yard and Mr Hole, in fact, the situation is ambiguous: both were individuals who had in the past objected to May-games and such festivities, and thus in one sense they were already culturally in conflict with the revellers. Yet they were also co-parishioners, neighbours, part of the same community, and the ridicule was directed against them because they had broken the rules of sexual propriety of that community.

Many of the unofficial punishment rituals of sixteenth- and seventeenth-century urban and village culture dated back to the Middle Ages. They had various functions: to shame or humiliate people whose violations of social or moral codes did not amount to crimes which would be dealt with by the legal system; to pre-empt legal action, functioning as an improvised form of local justice which prevented certain cases ever reaching the courts; and occasionally to articulate the protests of the relatively powerless against the powerful.

'Charivari' (known in the West Country as 'skimmington rides' or 'skimmingtons') were processions aimed at ridiculing members of the community in order to punish deviant behaviour. The lampooning of the unfortunately-named Mr Hole and Mrs Yard was an impromptu charivari which developed out of a more official and more benevolent event. But the charivari procession was more usually an end in itself in which men and women making discordant 'rough music' with pots, pans, spoons and ladles would parade through a town or village, focusing upon the house of the offender.[40]

Charivaris could be used for 'punishing' a variety of social misdemeanours. At times they had the effect of a political demonstration, as when they were used against landowners who enclosed common pasture land, or otherwise threatened customary rights. By far the most regular use of the charivari or skimmington, however, was as a way of reinforcing patriarchal authority and the rigid rules regarding gender roles. The most frequent victims of charivari were people who in one way or another had offended against sexual norms and *mores*: in particular, couples in which the woman was deemed to have achieved an undue degree of dominance in the relationship. Wives who beat their husbands were a favourite target, as were unfaithful wives. These two situations were frequently assumed to be connected: both showed evidence of unacceptable female dominance in the relationship. In such cases the henpecked or cuckolded husband was as much an object of the procession as the wife: his crime was failing to uphold patriarchal authority and thus letting the side down.

In addition to the procession and the rough music there were various symbols to represent the offence: in the case of infidelity the cuckold's horns played a prominent rôle. These are the symbolic horns of the deceived husband which are referred to so frequently in Elizabethan comedies. In the real-life ritual the horns could be displayed in a number of ways: perhaps perched on top of a pole, or left at the offenders' front door, attached to the victims' pew in church or hung about the neck of their horse. In the case of a scolding or violent wife, the whole scene of the offence might be acted out by surrogates – neighbours dressed up to represent both husband and wife, with the 'husband' riding backwards on a horse or ass while the 'wife', frequently a man dressed up in women's clothes to stress the 'unnaturalness' of her violence, berated or beat him.[41]

Charivari was thus, effectively, a form of street theatre in which a community would stage a ritual show acting out the rôles of those who offended against established norms. In this acting out there is a paradox. The charivari was aimed at enforcing society's expected gender rôles. It punished adultery, which threatened the stability of the patriarchal family; it ridiculed women whose violence towards their husbands showed them to be 'mannish', and men who, by allowing their wives to dominate or cheat them, failed to fulfil the patriarchal rôle assigned to them by society. Yet in order to enforce traditional rôles, men dress up as women – enacting as performance the very behaviour they are condemning. The staged event has an ambiguous relationship to the object of its disapproval.

The element of spectacle was thus central to the community's strategies for regulating itself in sixteenth- and seventeenth-century England. The unofficial punishments which these communities visited upon their members could in themselves be highly theatrical – as indeed could the official punishments imposed by the courts. The legal system of the period set much store by the public display and humiliation of lawbreakers and the accompanying rituals. Stocks and pillory were physically uncomfortable, painful and occasionally fatal punishments, but their real point lay in the public exposure to which the culprit was subjected. The wrongdoer was locked by the heels, or by head and hands, into a wooden frame, and exposed to the derision of the community. Since onlookers were also expected and encouraged to pelt the offender with dung, dirt, stones and refuse, the audience became participants and the community became implicated in the act of punishment.

In fact, the boundaries between official and unofficial punishments were ill-defined, and a sentence of this kind, ordered by the local magistrates, could often be accompanied by impromptu rough music. This was frequently the case with the 'carting' of whores – a ritual which, according to David Underdown, 'provided cathartic release for community tensions, gave its participants a virtuous sense of enforcing moral standards and was for all but the victim an enjoyable, festive occasion'.[42] This kind of 'festivity' has an inherently conservative function: the scapegoating of a victim allows the rest of the community to reaffirm its shared values.

Another official punishment which was close in spirit to charivari was the use of the ducking stool. This was another shaming ritual, whose function was once more to ensure conformity to fixed gender rôles. Most towns and many villages maintained one of these contraptions, and the town records for Coventry in 1597 are typical in their description of the use and purpose of the ducking- or cucking-stool:

> Whereas there are diverse and sundry disordered persons within this city that be scolds, brawlers, disturbers and disquieters of their neighbours, to the great offence of Almighty God and the breach of her Majesty's peace; for the reformation of such abuses it is ordered and enacted at this leet . . . they shall be committed to the cuckstool lately appointed for the punishment of such offenders, and thereupon be punished for their deserts, except they, or every one of them, do presently pay 3s 3d for their redemption from that punishment to the use of the poor of the city.[43]

The Coventry records use the gender-neutral term 'persons', but from the fifteenth century onwards the ducking-stool was mainly, if not entirely, used as a punishment for women who trespassed against the societal norms. Equally so was the branks, or 'scold's bridle', a form of gag used in the North of England, generally in conjunction with public exposure at market-cross or pillory.

The extent of Elizabethan and Jacobean anxieties concerning the maintenance of gender rôles and patriarchal authority is striking. They are expressed in the literature of the time – and not least in Shakespeare's comedies, which certainly have their fair share of unusually independent or unruly women – as well as in legislation and community rituals. These anxieties are part of a larger picture: they relate to a more general fear of breakdown in the social order which was felt by many people in the period. Writers, preachers and legislators in the late sixteenth and early seventeenth centuries shared an acute sense of living in a time of exceptional instability. This sense was not unjustified. Real changes were taking place in that society, and causes included an expanding population, a series of poor harvests resulting in bursts of inflation, vagrancy resulting from enclosures, the gradual but accelerating transition from a feudal to a capitalist economy, and increased social and geographical mobility. Traditional beliefs in an interlocking network of hierarchies, whereby the family was seen as a microcosm of the state, led to the projection of many of these more general anxieties onto the domestic situation. The fear of the breakdown of patriarchal authority was an integral part of larger societal fears. It was also local and immediate, and something could be done about it. Central to the culture's strategies for doing something about it was the element of spectacle and theatricality which characterized both the official and the unofficial punishments of the time.

Following the work of the French cultural theorist Michel Foucault,[44] much has been written about the dimension of spectacle in capital punishment during the early modern period, and the way in which public executions of criminals in the sixteenth, seventeenth and eighteenth centuries were stage-managed in order to inscribe and reinforce the authority of law. An analogy has been drawn by some literary critics between the theatricality of the public execution and the theatrical form of tragedy. The satirists who flourished in the final years of Elizabeth's reign drew their own analogies between their satires and judicial punishment in works with titles like *The Whipping of the Satyr* (1601) and *The Scourge of Villainy* (1598). In the same way analogies could also be drawn between the shaming spectacles so central to both unofficial and legal punishments – ducking-stool, branks, pillory and stocks – and some of the crueller dimensions of Elizabethan comedy.

Shakespeare's comedies occasionally take on dimensions of the charivari. One way of understanding *The Taming of the Shrew* might be to see it in terms of an elaborately-staged 'rough music' aimed at taming the unruly woman. Kate's first appearance in the play is announced by a play on words which links courtship to the rituals of shaming:

> *Baptista* If either of you both love Katherina,
> Because I know you well and love you well
> Leave shall you have to court her at your pleasure.
> *Gremio* To cart her rather. She's too rough for me.
> (*Shrew*, I, i, ll. 52–5)

Gremio's court/cart pun sets the tone for the rest of the play, which thus becomes a charivari stage-managed by Petruchio, in which the scolding woman is humiliated, silenced, displayed and finally brought to repentance.

Another comedy which is structured around a sequence of

punitive rituals, directed this time against a male sexual outlaw, is *The Merry Wives of Windsor.* Here, the would-be adulterer Sir John Falstaff's various defeats at the hands of Mistress Ford and Mistress Page are marked by a series of ritual humiliations which echo the structures of legal and communal punishments. In the first he is carried out of the house in dirty linen and dumped in the Thames, as if in a ducking-stool:

> *Falstaff*... Have I lived to be carried in a basket like a barrow of butcher's offal, and to be thrown into the Thames? Well, if I be served such another trick, I'll have my brains ta'en out and buttered, and give them to a dog for a New Year's gift. 'Sblood, the rogues slighted me into the river with as little remorse as they would have drowned a blind bitch's puppies, fifteen i' th' litter. And you may know by my size that I have a kind of alacrity in sinking.
>
> (*Merry Wives* III, v, ll. 4–12)

The second and third punishments amount to a kind of charivari in which he is both the subject and the principal actor. His failed attempts to cuckold Master Ford lead him to make an ungainly escape dressed as an old woman. In this disguise he is beaten out of the house by Ford, much to the amusement of Mistresses Ford and Page.

> *Ford*... Come down, you witch, you hag, you! Come down, I say!
>
> (*Enter Mistress Page, and Sir John Falstaff, disguised as an old woman. Ford makes towards them.*)
>
> *Mistress Ford* Nay, good sweet husband! – Good gentlemen, let him not strike the old woman.
>
> *Mistress Page* (*to Sir John*) Come, Mother Prat. Come, give me your hand.
>
> *Ford* I'll prat her!
>
> (*He beats Sir John*)
>
> Out of my door, you witch, you rag, you baggage, you polecat, you runnion! Out, out! I'll conjure you, I'll fortune-tell you.
>
> (*Merry Wives*, IV, iv, ll. 164–73)

The final complex indignity comes in the last scene. Tricked into a supposed assignation with both wives, Falstaff waits for them at Herne's oak. He is disguised as the mythical figure Herne the Hunter who supposedly haunts the park in the shape of a deer. Falstaff himself comments on how his disguise makes him resemble a famous mythological symbol of male fertility:

> *Falstaff*... Remember, Jove, thou wast a bull for thy Europa;

> love set on thy horns. O powerful love, that in some respects makes a beast a man, in some other a man a beast.
>
> (*Merry Wives*, V, v, ll. 3–5)

And on a more local level, Herne the Hunter is associated with Cernunnos, the 'horned god' of Celtic fertility myths.[45] Falstaff, in his own eyes, has become the horned god.

But such grandiose notions quickly collapse as the children of the town, disguised as fairies and hobgoblins, arrive to taunt the credulous knight, who believes them to be supernatural spirits indeed. The horns he is wearing turn out to be the badge not of potency but of humiliation: they are, after all, the cuckold's horns of the charivari. Falstaff is caught in his own trap, and jeered at by the citizens of Windsor. Once more the sexual outlaw is ridiculed by the laughter of the community whose codes he has sought to violate. If one subtext of comedy is carnival and celebration, another is that of punishment, regulation, and scapegoating.

Notes

1. J. M. Lothian and T. W. Craik, eds, *Twelfth Night* (London: Methuen, 1975), p. 44.
2. L. C. Knights, *The Importance of Scrutiny* (1964), p. 227, quoted in Moelwyn Merchant, *The Critical Idiom: Comedy* (London: Methuen, 1972).
3. Keith Thomas, 'The place of laughter in Tudor and Stuart England', *Times Literary Supplement*, 21 January 1977, p. 80.
4. Anon, *The Beauty of Women* (London, *c.* 1525), sigs. A2–A3.
5. P. M. Zall, *A Nest of Ninnies and Other Jestbooks of the Seventeenth Century* (Lincoln: University of Nebraska Press, 1970), p. x.
6. Thomas Dekker and George Wilkins, *Jests to Make You Merry* (London, 1607), 55th Jest.
7. Will Kempe, *Kempe's Nine-Day's Wonder* (London, 1600), sig. B3v.
8. Ibid., sig. Bv.
9. Thomas Wilson, *The Art of Rhetoric* (1553), quoted in Thomas, 'The place of laughter in Tudor and Stuart England', p. 78.
10. Sir Philip Sidney, *An Apology for Poetry or The Defence of Poesy* (1595) ed. Geoffrey Shepherd (Manchester: Manchester University Press, 1965), p. 136. For a fuller account of Sidney's and Jonson's ideas about comedy see below, Chapter 3.
11. Ben Jonson, *Timber, or Discoveries*, in C. H. Herford, P. and E. Simpson, *Ben Jonson* (Oxford: Clarendon Press, 1925–52), vol. 8, p. 644.
12. This is reprinted in Gregory de Rocher, *Rabelais' Laughers and Joubert's Traité du Ris* (Montgomery: University of Alabama Press, 1980).

13. de Rocher, *Rabelais' Laughters*, p. 17.
14. Ibid., p. 17.
15. Ibid., p. 22.
16. Ibid., p. 20.
17. Ibid., p. 19.
18. Ibid., p. 20.
19. See Enid Welsford, *The Fool: His Social and Literary History* (London: Faber and Faber, 1935).
20. Thomas, 'The place of laughter in Tudor and Stuart England', p. 78.
21. Philip Stubbes, *The Anatomy of Abuses*, ed. F. J. Furnivall (London: New Shakespeare Society, 1877–9), pp. 146–8.
22. Welsford, *The Fool*, p. 202.
23. David Wilkins, *Concilia Magnae Britanniae et Hiberniae* (London, 1737), vol. 3, p. 860.
24. Mikhail Bakhtin, *Rabelais and his World*, reprinted in D. J. Palmer, ed., *Comedy: Developments in Criticism* (London and Basingstoke: Macmillan, 1984), p. 95.
25. Bakhtin, *Rabelais and his World*, p. 95.
26. Ibid., p. 95.
27. Ibid., p. 101.
28. Ibid., p. 99.
29. Ibid., p. 95.
30. Stubbes, *The Anatomy of Abuses*, p. 148.
31. See Michael Bristol, *Carnival and Theater: Plebeian Culture and the Structure of Authority in Renaissance England* (London: Methuen, 1985), p. 22.
32. Welsford, *The Fool*, p. 204.
33. Ibid., p. 213.
34. Ibid., p. 215.
35. Stubbes, *The Anatomy of Abuses*, p. 147.
36. William Harrison, *A Description of England*, ed. F. J. Furnivall (London: New Shakespeare Society, 1877–81), pp. 133–4.
37. Sidney, *An Apology for Poetry*, p. 136.
38. David Underdown, *Revel, Riot and Rebellion* (Oxford: Oxford University Press, 1985) pp. 55–6.
39. Ibid., p. 55.
40. Articles and books describing various manifestations of the charivari include E. P. Thompson, '"Rough Music": le charivari anglais', *Annales ESC* XXVII (1972), pp. 283–312; J. Le Goff and J. C. Schmitt, eds, *Le Charivari* (Paris, 1981); David Underdown, 'The taming of the scold: the enforcement of patriarchal authority in early modern England', in Anthony Fletcher and John Stevenson, eds, *Order and Disorder in Early Modern England* (Cambridge: Cambridge University Press, 1985), pp. 116–36.
41. Underdown, 'The taming of the scold', pp. 128–9.

42. Ibid., p. 128.
43. Cited in E. J. Burford and Sandra Shulman, *Of Bridles and Burnings: the Punishment of Women* (New York: St Martin's Press, 1992, p. 96.
44. See Michel Foucault, *Discipline and Punish: The Birth of the Prison*, trans. Alan Sheridan (New York: Random House, 1978).
45. See William Anderson, *The Green Man: the Archetype of our Oneness with the Earth* (London and San Francisco: HarperCollins, 1990), p. 140.

2 Fools, clowns and jesters

Perhaps the most famous of all Shakespearean fool rôles is that of the unnamed 'boy' in *King Lear*, where the double-act between the Fool and the King during the early part of the play allows Shakespeare to move swiftly between different dramatic registers in his exploration of rationality and madness, language and power. But the fool is a stock character of Shakespearean comedy: Feste, Touchstone and Lavatch are paid retainers, charged with the providing of entertainment to aristocratic households. We have seen how, in charivaris, feasts and festivals, certain kinds of laughter were related to specific times, places and social events. In this chapter I want to turn from places and events to people: those paid entertainers who lived by laughter in various social contexts during the late medieval and early modern period. There are three reasons for this. Firstly, because of what the real-life fools, clowns and jesters can show about traditions of popular (and aristocratic) comic entertainment which were inherited by the Elizabethan theatre. Secondly, because Shakespeare repeatedly shows specific interest in them as characters, incorporating the figure of the fool into several of his plays. And thirdly, because their changing functions show, once more, significant points of contact between the theatrical world and the world of everyday reality.

There is, though, a problem of terminology. Much has been written about Shakespeare's fools, or Shakespeare's clowns, or even Shakespeare's jesters.[1] But there is also some confusion about these words and we need to look at each of them closely. Is it the case that the terms are synonymous and that they can be used interchangeably to refer to the same figure? Or are fool, jester and clown three separate entities?

In fact the three words do all have slightly different shades of meaning. However, it is not always easy to separate out these meanings in Shakespeare's plays, since there is a good deal of wordplay (especially on the part of the clowns, fools and jesters themselves) which depends on the ambiguities and double-meanings which reside in the words themselves. There is something quite fitting in this: Feste describes himself in *Twelfth Night* as a 'corrupter of words' (III, i, l. 34), so perhaps it is not surprising that any words used to describe the fool, clown or jester are themselves slippery, ambiguous and elusive. It is worth, however, attempting to unravel some of the different strands of meaning in the words in order to arrive at some definitions.

Jester and fool

'Jester' is perhaps the simplest and semantically the least rich of the three words. Yet even here there are shades of meaning which are not immediately available to us (although they would have been to Shakespeare and his contemporaries) and which may affect our understanding of the function of characters such as Feste and Touchstone. The word 'jester' (or 'gester') was originally used to refer to one who sang or told stories of great deeds. The Middle English word 'gest' could mean a notable deed or the narrative in which that deed was related. The meaning later developed to include any kind of story or tale. Thus the earliest 'gesters' were the professional and semi-professional story-tellers and minstrels of the medieval period, the singers of tales and romances. Chaucer refers to these story-tellers in his love poem *The House of Fame* (*c.* 1380), where he talks of 'all manner of minstrels, / And gesters, that tellen tales / Both of weeping and of game . . .' (III, ll. 1197–99).[2]

By Elizabethan times this meaning had not been lost, but the word had also come to refer more specifically to purveyors of merriment. A manuscript drawing of Richard Tarlton, Queen Elizabeth's jester, which is held in the British Library[3] is accompanied by an anonymous poem singing the praises of Tarlton 'who merry many made / When he appeard in sight / The grave and wise as well as rude / At him did take delight'. Written after his death, the poem praises Tarlton's skill as an actor, and goes on to state admiringly that 'Of all the Jesters in the lande / He bare the praise away'. The manuscript picture of Tarlton shows him playing a pipe and drum: even up to the time of Elizabeth's reign the jester still retains his association with music and minstrelsy.

The 'jester' has these dimensions to it: on the one hand a singer and story-teller, telling tales 'both of weeping and of game', and on the other hand a professional comedian. Yet while characters such as Touchstone and Feste are recognizably 'jesters' employed by rich houses, they are more usually referred to as 'fools' – a word which, in Shakespeare's use, is played upon obsessively. It seems that Shakespeare is temperamentally incapable of putting a motley fool on stage without playing on different meanings of the word 'fool'. The following routine from *Twelfth Night* provides a good example of this: it is an exchange between Olivia and Feste:

Feste God bless thee, lady.
Olivia (*to attendants*) Take the fool away.
Feste Do you not hear, fellows? Take away the lady . . .
Olivia Sir, I bade them take away you.
Feste Misprision in the highest degree! Lady, '*Cucullus non facit monachum*' – that's as much to say as I wear not motley in my brain. Good madonna, give me leave to prove you a fool.
Olivia Can you do it?
Feste Dexteriously, good madonna.
Olivia Make your proof.

(*Twelfth Night*, I, v, ll. 33–6, 50–7)

Feste goes on to establish through paradox that Olivia, not he, is the fool after all. These are the questions which the presence of the fool on the Shakespearean stage continually asks, both implicitly and explicitly: what is the relationship between the foolery of the professional comedian and the foolishness of others? The fool's central joke is this: who is the real fool? Feste makes the joke with bravado, Lear's Fool with bitterness:

Fool The lord that counselled thee
To give away thy land,
Come place him here by me;
Do thou for him stand.
The sweet and bitter fool
Will presently appear,
The one in motley here,
The other found out there.
Lear Dost thou call me fool, boy?
Fool All thy other titles thou hast given away. That thou wast born with.

(*King Lear*, quarto, I, iv, ll. 135–45)[4]

Feste and his colleagues in the motley repeat the joke time and again, throughout Shakespeare's plays. It is such a familiar gag that it is easy to ignore the fact that it masks a harsh historical truth that the European court fool of the Middle Ages and the Renaissance was frequently a fool in the original sense of the word: someone mentally deficient or handicapped. This is the sense of the word which Shakespeare's contemporary, the essayist Nicholas Breton, refers to in his definition of a fool:

A Fool is that abortive of wit, where Nature hath more power than reason, in bringing forth the fruit of imperfection. His actions are most in extremes, and the scope of his brain is but ignorance: only Nature hath taught him to feed, and Use, to labour without knowledge. He is a kind of shadow of a better substance, or, like the vision of a dream, that yields nothing awake. He is commonly known by one of two special names, as, from wilfull 'Will Fool', and 'Hodge', from hodge-podge. All meats are alike, all are one to a fool. His exercises are commonly divided into four parts: eating and drinking, sleeping and laughing. Four things are his chief loves: a bauble and a bell, a coxcomb and a pied-coat. He was begotten in unhappiness, born to no goodness, lives but in beastliness, and dies but in forgetfulness. In sum, he is the shame of Nature, the trouble of wit, the charge of charity, and the loss of liberality.[5]

The fool described in this essay, which veers uncertainly in tone between sympathy and contempt, might be a village idiot, or might be a paid retainer of a great man, kept around to be laughed at for his idiocy. Shakespeare's court jesters are witty, intelligent and rather well-read. They are artificial fools in that they are actually in full command of their faculties, but are putting on an act of folly in order to entertain or to make a point. The historical court fool in England and in the rest of Europe was just as likely to be such a person as Breton describes, someone with severe mental and/or physical disabilities. Enid Welsford, whose classic 1935 book *The Fool: His Social and Literary History* pioneered much research in this field, characterizes the 'natural' fool as one who

> . . . causes amusement . . . by mental deficiencies or physical deformities which deprive him both of rights and responsibilities and put him in the paradoxical position of virtual outlawry combined with utter dependence on the support of the social group to which he belongs. I have included physical deformity in my definition because it is not possible to draw a hard and fast distinction between the court-fool and the court-dwarf, since they both had much the same function in society, and since both types of infirmity were frequently found in the same person.[6]

When Welsford talks about the fool's 'paradoxical position of virtual outlawry combined with utter dependence' it strikes a chord, for this is a good description of the position not only of Feste and Touchstone but also of the typical Elizabethan player. Caught between the vagrancy laws on the one hand and the possibility of court patronage on the other, the Elizabethan actor had much in common with the traditional situation of the fool.

Welsford explores cross-cultural examples of the fool phenomenon, ranging from Martial's accounts of slave-buying in ancient Rome, to the Vidusaka, the 'misshapen dwarf' of fourth-century

Indian culture, and she asks about the mixed motives which led people to keep idiots and deformed persons in their houses. She makes various suggestions: that it was done originally for magical purposes (since such persons were seen as lucky, being immune from the Evil Eye); that it was due to a general human fascination with the unusual or the grotesque; that it was a superstitious tactic to defend against the sin of *hubris* (excessive pride) and the ensuing cosmic punishment. She suggests that it had derived in part from ancient tribal scapegoat rites, and she stresses similarities between customs and rituals associated with fools and those associated with the slaying of the priest-king which James Frazer details in *The Golden Bough.*[7]

Most scholarly studies of the fool tradition follow Welsford's lead; there is ample evidence to show the widespread use of the disabled, the maimed, the disfigured and the simple as figures of fun. William Willeford, for example, talks of

> the earliest jester of whom we have any knowledge . . . a dwarf at the court of the Egyptian Pharaoh Pepi (or Papi) I. There were dwarf jesters in China in the earliest days, and in both areas of high civilization in pre-Columbian America dwarfs and hunchbacks served as court jesters. Cripples and freaks were sold in Roman markets, and dwarfs ran about naked in the salons of Roman ladies. This aristocratic appreciation of human monstrosities flourished as late as 1566, when thirty-four dwarfs, almost all deformed, served at the banquet given by Cardinal Vitelli in Rome. In the courts of Christian Europe dwarfs and other freaks served as jesters, as they had earlier. The first court dwarf in England was Xit, in the reign of Edward VI, and the last was Copperin, dwarf of the Princess (Augusta) of Wales, mother of George III.[8]

We might read into these cruel details an implicit continuity between earlier cultures and our own: to recognize in them our own readiness to laugh at the misfortunes of others, to see other people's differences as a fit subject for mirth. We might also see in them the distance which exists between our culture and that of medieval and Renaissance Europe. Without overstating the case or being too optimistic, it could be suggested that these cultures show significant differences from our own in the ways in which they react to 'deformity', 'freaks', 'monstrosities', 'grotesqueness', 'mental deficiency'; and that our own cultural norms mean that it is no longer entirely comfortable for most of us to laugh at the disabilities, mental or physical, of other people.

The point of this is not to take the moral high ground on this matter or to assume the ethical superiority of 'our' culture over an earlier one, but to establish that the fools of Shakespeare's plays were related to a family, not just of courtiers, nor of philosophers, but also of 'natural fools'. It is also to stress a dimension of Shakespeare's repeated pun which is often missed, precisely because we are so familiar with the stage figure of the witty fool. We no longer see Feste or Touchstone or Lear's boy as being kin to what the twentieth century has referred to variously as the 'congenital idiot', the 'retard', the 'mentally handicapped', or the 'person with learning difficulties'. And so it is easy for us to forget the extent to which their wit goes against the grain, and that the speaker is having to overturn deep-seated prejudices in order to be heard at all. Shakespeare's fools inhabit a deliberately ambiguous zone between two meanings of the word, and the repeated joke about 'who is the real fool?' is a deeper and darker one than it may seem.

Many noble English houses during the fourteenth, fifteenth and sixteenth centuries employed fools as part of their household retinue, and many of these were just such 'natural fools'. It is, however, the names of the 'artificial fools' which have come down to posterity – the professional comedians whose job it was to keep the monarchy and the aristocracy amused. What sort of social position was held by these real-life court fools? This question is worth asking not only for its own sake, but because of the implications it may have for an understanding of Shakespeare's fools. A series of critical assumptions have grown up around the figure of the fool in Shakespeare's plays: according to this critical tradition figures like Lear's Fool and Feste are typically seen as the outsiders in the corridors of power, as marginalized figures, hovering between the Council Chamber and the servants' quarters. This very marginality, however, allows the court fool a perspective from which to speak which amounts to a kind of wisdom. His rôle is that of the witty, sardonic servant whose seemingly meaningless words conceal profound thoughts and 'whose apparent simplicity disguises a shrewd understanding of the cruelty and harshness of the world'.[9] Thus through his seeming folly he speaks occasional words of devastating and radical insight, subverting the power structures of the court and threatening the status quo. By an easy kind of slippage, too, it has been assumed by some writers that the real-life fools of monarchs and nobles fulfilled similar functions.

More recently these readings of the function of the court fool have been challenged on both literary and historical counts. The American scholar Theodore B. Leinwand places characters such as Lear's Fool and Touchstone in a much more conservative light, seeing them not as subverters of the *status quo* but as supporters of it.[10] By examining the career of James I's real-life fool Archy Armstrong, Leinwand argues forcibly that the social determinants which conditioned the position of real-life fools and jesters at court and in the great houses of Renaissance England ensured that they were, effectively, minions of the house. Archy Armstrong was by no means a marginalized figure. He wore the King's livery, and involved himself in matters of state. He used his influence at court to further both his own interests and those of his political and religious allies. His fierce anti-Catholicism took him to Spain as a member of the King's household, and there he was a central figure in the failure of the proposed marriage negotiations between Prince Charles and the Spanish Infanta. It also eventually led to his own downfall: in 1637 he took on an enemy too powerful for him, and Archbishop Laud secured his exile from the court. Archy Armstrong, then, seems to have been a figure of some centrality to the court of King James. Rather than someone who stood outside the hierarchies and power struggles of the day and commented on them, he was thoroughly implicated in their dealings. Leinwand argues that this is the true model for the court fools in Shakespeare's plays, and that Touchstone and Lear's Fool should be seen in this light: as conservative figures, not radicals; as servants of the court not as reformers of it.

Leinwand's argument is a valuable antidote to the tendency of some critics to sentimentalize figures such as Touchstone or Lear's Fool. They are not, after all, radical reformers, offering a thoroughgoing critique of the power structures of the day. They know on which side their bread is buttered, and for all their criticisms of their employers, they are dependent upon them. Yet they *do* at times oppose them, and in doing so they act against their own most obvious self-interest: Lear's Fool speaks from a position which is anything but comfortable in relation to the power structures with which he has to deal.

> I marvel what kin thou and thy daughters are. They'll have me whipped for telling the truth, thou'lt have me whipped for lying, and sometimes I am whipped for holding my peace. I had rather be any kind of thing than a fool . . .
>
> (*King Lear*, I, iv, ll. 163–7)

And in *As You Like It* Touchstone rebels against his master, the usurping Duke Frederick, in order to ally himself with the outlawed Rosalind and the exiled Celia. If the courtier-fool Archy Armstrong is a typical real-life fool, what is significant is not the similarities between him and Shakespeare's court fools but the differences.

Armstrong, in any case, is unlikely to have been a direct model for any of the court fools of Shakespeare's plays. He did not arrive on the English court scene until 1603, when he accompanied King James down from Scotland on James's accession to the English throne. By then Touchstone and Feste were already established characters on the London stage. Moreover, Armstrong's years of greatest political influence and centrality actually occurred after Shakespeare's writing career was over. The tradition of real-life fools and jesters upon which Shakespeare drew contained figures besides Armstrong. To find the more immediate real-life counterparts to Shakespeare's clowns and jesters we need to turn back to Armstrong's predecessors.

What we see is a history of a changing figure which is neither like the traditional picture of the fool as witty outsider, nor completely like Leinwand's revisionist view of the fool as fully implicated in the stratagems of the court. Indeed, the position of the European court fool changed during medieval and Renaissance times, showing a gradual increase in status. If by the time of Archy Armstrong the court fool could become something akin to a statesman, we have already seen that it began its career as something more like a pet.

Henry VIII's jester Will Somers (or Summers) was famous enough in his own lifetime but achieved further fame posthumously when he became a fictional character in an entertainment by Thomas Nashe, entitled *Summer's Last Will and Testament*,[11] and again in William Rowley's play *When You See Me You Know Me.*[12] In this latter play he was portrayed not only as entertainer but also as hero, exposing the greedy machinations of the Catholic Cardinal Wolsey and thereby saving the Protestant King Henry. He was further immortalized by one of his own successors Robert Armin, who, in the early years of the seventeenth century, published a volume of anecdotes about fools entitled, aptly enough, *Fool Upon Fool.* In the following extract, which gives a flavour both of the volume and of Will's professional style and character, he is trying to cheer up King Henry by asking him a series of riddles:

> 'Now tell me,' says Will 'if you can, what it is that being born without life, head, nose, lip or eye, and yet runs terribly roaring through the world till it dies?'
>
> 'This is a wonder,' quoth the King, 'and no question, and I know it not.'
>
> 'Why,' quoth Will, 'it is a fart.'
>
> At this the King laughed heartily, and was exceeding merry, and bids Will ask any reasonable thing and he would grant it.
>
> 'Thanks, Harry,' says he, 'now against I want I know where

to find; for yet I need nothing, but one day I shall, for every man sees his latter end, but knows not his beginning.'

The King understood his meaning, and so pleasantly departed for that season, and Will lays him down among the spaniels to sleep.[13]

This combination of crudeness and wisdom, cheap jokes and philosophy is not so far in spirit from the typical Shakespearean fool, and it might be thought that he was the prototype for some of the fool figures in the plays. Yet this Will is the product of a narrative, too. In the process of being written into stories he has become a fictional character himself – and moreover, one whose story is being told by Robert Armin, the actor who played the fool rôles for Shakespeare. It is just as possible, therefore, that the stage fool of Shakespeare's plays influenced Armin's 'creation' of Will Somers.

Richard Tarlton, jester to Elizabeth I, also found a kind of literary fame by living on in the popular imagination as the supposed author of a published jest-book. *Tarlton's Jests* (1611) is attributed to him, but is in fact of dubious authorship, and probably written about twenty years after his death by someone attempting to capitalize on the memory of the famous entertainer. It consists largely of stories of the jester's own exploits, both on and off the stage. The tales are crude in structure and often in content as well; their typical subject matter is the way in which the jester, having seemingly been put down by an antagonist or rival, rallies to triumph over his opponent. The following short story is typical of the collection.

How Tarlton Deceived the Watch in Fleet Street

Tarlton having been late at Court and coming homewards through Fleet Street, he espied the Watch and not knowing how to pass them he went very fast, thinking by that means to go unexamined. But the Watchmen, perceiving that he shunned them, stepped to him and commanded him in the Queen's name to stand. 'Stand!' quoth Tarlton. 'Let them stand that can, for I cannot.' So falling down as though he had been drunk, they helped him up and so let him pass.[14]

Between the careers of Somers and Tarlton we can see the changes in status which were taking place during the sixteenth century. Will Somers was Henry VIII's permanent servant and their relationship seems to have been a feudal one. Sandra Billington describes it as follows:

Somers' reputation earned him a place in plays and . . . his

> talents were of the standard of a professional Fool, but the period in which Somers lived was too early for him to have had the freedom to entertain in public. Fools were still owned by their masters, and despite Somers' intelligence and the respect Henry showed for him, Somers' life was bounded by the court: amusing the King and eating and sleeping with the spaniels.[15]

But if Henry VIII effectively maintained a master-slave relationship with his jester, for whom there was no question of pursuing an independent career as a professional public entertainer, things changed rapidly in the middle years of the century. For by the time of Elizabeth's reign, this was precisely what was expected of a royal jester. Tarlton's predecessor in Elizabeth's service, an entertainer known simply as Lockwood, enjoyed royal patronage, but he also travelled all around the country giving performances as a solo entertainer. And Tarlton himself, whom history describes as 'Elizabeth's jester', seems to have lived a triple life. He was, predominantly, a professional actor, a member (inevitably enough) of the Queen's Men who sang, improvised and performed clown's rôles with them, both in London and on tour in the provinces. He was also an innkeeper, with hostelries in Gracechurch Street and Paternoster Row. In fact his main function at court seems to have been an occasional one; rather than living as a resident servant, like Somers, he was actually engaged for special occasions. David Wiles describes Tarlton's rôle at court as follows:

> At court and in private houses, Tarlton's function was to appear at banquets. No common guest, 'he was there of purpose to jest amongst them' (A2v), and he usually stayed until the small hours. When Burleigh entertained the Queen at his house in the Strand, Tarlton appeared 'in his clown's apparel' (A3) – so his rôle as a jester was clearly formalized . . . Crushing personal attacks were interspersed with other types of verbal wit. Singing was central to Tarlton's act . . . and the rhymes which men gave him to cap were often sung rather than spoken.[16]

Thus if Archy Armstrong is unlike the traditional stage image of the Shakespearean fool because he is so much at the centre of court life, Tarlton is unlike it for precisely the opposite reason. Unlike Lear's Fool, or Feste or Touchstone, who are continually on hand to tease or scold their master or mistress, Tarlton, it seems, was wheeled in for special occasions when he was not appearing in a show somewhere else, or busy pulling pints in

Paternoster Row. The Elizabethan and Jacobean period seems to have been a time of the privatization of foolery.

'Invest me in my motley': stage clowns and fool rôles

The Shakespearean fool, then, is not entirely like any single one of the available real-life models. Rather he comprises an amalgamation of traits drawn from all of them. Neither as feudal as Will Somers, nor as financially self-sufficient as Richard Tarlton; not as central to the court as Archy Armstrong, nor as much of an outsider as Lockwood, Feste, Touchstone, Lavatch and Lear's boy retain a critical distance from the hands that feed them, and spend much time testing the limitations of licence.

As regards terminology, fools and jesters are not precisely the same, yet they and their functions overlap. There is a continuum which encompasses the 'natural' village idiot, the simple-minded servant kept about a court expressly to provide amusement and/or a scapegoat, the artificial fool who lives by his wits in counterfeiting folly, and the court entertainer, maintained to tell jokes and stories and to sing songs. Neither in the real-life courts of Europe nor in the plays of Shakespeare can hard and fast distinctions be made between one function and another.

A third term, however, adds another dimension to the problems and confusions of terminology. In *Twelfth Night,* for example, Feste refers to himself throughout as 'fool', and his mistress Olivia uses the phrase 'an allowed fool' (I, v, l. 93) – a term which reminds us of the ever-present relationship between jesting and power. Curio, on the other hand, talks of him as 'Feste the jester' (II, iv, l. 11). In the words which the audience hear, therefore, Feste is both jester and fool. In the earliest printed texts of the play, however, in stage directions, in the *dramatis personae* and in the character's speech tag he is continually referred to as 'Clown'.

Our own contemporary image of the clown is derived primarily from the European and American circus and pantomime traditions of the nineteenth and early twentieth centuries. The figure we recognize as 'the clown', with his (rarely her!) stylized make-up, his pratfalls and his slapstick, was first made famous by such figures as Joseph Grimaldi in the early nineteenth century and later developed by such well-known circus clowns as Coco. But the word has a very different meaning in the second half of the sixteenth century, when it first appears in the English language: it means 'rustic' or 'countryman'.

This sudden appearance of the word in the language is significant – as is the way its meaning developed. It referred in the first instance simply to someone from the countryside and could be used, potentially at least, as a neutral term, implying no particular attitude on the part of the speaker. Ben Jonson uses it this way in his country-house poem 'To Penshurst', when he envisages all the local villagers, 'the farmer and the clown', coming to Penshurst 'to salute / Thy lord and lady' (ll. 48–50).[17] Sixteenth- and seventeenth-century scholars even invented a false etymology for the word, deriving it from the Latin 'Colonus, one that plougheth the ground'.[18] Thus Richard Tarlton was both jester and clown. Or, perhaps more precisely, as a contemporary rhyme about him explains, he would habitually 'counterfeit' . . . [a] Clown with coat of russet hue'.[19] This russet countryman's coat suggests an important change of meaning between the Elizabethan sense of the word 'clown' and our twentieth-century understanding of it.

The Elizabethan sense of the word, however, was not entirely stable either. Almost immediately it took on a secondary meaning: a 'clown' was someone slow-witted, ignorant, crass or boorish. And on the stage, actors like Richard Tarlton counterfeited the clown and turned the countryman into a figure of fun. This is, to some extent, a feature of the age-old antagonism between city and country: the slow and simple country bumpkin seems to have been a favourite butt of jokes for city-dwellers for as long as cities have stood.

There is also, though, something historically specific about this double meaning of the word. This sense of 'clown' to mean 'rustic' is particularly pertinent to the way the word is used in Elizabethan drama: the Elizabethan theatre, largely based as it was on the south bank of the Thames, was an essentially urban phenomenon. The growth of London as a cultural and economic centre meant that there was a newly expanded, self-confident urban population, happy to laugh at passing rustics up for a day's or a week's trading. While there were few other towns of any size in Elizabethan England, London was the home for about 5 per cent of the country's population by 1600; its own population had increased by (at the most conservative estimate) 150 per cent in sixty years and it was, by the time of Elizabeth's death, the fourth largest city in Europe. 'The city' in the context of Elizabethan and Jacobean England means simply London; there were no others. 'The country' means everywhere else.

Moreover, this expansion of London was in part brought about by a vast migration of country people to the city, driven by a mixture of economic and social pressures. There was, therefore, no shortage of countrymen come up from the provinces – as the young Shakespeare himself had once done from his home in the Midlands. The stereotype of the slow-witted countryman allowed the city-folk of Elizabethan London to pride themselves on their own comparative intelligence and sharpness: it is unlikely that the fact that many of them had once been 'clowns' themselves would have diminished their laughter.

The development of the clown as a figure of fun in English professional comedy parallels similar theatrical developments in mainland Europe. The professional comedians of the Italian *commedia dell'arte*, for example, had developed a series of comic routines based around the masks of the *zanni* – from which we get the modern English word 'zany'. '*Zanni*' (short for Giovanni, or John) was the sixteenth-century Venetian nickname for the Bergamese peasants of the Po valley, who flooded into the towns after Bergamo was conquered by Venice. This was the result of Venice's policy of colonial expansion, sponsored by the great banking families, and as a consequence the influx of cheap foodstuffs from newly conquered lands meant that the Bergamese *zanni* were unable to sell their own produce. Effectively bankrupted, threatened by famine, thousands left their lands and moved to the city in search of work to keep themselves from starving. A contemporary commentator noted that they are

> coarse fellows, simple and good natured enough, who come down from the mountains of Bergamo to fetch and carry for the rest of mankind . . . Their dress is utterly uncivilized, and you can smell their sacking miles away. Their speech is so grotesque that the *zanni* who are like magpies to mimic a pronunciation or any other characteristic have adopted it in their comedies to entertain the crowd.[20]

The *zanni* thus became comic characters, often servants in the plot, and notable for their ignorance and buffoonery. A broad strand of the comic tradition in European theatre seems to derive from the townsman's finding the countryman terribly amusing.

In *A Midsummer Night's Dream* most of the last act is taken up with laughing at 'clowns', as Bottom and his companions attempt with indifferent success to stage the story of Pyramus and Thisbe. Here the historical connections between Shakespeare's mechanicals and the bumpkin *zanni* of the *commedia dell'arte* are made in an unexpected way during the closing moments of the act. Having starred in the tragedy of 'Pyramus and Thisbe', Bottom turns to the assembled aristocrats and asks 'Will it please you to see the epilogue or to hear a bergomask dance between two of our company?' (*Dream,* V, i, ll. 346–8). Duke Theseus declines the epilogue and opts for the 'bergomask dance'. Most modern productions play this as a bit of rather ill-performed country dancing – and their instinct is quite right. The Oxford English Dictionary defines a bergomask as 'a rustic dance, framed in imitation of the people of Bergamo (a province in the state of Venice) ridiculed as clownish in their manners and dialect'.[21] The roots of this joke run deep.

As it happens, Bottom and his friends are Athenian artisans, and that, in the world of *A Midsummer Night's Dream* makes them city-dwellers rather than countrymen. Even so, they are still, strictly speaking, clowns. I am using the word not just to describe how they come across (i.e. as funny), but how they function in the play. And, indeed, in some scenes in the Quarto and the Folio editions of the play, Bottom – like Feste – is referred to in the stage directions as 'Clowne'.

This is, in part, a reflection of a social change which the play acknowledges. By the 1590s the regional antagonism between country and city which is implicit in the original use of the term was being assimilated into the more complex tensions and antagonisms between different social groupings within the city itself. And so, just as the word 'clown' changed from its original meaning of, simply, 'a countryman' to its more general one of 'an ill-educated, boorish, ignorant person', so the figure of the clown changed and developed; it was no longer necessary for him to be literally a country-dweller. Like his real-life counterparts, he could be transposed to the city and still serve his original function. Or, as a later culture put it: 'you can take the boy out of the country, but you can't take the country out of the boy'. The Elizabethan satirist Samuel Rowlands, writing in 1599, makes the point that by the end of the century at least, comic stereotypes based purely on rustic boorishness are rather out-of-date. He takes to task two contemporary actors:

> . . . What means Singer then
> And Pope the clown to speak so boorish, when
> They counterfeit the clowns upon the stage?
> Since country fellows grow in this same age
> To be so quaint in their new-printed speech
> That cloth will now compare with velvet breech.[22]

The changing meaning of the word clown, however, had as much to do with the organization of the Elizabethan acting company as it did with urban class conflict. Feste and Bottom are very different kinds of character, and yet, as pointed out above, in stage directions they are both called 'Clowns'. And this is an important point: the word 'clown' is frequently found in the stage directions of plays of the period, but hardly ever in the dialogue. This is because in the Elizabethan theatre the word is used to designate not a character, but an actor. The 'Clown' referred to in the stage directions and the speech-tags is the particular member of the acting company who will say the lines and play the part: the member of the company who specializes in comic rôles – the company clown. As David Wiles has shown in his book *Shakespeare's Clown: Actor and Text in the Elizabethan Playhouse*,[23] professional companies would employ (or include as a shareholding partner) one or more actors whose function was specifically to take on these clown rôles and, often, to write and perform a 'jig' at the end of the play.

The word thus becomes an increasingly technical one in the theatrical vocabulary of the period, developing through a series of meanings. Originally a synonym for countryman, then a word for an ignorant boor, the word 'clown' rapidly becomes part of playhouse terminology, referring to a highly skilled specialist member of the personnel, as important in his own way as the leading actor – or the playwright.

'No more than is set down for them': improvisation, jigs and drolls

In *Hamlet* the Prince, famously, gives the travelling players a lecture on drama; one of his rules is that an acting company should

> let those that play the clowns speak no more than is set down for them; for there be of them that will themselves laugh to set on some quantity of barren spectators to laugh too, though in the mean time some necessary question of the play be then to be considered. That's villainous, and shows a most pitiful ambition in the fool that uses it.
>
> (*Hamlet*, III, ii, ll. 38–45)

It is sometimes suggested that here we have Shakespeare the writer speaking through Hamlet the character in order to articulate his own professional grievance against the 'low' humour of the clowns and their tendency to detract from the serious business of the verse. In fact, this is rather an oversimplification. Shakespeare, after all, was a practical man of the theatre as well as a playwright, and a shareholder in the Lord Chamberlain's Men. As a playwright, certainly, he had reason enough to want to look after the words he wrote; but he had no reason for seeing these words as sacrosanct, as later generations of scholars and critics have done. He would have needed to understand as well as anyone the importance of the clown's improvisatory skills in the success of a company, even when the company was putting on a tragedy. Hamlet's words are spoken by a novice playwright lecturing professional actors on the ethics of their craft, and doing so for very particular reasons: the play's words, after all, are designed to 'catch the conscience of the King' (*Hamlet*, II, ii, l. 606). It is not necessary to read this moment as a manifesto of Shakespeare's own attitudes towards clowns and the skills of improvisation.

Nonetheless, the speech clearly suggests a potential tension in the Elizabethan theatre company, to which Shakespeare might not have been totally immune: the tension between the conflicting demands of the clown and the playwright, between the high-art aesthetic which privileged the written word, and the popular tradition of performance which valued clowning and improvisation. Hamlet, after all, was not entirely wrong: the skill of the clown was first and foremost the skill of improvisation, as the following anecdote from *Tarlton's Jests* illustrates.

> It chanced that in the midst of a play, after long expectation for Tarlton, being much desired of the people, at length he came forth, where (at his entrance) one in the gallery pointed his finger at him, saying to a friend that had never seen him, 'That is he.'
>
> Tarlton, to make sport at the least occasion given him, and seeing the man point with the finger, he in love again held up two fingers. The captious fellow, jealous of his wife (for he was married) and because a player did it, took the matter more heinously and asked him why he made horns at him. 'No,' quoth Tarlton, 'they be fingers . . .'
>
> 'No, no,' says the fellow, 'you gave me the horns.'
>
> 'True,' says Tarlton, 'for my fingers are tipped with nails which are like horns, and I must make a show of that which you are sure of.'
>
> This matter grew so, that the more he meddled, the more it was for his disgrace; wherefore the standers-by counseled him to depart, both he and his horns, lest his cause grow desperate.[24]

The story may be apocryphal, as many in *Tarlton's Jests* are, but it suggests the directness of the playhouse relationship between a clown and his audience. Not just a speaker of other men's lines, Tarlton looks 'to make sport at the least occasion given him' and has no qualms about entering into dialogue – and even confrontation – with the audience. The play, meanwhile, takes second place. The tension which Hamlet suggests between the demands of the text and the demands of the comic performer is illustrated in this anecdote of the early Elizabethan theatre.

As the Elizabethan theatre developed, however, theatre companies found a way of negotiating this tension. During the 1590s the custom arose of allowing the clown the freedom of the stage after the play was over, thereby giving him an area in which to allow his skills full rein. Thus there grew up within the Elizabethan theatre a tradition of 'postludes', events after the play, in which the clown played a central part. Initiated by Richard Tarlton as simple encores, in which he would improvise verses and songs in dialogue with the audience, these postludes grew into entertainments in their own right, known as jigs.[25]

In current English usage the word 'jig' means a dance, but the performance which took place in the Elizabethan theatre was much more than this. It was, in effect, a small playlet, a sketch or pantomime, sometimes a solo piece for the clown alone, sometimes for other actors as well. Although few examples of Elizabethan jigs survive, some of them, mainly those which were written or performed by a famous clown, were licensed for publication. Thus in the Stationer's Register in the 1590s we find the following entries relating to jigs by Will Kempe.

> 28 December (1591)
> *Thomas Gosson* Entered for his copy under the hand of Mr Watkins, the third and last part of Kempe's Jig, so it appertain not to any other.
>
> ii^{do} die Maii (1595)
> *William Blackwall* Entered for his copy under Mr Warden Bing's hand, a ballad, of Mr Kempe's New Jig of the Kitchen-Stuff Woman.
>
> 21 October (1595)
> *Tho. Gosson* Entered for his copy under the hand of the Wardens, a Ballad called Kempe's New Jig betwixt a soldier and a miser and Sym the clown.[26]

The Elizabethan jig included both music and dancing, but it also contained dialogue, which was probably sung, and it told a story, usually a bawdy one (the word 'jig' itself has an obscene meaning in Elizabethan slang). Whether or not their introduction into the evening's entertainment did, as Wiles suggests, resolve the tension between playwright and clown is a matter for conjecture. Inevitably jigs attracted the attention and the abuse of Puritan inveighers against the theatre, but playwrights also continue, throughout the period, to make slighting references to the custom. Marlowe speaks of offering an alternative to the 'jigging veins of rhyming mother wits / And such conceits as clownage keeps in pay';[27] Jonson makes slighting reference to 'the concupiscence of jigs and dances';[28] and Thomas Dekker complains about audiences who prefer 'a nasty bawdy jig' to 'some worthy tragedy'.[29] Shakespeare has Hamlet insult Polonius by saying to him that he would rather see 'a jig or a tale of bawdry' (*Hamlet*, II, ii, l. 502) than a good play.

The jig, however, was a popular feature with the audiences in the Elizabethan playhouses – so much so, in fact, that it eventually became a victim of its own success. In 1612 the magistrates at the Middlesex General Session of the Peace issued 'An Order for suppressing of Jigges at the ende of Playes':

> Whereas complaint have been made at this last General Sessions, that by reason of certain lewd jigs, songs and dances used and accustomed at the playhouse called The Fortune in Goulding Lane, diverse cutpurses and other lewd and ill-disposed persons in great multitudes do resort thither at the end of every play, many times causing tumults and outrages.[30]

The magistrates are responding not merely to the threat of public morality caused by the contents of the performances themselves, but also the threat to public order caused by their popularity – especially among 'lewd and ill-disposed persons'. This popularity might have been at least partially due to the theatre managements' custom of allowing customers free or much-reduced entry for this part of the programme. At any rate, the popularity of the jigs led to steps being taken to suppress them.

The texts of some Elizabethan jigs have come down to us, although the verbal skeleton they provide gives us only a shadowy idea of the comic performance which they generated. *Singing Simpkin*, for example, is a jig probably performed by, though not written by, Will Kempe. In it Simpkin is trying to woo the wife of an old man. Bluster, his rival, appears at the house and Simpkin is forced to hide in a chest, from where he comments ironically on Bluster's unsuccessful wooing. The woman's husband then also arrives home; Bluster attempts unsuccessfully to hide in the same chest as Simpkin. The wife concocts a tale to satisfy her husband whereby Bluster pretends to be searching for a thief. When Simpkin climbs out of the chest, he continues his attempted seduction of the wife, but the old man overhears, and beats him out of the house. The following short extract gives a flavour of the piece: it is the moment when the husband returns to interrupt Bluster's wooing of the wife; Simpkin is hiding in the chest, and the lines he speaks are audible only to the audience.

> *Wife* I have a place behind here,

Which yet is known to no man
Simpkin She has a place before, too,
But that is all too common

(*Old man within*)

Old Man Wife, wherefore is the door thus barr'd
What mean you pray by this?
Wife Alas, it is my husband
Simpkin I laugh now till I piss.
Bluster Open the chest, I'll into it
My life else it may cost.
Wife Alas I cannot open it.
Simpkin I believe the key is lost.[31]

The humour stems both from the situation, which is the stock one of sexual infidelity, and from the verbal innuendos. Simpkin addresses the audience directly in a series of asides designed to let them in on the joke. The doggerel rhythms of the verses keep the story trotting along at a fast pace; they are regular and strictly scripted. Improvisation, in fact, has turned back into performance of written text, for the jig as a whole is fully scripted, set to music and sung.

The function of the jig was, on one level, to act as an afterpiece to the play – be it comedy or tragedy – and to send the audience home laughing. It also allowed a modulation between the world of the play and the world of everyday reality, inhabiting an ambiguous ground which contained elements of both popular and high-art traditions of entertainment. The jig was both separate from, but also an integral part of, the dramatic performance. In some ways it must be seen to relate to the play-world itself. The problem is that we cannot tell quite how this relation might have worked, since we do not know which jigs were played at the end of which plays. If *Singing Simpkin* were to be played after a performance of *Julius Caesar* it would have a markedly different effect from if it were played after *The Merry Wives of Windsor.* Indeed, since *The Merry Wives* itself contains farcical scenes of would-be adulterers attempting to hide from jealous husbands, the effect there would probably have been simply rather repetitive! Similarly, *Attowell's Jig* repeats elements of the plot of *All's Well That End's Well.*[32] Thus there is no absolute distinction between the jig and the play 'proper': they were able to share elements, and comedies in particular were able to reassimilate into themselves narrative lines which were derived from the clown's jig. Perhaps this, too, was a way of negotiating a tension between clown and playwright.

It has been argued that the jig purveyed a world of anarchy, which counterbalanced the harmonies of the world of the main play.[33] Attractive though the idea is, it does not ring entirely true: for one thing, not all the main plays of the period end in harmony. Equally, the jig does not necessarily embody anarchy. *Singing Simpkin,* typically, is bawdy and farcical, but it is hardly anarchic. It treads familiar comic ground (old men with young wives, lovers hiding from husbands) and ends in a way which offers no threat to conventional morality: Simpkin is beaten away by the husband and his attempted seduction fails.

We simply do not know what effect the jig would have had on any single performance. It is important, though, that we remember that it existed. In Shakespeare's theatre, the end of the play might not be the end of the evening's entertainment. After the final speeches, the applause, the epilogue, the clearing of the stage, there is a further element – the unknown jig which for Elizabethan theatre-goers was the true completion of the performance.

The jig, then, shares the stage with the comedy (or the tragedy!), and developed in response to the problem which Hamlet articulates about clowns speaking more than is set down for them. Another dramatic form which developed rather later in relation to comic theatrical conventions is the droll. Hamlet's remarks are relevant to this, too, and although the droll strictly belongs to a later chapter in theatrical history, it is worth considering briefly here; for in the development of the droll some of the Prince's worst fears were realized. Hamlet is concerned, in effect, about the way in which laughter can take over the stage: he sees this as a threat to the seriousness of his drama – a pandering to the lowest common denominator. Yet it can be seen in other ways, too.

When Civil War broke out in England in 1642, all the theatres were closed, and remained so throughout the time of the Commonwealth until the Restoration of Charles II in 1660. What was initially a temporary measure at a time of crisis became a more permanent legislative fact in 1647 when the victorious Parliamentarians, their ranks swelled by Puritans long hostile to the theatre, outlawed the staging of plays and performances by decree. In fact, like so many attempts to curb art by means of the law, the legislation was only partly effective. Throughout the period of the closure of the theatres, surreptitious performances were given in private houses, in fairgrounds and taverns, and occasionally in the old closed theatres themselves. Often broken up by soldiers, these clandestine performances needed, by their very nature, to be portable, makeshift and short. Rarely was a full play performed; instead there grew up an 'underground' dramatic genre called the 'droll', which consisted of extracts from old plays, simplified and adapted for these new illegal playing conditions. This meant, in effect, that they were short comic interludes, suitable to be played quickly, so that the actors could make a quick profit and then disappear. While the anti-theatrical laws were repealed in 1660, and licensed performances once again allowed, these unofficial theatrical performances continued until the end of the eighteenth century, long after the disappearance of those conditions which had originally made them necessary.

There are records of the existence of three Shakespearean drolls of the Commonwealth period, although more may have been played which have since vanished. In 1662 a printer and bookseller called Henry Marsh took advantage of the new liberalism to bring out a printed edition of some of these drolls, which had previously existed only in manuscript. Edited by Francis Kirkman, the volume was entitled *The Wits, or Sport Upon Sport*,[34] and it contained twenty-six drolls in all, including 'The Merry Conceits of Bottom the Weaver' which was based upon *A Midsummer Night's Dream* and 'The Bouncing Knight' derived from the *Henry IV* plays – the knight of the title being, of course, Falstaff. An illustration in this collection shows Falstaff drinking downstage with 'the Hostess' (Mistress Quickly), on a stage also peopled by characters from other drolls based on plays by Fletcher, Massinger, Middleton, Rowley and others. From behind a curtain peeps a fool, uttering the words 'Tu quoque' ('You too are a fool'). Because this illustration is a composite and not intended to represent a single performance, we cannot draw firm conclusions from it regarding the staging, yet the mood of it is unmistakeable: these are characters turned into grotesques. As their titles might suggest, these drolls took as their centrepiece the most obviously clownish scenes from the plays; Bottom and Falstaff are such well-known Shakespearean comic characters that we need not be greatly surprised that they formed the centrepiece of these entertainments. More surprising, perhaps, is the third one: 'The Grave-Makers' is based on *Hamlet*. The Prince who lectured the players so austerely against playing for laughs would have been aghast to find his own story shrunk to a clowning routine.

Clowns who speak more than is set down for them; bastardized versions of tragedies and histories turned into comic interludes: looked at in one way these are simply what semioticians would describe as 'noise' – irrelevant and irritating distractions which prevent the 'true' meanings of great works like *Hamlet*, *Henry IV*, or *A Midsummer Night's Dream* from getting through to us. Looked at in another way, however, they can be seen as a repeated tendency of comedy, of laughter, to shoulder its way into the limelight, to upstage art and seriousness. When John Manningham, a student at one of the Inns of Court, went to see The Lord Chamberlain's Men play *Twelfth Night* in 1602, what he remembered most was Malvolio's silly smile and funny costume.[35] When the Swiss traveller Thomas Platter went to see *Julius Caesar* at the Globe Theatre in 1599, his most vivid memory of it was that 'when the play was over, they danced very marvellously and gracefully together as is their wont, two dressed as men and two as women'.[36]

In Shakespeare's comedies, there is a repeated movement of *displacement*. The clowns, as Hamlet feared they might, get to take over. Like festivals of inversion, these are places where the marginalized, the oppressed, the suppressed and the subservient may occasionally take centre stage, and where the clowns may speak more than is set down for them. No wonder, then, that Hamlet was worried. To anyone concerned with controlling established meanings the clown, and all he stands for, pose a threat. To this extent the Danish Prince is in unlikely alliance with those Middlesex magistrates who published the order suppressing jigs, with Malvolio who detests such 'set kind of fools' (*Twelfth Night*, I, v, l. 85) as Feste, and with Malvolio's real-life counterparts, the moralists of all persuasions who agreed in condemning 'Clowns clad as well with country condition as in rough russet . . . [and] Fools as fond as might be'.[37]

These Elizabethans are heir to a medieval tradition which is deeply suspicious of fools and folly. Many polytheistic cultures have trickster-gods: Hermes in Greece and the North American animal tricksters are good examples. But monotheistic religions have tended to exclude this attribute of the deity. A monotheistic God does not play jokes upon his subjects, and fools and tricksters in the Christian tradition have often been seen as diabolical rather than divine. Thus one official theological attitude towards the fool during the Middle Ages and the Renaissance was one of disapproval: folly and foolery came to be associated with the devil. When Erasmus wrote his playful and ironic *Praise of Folly*[38] in the sixteenth century, he sailed very close to the wind of blasphemy.

Yet Erasmus could refer back to an existing image which was kept alive despite this official disapproval: the image of the holy fool. In the Greek there is available a play on the words 'Christos' (Christ) and 'chrestos' (fool). St Paul in his first Epistle to the Corinthians talks of Christians becoming 'fools for Christ's sake', 'for the wisdom of the world is foolishness with God' and 'the foolishness of God is wiser than men'[39] and plays with the familiar paradox of the need to become foolish in order to learn wisdom. More importantly, as Sandra Billington shows in her book *A Social*

History of the Fool,[40] mystery plays frequently made the association between Christ and the fool: in the trial and torture scenes of the York cycle, for example, Herod and his soldiers treat Christ as the seasonal Christmas fool, the entertainer in Yuletide revelries. Like the fools and clowns in Shakespeare's works, the historical fool is a thing of paradox which dramatizes the truism that at the limits of discursive reason, wisdom and foolery are not easily distinguished. I am writing this on Friday 1 April 1994, which is both Good Friday and All Fool's Day.

Notes

1. See, for example, Roberta Mullini, 'Playing the fool: the pragmatic status of Shakespeare's clowns' *New Theatre Quarterly* I (1985), pp. 98–104; David Wiles, *Shakespeare's Clown: Actor and Text in the Elizabethan Playhouse* (Cambridge: Cambridge University Press, 1987); Guy Butler, 'Shakespeare and the two jesters', *Hebrew University Studies in Literature and the Arts,* 11 (1983), pp. 161–204; C. S. Felver, *Robert Armin, Shakespeare's Fool* (Kent: Ohio University Press, 1961).
2. Chaucer, *The House of Fame,* in *Works,* ed. F. N. Robinson (London: Oxford University Press, 1957), pp. 280–302.
3. Harley Ms. 3885, fol. 19.
4. In the Oxford edition of Shakespeare's *Complete Works,* the folio and quarto versions of *King Lear* are both printed separately, rather than being conflated, as is more usual editorial practice. The quarto edition is the only one in which these lines appear.
5. Nicholas Breton, *The Good and the Bad, or Descriptions of the Worthies and Unworthies of this Age* (London, 1616), sig. D4.
6. Enid Welsford, *The Fool: His Social and Literary History* (London: Faber and Faber, 1935).
7. Sir James Frazer, *The Golden Bough,* 3rd edn, revised and enlarged (London: Macmillan, 1911–15).
8. William Willeford, *The Fool and His Sceptre* (London: Edward Arnold, 1969), p. 14.
9. Sandra Clark, *A Shakespeare Dictionary* (London: Century Hutchinson, 1986), p. 140.
10. Theodore B. Leinwand, 'Conservative fools in James's court and Shakespeare's plays', *Shakespeare Studies* 19, pp. 219–37.
11. Thomas Nashe, *Summer's Last Will and Testament* (London, 1600).
12. William Rowley, *When You See Me You Know Me* (London, 1604).
13. H. F. Lippincott, ed., *A Shakespeare Jestbook: Robert Armin's Foole Upon Foole (1600)* (Salzburg: Institut für Englische Sprache, 1973), p. 128.
14. P. M. Zall, ed., *A Nest of Ninnies and Other English Jestbooks of the Seventeenth Century* (Lincoln: University of Nebraska Press, 1970), pp. 91–2.

15. Sandra Billington, *A Social History of the Fool* (Brighton: Harvester Press, 1984), p. 35.
16. Wiles, *Shakespeare's Clown*, p. 15.
17. Ben Jonson, 'To Penshurst', in Ian Donaldson, ed., *Ben Jonson* (Oxford: Oxford University Press, 1985), p. 283.
18. Thomas Fuller, *History of the Worthies of England* (London, 1662), vol. 2, p. 177.
19. Harley Ms. 3885, fol. 19.
20. T. Garzoni, *Piazza Universale* (1585), quoted by John Rudlin in *Commedia dell' arte: an Actor's Handbook* (London: Routledge, 1994), p. 68.
21. *The Compact Edition of the Oxford English Dictionary* (Oxford: Oxford University Press, 1971), p. 203.
22. Samuel Rowlands, *The Letting of Humour's Blood in the Head-Vein* (1599), reprinted in S. J. Herrtage, ed., *Complete Works* (Glasgow: Hunterian Club, 1880), vol. 1, p. 63.
23. Wiles, *Shakespeare's Clown*, pp. 61–72.
24. Zall, *A Nest of Ninnies*, p. 92.
25. Wiles, *Shakespeare's Clown*, pp. 43–60.
26. Cited in Chris Harris, *Will Kempe: Shakespeare's Forgotten Clown* (Waddesdon, Bucks: Kylin Press, 1983), p. 14.
27. Christopher Marlowe, *Tamburlaine*, Prologue, ll. 1–2, in E. D. Pendry and J. C. Maxwell, eds, *Complete Plays and Poems* (London: J. M. Dent, 1976).
28. Ben Jonson, *Bartholomew Fair*, Induction, ll. 126–7, ed. G. R. Hibbard (London: Ernest Benn, 1977), p. 12.
29. Thomas Dekker, *A Strange Horse-Race* (1613), in A. B. Grosart, ed., *The Non-Dramatic Works* (London: Hazell Watson and Viney, 1884–6), vol. 3, p. 340.
30. Cited in Andrew Gurr, *Playgoing in Shakespeare's London* (Cambridge: Cambridge University Press, 1987), pp. 225–6.
31. Reprinted in Harris, *Will Kempe*, p. 17.
32. Reprinted in G. Blakemore Evans, ed., *Elizabethan-Jacobean Drama* (London: A. & C. Black, 1987), pp. 365–71.
33. Wiles, *Shakespeare's Clown*, p. 43ff.
34. Francis Kirkman, *The Wits, or Sport Upon Sport* (London: Henry Marsh, 1662).
35. Reprinted in J. M. Lothian and T. W. Craik, eds, *Twelfth Night* (London: Methuen, 1975), p. xxvi.
36. Reprinted in Blakemore Evans, *Elizabethan-Jacobean Drama*, pp. 56–7.
37. William Rankins, *A Mirror of Monsters* (London, 1587), p. 7.
38. Desiderius Erasmus, *The Praise of Folly* (1511), ed. P. S. Allen (Oxford: Clarendon Press, 1910).
39. I Corinthians 4:10, 3:19, 1:25.
40. Billington, *A Social History of the Fool*, p. 35.

3 An audience for comedy

Stage and audience

Sitting alone, reading something funny, we may smile or chuckle. In company, hearing a joke, we may laugh more loudly, sharing the laughter, being infected by it and using it to communicate our own pleasure. Laughter, as we know, depends upon context. Well-funded psychological research into humour and laughter has foundered because the subjects were tested under laboratory conditions: 'Please sit down, look at this joke, on a funniness scale of one to ten, where would you rate it?' Humour is precisely that which escapes laboratory conditions. It exists as a function of the human relationships which engender it. In the same vein, dramatic texts – scripts – have their existence primarily in a public context: the moment of meeting between stage and audience. This is not to say that an audience always creates the conditions which make laughter possible. The very reverse may be the case: sitting in a theatre, seeing something we find amusing, we may suppress a laugh because no-one else is laughing; or else we may be carried away by the hilarity of others, laughing uproariously at something which in another context would have not seemed in the least bit funny. The dimension of the audience in theatre is something which is becoming more clearly understood; in this section I want to look at the experience of Elizabethan theatre-going in order to suggest ways in which it contributes to elements of Shakespearean comedy.

First of all, we need to remember that while we can construct a general picture of the Elizabethan theatre and its audience, there was in fact a great variety of different theatres, different kinds of performance events, and different kinds of audiences. The problem with trying to recreate a sense of Elizabethan playing and audience conditions is that it often seems rather reductive, rather static – as if there was a single typical way of doing things and that it was always more or less like that. The truth is that during the period which we often call for convenience the Elizabethan and Jacobean age, and which actually comprises the years between the opening of London's first purpose-built commercial playhouse (the Theatre in Shoreditch) in 1576 and the closing of all the playhouses at the time of Civil War in 1642, most things about the theatre were continually changing: designs of buildings, patterns of theatre-going, playwriting techniques and acting styles were developing all the time.

Nor, at any one time, was there a single 'typical' audience. Audiences in the Elizabethan theatre differed one from another, as they do now. In contemporary terms we might think about the differences between the audience at the first night of a new play at the National Theatre, the audience at a star-studded pantomime in a provincial repertory theatre just after Christmas, the audience at an amateur production of an Agatha Christie whodunnit, the audience for a stand-up comic at a working men's club in Chorlton-cum-Hardy and so forth. All these are distinct entities, each with their own codes, understandings and expectations. The theatre of Shakespeare's time also catered for diverse audiences, and the most recent research into patterns of playgoing during the late sixteenth and early seventeenth centuries suggests that between 1576 and 1642, different theatres came to cater for different tastes, with audiences at those theatres in the north of London having a reputation for being on the whole less well-educated and less discerning than their equivalents on Bankside.[1] Playhouses began to develop reputations for presenting particular kinds of plays, addressing perhaps particular kinds of audiences. A contemporary poem, for example, extols the virtues of the 'manly' plays to be seen at the Bull, as opposed to the soppy romances of the Globe and the Swan:

> The players of the Bankside
> The round Globe and the Swan
> Will teach you idle tricks of love,
> But the Bull will play the man.[2]

Shakespeare learned about these different audiences early on. His earliest comedies were written freelance, and staged by various companies at various theatres. After 1594, however, he was writing exclusively for the Lord Chamberlain's Men who were playing primarily at the Theatre in Shoreditch. Thus he had a chance to develop a longer-term relationship with a particular theatre audience – an experience which was repeated when the Lord Chamberlain's Men moved in 1599 to the Globe on Bankside. Some of the middle comedies date from this period and they do fit the description of the 'idle tricks of love' mentioned in the poem. By the time Shakespeare was working on his 'late plays' the company, by now known as the King's Men, was also playing at the smaller, more elaborately equipped and more expensive indoor theatre in Blackfriars which the Burbage family had acquired years earlier, and which in 1608 was finally licensed for their performances.

But as well as their permanent London theatres, the Lord Chamberlain's Men/Kings Men – like other London acting companies – would also have performed in a variety of other venues, and would have needed to be able to address a variety of audiences. They regularly played at court, for an audience of royalty and courtiers by the command of the Master of the Revels (who is parodied in the character of Philostrate in *A Midsummer Night's Dream*). They provided entertainment at feasts and celebrations for important municipal or professional bodies, such as the various Inns of Court. For the wealthy private individual, too, it was possible to hire a professional company to play at a wedding feast, just as Duke Theseus commissions a dramatic entertainment for his wedding night in *A Midsummer Night's Dream.*

While the theatre profession was usually completely London-based, there were times when theatres in the capital were closed down by the authorities because of the perceived risk of contagion in times of plague. Even before the proliferation of the commercial public theatres, the (not unjustified) fear that large gatherings of people would encourage the pestilence to spread led to exhortations such as the following:

> . . . the present time requireth you to have good care and use good means touching the contagion of sickness, that the sick be kept from the whole, that the places of persons infected be made plain to be known, and the more relieved . . . that unnecessary and scarcely honest resorts to plays, to shows, to the occasions of throngs and press . . . may be avoided.[3]

When the number of plague deaths rose to forty per week the theatres were closed by decree. This could involve a closure of a few weeks – or of much longer duration. In the summer of 1592 London was hit by a devastating epidemic which caused the deaths of over twenty thousand people. The theatres were closed more or less completely until the middle of 1594. The loss of the regular audience in the capital meant that major London companies were often obliged to seek an alternative audience in the provinces, joining the ranks of travelling players on the road and taking a reduced cast on tour. Touring was harder work and much less profitable than London playing: audiences tended to be smaller (not least for fear of contamination by plague-carrying Londoners), there was the difficulty of the continual travelling and setting-up, and there were the extra expenses of accommodation. Nonetheless, these tours provided much-needed supplementary income for the company. Some of the venues, too, were relatively prestigious: major companies would frequently play at great houses, or at the universities of Oxford and Cambridge.

In London and elsewhere (but particularly in the capital) Elizabethan theatre audiences frequently received a bad press. Whereas today theatre-going – especially to see a play by Marlowe or Jonson or Shakespeare – is afforded the stamp of approval of high culture, that was by no means the case in Elizabethan England. In 1594 the Lord Mayor of London made no secret of his opinion of

> . . . the quality of such as frequent the said plays, being the ordinary places of meeting for all vagrant persons and masterless men that hang about the City: thieves, horse-stealers, whoremongers, cozeners, conycatching persons, practisers of treason, and other such like . . . [4]

This kind of rhetoric could be heard from many of the anti-stage propagandists, Puritans and others, whose argument was not only that theatres attracted reprobates, but that they created them; that sex and violence in the media were responsible for many of the ills of society, and that the representation of vice on the stage would lead to its inevitable increase in society:

> If you will learn how to be false and deceive your husbands, or husbands their wives, how to play the harlots, to obtain one's love, how to ravish, how to beguile, how to betray, to flatter, lie, swear, forswear, how to allure to whoredom, how to murder, how to poison, how to disobey and rebel against princes, to consume treasures prodigally, to move to lusts, to ransack and spoil cities and towns, to be idle, to blaspheme, to sing filthy songs of love, to speak filthily, to be proud, how to mock, scoff and deride any nation . . . shall you not learn, then, at such interludes how to practise them?[5]

These are the same voices as those who condemned the traditions of carnival, the May-games and misrule of the calendary festivals. A moral disapproval of theatre-going is linked with an even more strenuous disapproval of the actors, playhouse-owners and playwrights – with the whole business of presenting dramatic fictions. At their most extreme such critics would argue that there is no difference between a stage portrayal of a crime and the crime itself; that the actors are as wicked in themselves as any of the vicious characters they portray.

> Are they not notoriously known to be those men in their life abroad as they are on stage: roisters, brawlers, ill-dealers, boasters, lovers, loiterers, ruffians? So that, they are always exercised

> in playing their parts and practising wickedness, making that an art, to the end they might better gesture in their parts. For who can better play the ruffian than a very ruffian? Who better the lover than they who make it a common exercise?[6]

Even those who might, in other circumstances, have been quite tolerant of the theatre, resisted the notion that one should be opened in their backyard. When the Burbage family first acquired the Blackfriars property and applied for planning permission to convert it into a theatre, the local residents got up a successful petition to the Privy Council to prevent it. They complained to the authorities that:

> the said Burbage is now altering and meaneth very shortly to convert and turn the same into a common playhouse, which will grow to be a very great annoyance and trouble, not only to all the noblemen and gentlemen thereabout inhabiting, but also a general inconvenience to all the inhabitants of the same precinct, both by reason of the great resort and gathering together of all manner of vagrant and lewd persons that, under colour of resorting to the plays, will come thither and work all manner of mischief, and also to the great pestering and filling up of the same precinct, if it should please God to send any visitation of sickness . . . and besides, that the same playhouse is so near the Church that the noise of the drums and trumpets will greatly disturb and hinder both the ministers and parishioners in time of divine service and sermons.[7]

The residents of Blackfriars show themselves to be about as enthusiastic about having theatre crowds in the neighbourhood as contemporary middle-class homeowners might be about football crowds or a rock festival. There is, perhaps, a double standard at work here – or at least, a double perspective. As individuals, Elizabethan theatre-goers might cover a broad spectrum of age, class, income and respectability. As a mass, though, they are regarded by the good citizens of Blackfriars (some of whom might, after all, have occasionally themselves gone to playhouses) as a large, dangerous, rowdy, volatile and potentially criminal multitude.

The audience in the theatre

Eyewitness accounts by visitors to London during this period allow us to build up certain images of the theatre-going experience. In the 1590s admission prices were comparatively low: entrance to the pit, or standing-room at the Globe cost one penny; if you wanted a seat you progressed from the pit into the gallery, paying an extra penny as you entered; or if you wanted the most comfortable seats, you paid another penny again and proceeded to the 'lord's room'. These admission prices of between one and three pennies come at a time when a London artisan's wages – a builder or joiner, for example – would be in the region of six shillings and eight shillings per week (72 pence and 96 pence per week). Theatre prices, therefore, started at about $1\frac{1}{2}$ per cent of a worker's weekly income, or, perhaps more pertinently, the price of two pints of ordinary beer. Like everything else, this was subject to variation. Indoor performances at theatres such as Blackfriars were significantly more expensive than outdoor ones, while inflation hit the open-air theatres as well as other sectors of the economy. By 1614 Jonson talks of prices up to half a crown (30 pence) in the newly-opened Hope Theatre.

While the 'lord's room' provided the most comfortable seating in the open-air playhouse, there was a place which could be had for a few extra pennies which some theatre-goers saw as even more desirable – a stool on the stage itself. Thomas Dekker's *The Gull's Horn-Book* is an ironic conduct-book which gives tongue-in-cheek instructions to a young man of fashion as to how he should behave. There is, of course, a chapter in it on theatre-going. The really stylish thing to do, Dekker advises, is to sit, not in the best seats in the auditorium, but on the stage itself:

> For do but cast up a reckoning, what large comings-in are pursed up by sitting on the stage? First, a conspicuous eminence is gotten, by which means the best and most essential parts of a gallant (good clothes, a proportionable leg, white hand, the Persian lock and a tolerable beard) are perfectly revealed . . . By sitting on the stage you may (without travelling for it) at the very next door ask whose play it is; and . . . if you know not the author you may rail at him, and peradventure, so behave yourself, that you may enforce the author to know you . . . It shall crown you with rich commendation to laugh aloud in the midst of the most serious and saddest scene of the terriblest tragedy; and to let that clapper (your tongue) be tossed so high that all the house may ring of it. [If you have a grudge against the author] you shall disgrace him worse than by tossing him in a blanket, or giving him the bastinado in a tavern, if in the middle of his play (be it pastoral or comedy, moral or tragedy), you rise with a screwed and discontented face from your stool to be gone. No matter whether the scenes be good, or no; the better they are the worse you do distaste them; and, being on your feet, sneak not away like a coward,

> but salute all your gentle acquaintance, that are spread either on the rushes, or on stools about you, and draw what troop you can from the stage with you . . . Marry, if either the company or indisposition of the weather bind you to sit it out, my counsel is then that you turn plain ape: take up a rush and tickle the earnest ears of your fellow gallants, to make other fools fall a-laughing; mew at passionate speeches, blare at merry, find fault with the music, whew at the children's action, whistle at the songs, and above all, curse the sharers . . . [8]

The theatre could thus be a place to be seen as well as to see: indeed for Dekker's gull that becomes its primary function. Not only by placing himself in the most prominent position, but by his subsequent behaviour, he does all he can to draw attention from the play to himself, railing against the author and the sharers (the theatre management), distracting the actors and audience alike, and generally showing off.

Dekker is being particularly sour here. He was a playwright himself and presumably he had had experience of his own plays being interrupted by this kind of behaviour. He is also, almost certainly, exaggerating: not all performances would have been subject to such interruptions. But the point which we must take from his account is this: that the dividing line between stage and audience was much less clear than it is today. If you were willing to pay the money you could purchase a stool on stage – becoming part of the spectacle, writing yourself, as it were, into the play.

Even at the best of times, the Elizabethan actor could hardly count on a docile audience. (The analogies with a modern-day sports crowd or rock audience which were suggested earlier are still pertinent here.) Quite what effect this had on actors' performance styles is unclear. There has been much scholarly debate about acting styles in the Elizabethan theatre. Were they comparatively naturalistic? Were they at all like modern acting styles? Were they capable of showing subtle psychological nuances? Or were they stylized and rhetorical, as might be needed to fill large open-air theatres? One thing that most scholars are agreed on is that a quiet, introverted delivery would have been lost at the Globe or the Theatre. This does not necessarily mean that the normal acting style of the period always involved huge displays of histrionics; the way in which Shakespeare parodies such over-the-top displays in Nick Bottom's acting in *A Midsummer Night's Dream* suggests that the theatre had moved beyond that by the mid-1590s. It is more likely that the Elizabethan actor learned how to be large and bombastic when necessary, and more low-key and subtle when he could get away with it. During the 1590s, as the theatre developed, so audiences developed as well, and learned to respond with great sophistication to the increasingly complex theatrical techniques of the playwrights of the time.

Nonetheless, the Elizabethan actor needed to keep the presence of the audience continually in mind, and to be master of a presentational acting style which spoke out to the audience, telling them a story and engaging their interest by means of direct contact. With this in mind it becomes clearer, perhaps, why the clown's skills of improvisation and direct address, discussed in the previous chapter, were so important in the Elizabethan theatre. A Tarlton, a Kempe or an Armin was capable of engaging an audience's attention by virtue of their own personality (or *persona*) as much as by that of the lines they spoke as Launce or Touchstone; and their apprenticeship had been served in Renaissance stand-up routines and battles of wit and improvisation with an audience. The techniques of the comedian, however, are not wholly separate from those of the tragedian, for whom the aside and the direct monologue address to the audience are two of the key registers of dramatic speech of the period.

Dekker, in a more forgiving mood than he was in *The Gull's Horn-Book*, may have contributed to the following description of an audience as it looked from the stage, and from an actor's point of view. It comes from *The Roaring Girl*, a collaborative work by Dekker and Thomas Middleton dating from about 1608, and it gives a sense of the variety and vitality of an Elizabethan auditorium.

> Now, when you look into my galleries,
> How bravely they're trimmed up, you all shall swear
> You're highly pleased to see what's set down there:
> Stories of men and women, mix'd together,
> Fair ones with foul, like sunshine in wet weather;
> Within one square a thousand heads are laid,
> So close that all of heads the room seems made;
> As many faces there, fill'd with blithe looks,
> Shew like the promising titles of new books
> Writ merrily, the readers being their own eyes,
> Which seem to move and to give plaudities;
> And here and there, whilst with obsequious ears
> Throng'd heaps do listen, a cut-purse thrusts and leers
> With hawk's eyes for his prey, I need not shew him;
> By a hanging, villainous look yourselves may know him,
> The face is drawn so rarely: then, sir, below,
> The very floor, as 'twere, waves to and fro,

And, like a floating island, seems to move
Upon a sea bound in with shores above.[9]

Audience on stage

A common theme which runs through so many accounts of the Elizabethan/Jacobean theatre is this: that the boundary between stage and reality was not a rigid one, but one which could be breached from both directions. In the open-air theatre, illuminated by daylight, the audience is not plunged into darkness at the start of the play, nor is there any pretence that the audience is not there. Acting styles demand immediacy and direct contact with the audience; clowns slip from rôle into their own persons in order to exchange banter with the crowd; gallants sit on the stage and make themselves part of the spectacle; Puritans complain that theatres are not only places which show immorality but where immorality takes place, that actors themselves are as degenerate as the characters they portray. There is a continual slippage of meaning between stage and audience.

It is because of this that Shakespearean comedy insists on foregrounding in the way it does an awareness of the stage's own fictionality. One convention of the stage demands that an audience 'believe' in the reality of that which is being represented; another simultaneous convention stresses the importance of remembering that what is happening is indeed a performance. In Shakespeare's comedies these two apparently opposing conventions are repeatedly played off against each other, and the resulting incongruity is exploited. Incongruity is classically one of the great sources of laughter: the incongruity between supposed dignity and the indignity of the custard pie, between how people are supposed to behave and how they actually do, between the two meanings of a punned-upon word. Shakespearean comedy – and Shakespearean dramaturgy in general – plays frequently upon the incongruity between the fantasy world to which the stage intends to transport us, and the tacky actuality of the canvas and hardboard which are its means to do so. The point is most tellingly made in one of the history plays: in *Henry V* Shakespeare outlines the dialectic between fantasy and materiality which is the prerequisite for theatrical creation. He begs the audience to:

Piece out our imperfections with your thoughts:
Into a thousand parts divide one man,
And make imaginary puissance.
Think, when we talk of horses, that you see them,
Printing their proud hoofs i'th' receiving earth;

For 'tis your thoughts that now must deck our kings . . .
(*Henry V*, Prologue, ll. 23–8)

In this famous speech, the tone is one of supplication: the author craves the audience's indulgence, its gracious participation in the great creative collaboration. Modern theatre semiotics stresses the importance of synecdoche in drama; by this is meant that what the audience sees on stage is often a small part of something much larger, whose presence the audience is meant to imagine for themselves. Thus a sofa may represent an entire living-room, a couple of trees a forest, or, as Shakespeare's example has it, a single man may represent a whole army. At times, and especially when the emotional temperature on stage is high, it may be important to suppress an awareness of these disparities – although it is notable that in his tragedies and history plays, too, Shakespeare repeatedly exposes the theatrical and fictional nature of his dramas. It is in the comedies, though, that he plays most frequently with the theme of stage illusion. *A Midsummer Night's Dream* and *Love's Labours Lost* contain plays within plays; *The Taming of the Shrew is* a play-within-a-play; the Masque of Hymen in *As You Like It*, like that of the Goddesses in *The Tempest*, exists in an ambiguous zone somewhere between stage spectacle and supernatural apparition. In playing with the idea of playing, Shakespeare most frequently seems to express an amusement that such collaborations between stage and audience can and do take place. And so, in the same year that he writes an intensely moving tragedy of young love, *Romeo and Juliet*, a story which becomes almost a byword for doomed romance, he also mercilessly parodies the whole business of theatrical communication by retelling almost the same story in the 'Pyramus and Thisbe' sequence of *A Midsummer Night's Dream*, and showing inept actors repeatedly failing to find that moment of creative collaboration. He writes plays which depend upon the fiction that a girl might be mistaken for a boy, and epilogues and asides which send up the whole idea. One of the sources of laughter in the comedies is the stage-audience relationship itself.

Shakespeare was not alone in his fascination with questions about the audience and its relation to the stage action. The Elizabethan stage is famously self-aware and self-reflexive. It constantly reminds the audience that it is in the presence of play-making and illusion. At a time when the English stage was re-inventing itself, and finding for itself a new social, economic and cultural role, it is hardly surprising that playwrights repeatedly wove into their stories devices which enabled them to ask questions about the ways in which meanings are made on stage. The

Elizabethans could trace the convention of the play-within-the-play, for example, back to Seneca, and it was popularized by Thomas Kyd, whose *Spanish Tragedy*[10] (*c.* 1585) provides an early example of a sophisticated use of the convention.

At times Elizabethan plays can seem quite postmodernist in their acknowledgement of the processes of spectatorship and their knowing references to their own fictionality. But it needs to be stressed that the Elizabethan stage was doing nothing new in this; on the contrary, it is following a convention which is surprisingly well-established in the native English dramatic tradition. From the Middle Ages onwards the theatre had been aware of, and had taken into account, the presence of the audience. The medieval guild plays which were performed at feast days throughout the year had treated their audiences as participants rather than as onlookers, assigning to them rôles within the action, just as a modern pantomime audience might be enjoined to warn the hero of the villain's approach. Guild plays, in any case, were staged by amateurs to an audience of friends and neighbours, and the stories they told were generally familiar ones. The divide between stage and audience was not great to begin with, and a play could easily enlist the audience as part of its own reality. As professional and semi-professional acting companies began to emerge in the late fifteenth and early sixteenth centuries, however, stratagems were needed to cope with a new relationship between stage and audience. Again, this was frequently done not by ignoring the audience, but by acknowledging it or its representatives. For example, one of the earliest Tudor interludes, Henry Medwall's *Fulgens and Lucrece,* begins with two servants (called simply A and B), one of whom has got wind of the fact that a play is about to be performed by a band of players. His companion suspects that the servant is himself one of the actors:

A I trow your own self be one
Of them that shall play.
B Nay I am none;
I trow thou speakest in derision
To liken me thereto.
A Nay, I mock not, wot ye well,
For I thought verily by your apparel
That ye had been a player.
B Nay, never a dell.
A Then I cry you mercy,
I was to blame, lo therefore I say.
There is so much nice array
Amongst these gallants nowaday,

> That a man shall not lightly
> Know a player from another man.[11]

Reassured, A and B start to watch the action of the 'play proper'. When, shortly after the start of this, one of the main characters declares that he needs a 'wise fellow' to assist him in his wooing of Lucrece, he turns to the audience and asks for volunteers:

> *Publius Cornelius* So many good fellows as been in this hall,
> And is there none, sirs, among you all
> That will enterprise this gear?
> Some of you can do it if ye lust;
> But if ye will not, then I must
> Go seek a man elsewhere.[12]

It comes as no surprise, perhaps, to find that A and B decide to accept his invitation and join in the action of the play. Thus Medwall allows the audience into the spectacle – but in a limited way, through their surrogates, the two servants.

Fulgens and Lucrece dates from 1497 and was written by a chaplain to the Archbishop of Canterbury. One hundred years later, Shakespeare's generation of professional playwrights was using versions of the same routine and many of the same gags: the pretence that the play is not a play, the blurring of the distinction between stage action and audience 'reality', the satirical remarks about how hard it is to tell players from honest men. The Elizabethan theatre's well-known obsession with its own theatricality was not an innovation but a convention, one which it had inherited from previous centuries.

This is not to say, however, that there was nothing new about it. The material relationship between the audience and the stage was very different in the Elizabethan period from what it had been in previous eras: it was now a commercial relationship, governed by the equivalent of the box-office. Ben Jonson refers ironically to this in his Induction to *Bartholomew Fair*:

> It is covenanted and agreed, by and between the parties abovesaid, and the said spectators and hearers, as well the curious and the envious as the favouring and judicious, as also the grounded judgements and under-standings do for themselves severally covenant and agree, to remain in the places their money or friends have put them in, with patience, for the space of two hours and a half and somewhat more. In which time the author promiseth to present them, by us, with a new sufficient play called *Barthol'mew Fair*, merry and as full of noise as sport, made to delight all and to offend none; provided they have either the wit or the honesty to think well of themselves.

> It is further agreed that every person here have his or their free-will of censure, to like or dislike at their own charge, the author having now departed with his right: it shall be lawful for every man to judge his six pen'orth, his twelve pen'orth, so to his eighteen pence, two shillings, half a crown, to the value of his place; provided always his place get not above his wit. And if he pay for half a dozen, he may censure for all them too, so that he will undertake that they shall be silent.[13]

The traditional trope of the blurring of stage and audience has been put to a new use to suit the new conditions. The contract between stage and audience was now a financial one. Jonson's Induction takes this to its logical conclusion: the amount you have paid correlates directly with the amount of censure you are allowed.

Beaumont and Fletcher's play *The Knight of the Burning Pestle* plays a similar game to *Fulgens and Lucrece:* in its opening scenes it shows a 'Citizen' and his wife in the audience, watching a play called, initially, 'The London Merchant'. They interrupt and challenge the on-stage action, demanding a different play, one 'in honour of the commons of the City'.[14] They end up by coming onto the stage to rewrite the entire play as they wish to see it, with their apprentice Rafe in the lead rôle. The significant difference between this Jacobean play and the medieval one is that the audience are now not 'servants' who respond to an invitation to join in, but citizens and paying customers, demanding that the product be tailored to suit their tastes. The theatre is beginning to suspect that the customer may always be right.

The Knight of the Burning Pestle is, of course, satirical, and the citizen's interruption is itself a fiction. But perhaps the satire is not so far from the truth. The following anecdote by Edward Gayton refers to the author's experiences of theatre-going in the first twenty years of the seventeenth century:

> . . . if it be on holidays, when sailors, watermen, shoemakers, butchers, and apprentices are at leisure, then it is good policy to amaze those violent spirits with some tearing tragedy full of fights and skirmishes . . . (with) the spectators frequently mounting the stage and making a more bloody Catastrophe amongst themselves than the players did. I have known upon one of these festivals, but especially at Shrovetide, where the players have been appointed, notwithstanding their bills to the contrary, to act what a major part of the company had a mind to; sometimes *Tamburlaine,* sometimes *Jugurth,* sometimes *The Jew of Malta,* and sometimes parts of all these; and, at last, none of the three taking, they were forced to undress and put

off their tragic habits, and conclude the day with *The Merry Milkmaids*.[15]

Dekker's gull merely wanted to upstage the actors; these spectators, like the citizen and his wife, want to hijack the whole performance. Gayton's image of the actors switching from play to play, from *Tamburlaine* to *The Merry Milkmaids*, in an attempt to find something which the crowd will tolerate, is a vivid image of an emerging consumer power in the Renaissance public theatre.

It is an image, too, of a relationship between audience and stage which includes an element of confrontation. Part of the clown's skill, as we saw in the previous chapter, might be to engineer and then win a minor skirmish between the stage and the audience. But in a larger context, if we look at images of audiences as they appear in plays of the period, we see that one of the things which they most frequently do is interrupt. The citizen and his wife in *The Knight of the Burning Pestle* are in good company: in *Hamlet* Claudius interrupts 'The Murder of Gonzago' terminally when he gets up and goes. Theseus and his courtiers in *A Midsummer Night's Dream* almost prevent Peter Quince's company from struggling through 'Pyramus and Thisbe'. And in *Bartholomew Fair* a Puritan preacher in the audience of a fairground booth show interrupts the action in order to debate the rights and wrongs of stage representation with a puppet.[16] The Elizabethan and Jacobean theatre might sometimes woo its audience into cooperation with gentle requests such as those voiced in the Prologue to *Henry V*, but it does so knowing that that cooperative relationship has to be negotiated. It is not something which can always be taken for granted.

Women in the Elizabethan theatre audience

It is a commonplace of theatre history that women played little or no part in the English theatrical tradition before the Restoration of King Charles II in 1660. At that point, with the return of the cavalier court from continental Europe, where it had developed a taste for watching women rather than boys playing female parts on the stage, it became possible for a woman to make a theatrical career: first of all as an actress, then as a playwright, and quite soon afterwards as a sharer in and even manager of a theatre. The Elizabethan, Jacobean and Caroline theatre, however, was controlled entirely by men, and women were entirely excluded from the process of playmaking.

In fact this is rather an oversimplification. It is not entirely true that there were no women on the English stage before the time of the Restoration. From the medieval period through into the sixteenth and seventeenth centuries women had participated in theatre in various ways. For example, the earliest stirrings of the English theatre were seen in medieval liturgical drama: the origins probably lay in the enacting of the visit to Jesus' tomb by the three Marys. Parish, civic and cathedral records show that these parts were sometimes played by women. There are records, too, of women taking part in the predominantly male guild dramas. These were amateur street and church theatricals, sometimes but not always religious in flavour, which were organized by groups of various kinds of workers, and which were descended from the mystery plays. Women also took part in various parish entertainments with a mimetic element: dancing, mumming, pageants and May-games. At one end of the social scale they were able to make a living as travelling entertainers: fiddlers, tumblers and acrobats; at the other they functioned as patrons of the arts, hiring minstrels, commissioning masques – and sometimes appearing in them too. There are even references of visiting companies of women actors from the Continent playing on the public stage in Elizabethan London. Women were more central to the development of a dramatic tradition in England than is often supposed.[17]

Nonetheless, women's influence on the growth of the drama had been severely limited, and was probably at its lowest ebb in the period 1570–1640. No women were members of the licensed professional acting companies which dominated the London-based Elizabethan theatre. The parts of Rosalind, Kate, Beatrice and Viola – along with Perdita, Ophelia and Lady Macbeth – were all written to be played by boy actors. It was men, not women, who wrote the plays, owned the playhouses and played all the parts – including the female rôles.

But if women were excluded from the professional stage, they were not, however, excluded from the theatres. The theatrical audience which was such an important element in the dynamic of the Elizabethan theatre was composed of both women and men. When the boy actor playing the part of Rosalind, at the end of *As You Like It*, steps forward and addresses the audience, he speaks (appropriately enough) to both the men and the women in the crowd before him:

> My way is to conjure you; and I'll begin with the women. I charge you, O women, for the love you bear to men, to like as much of this play as please you. And I charge you, O men, for the love you bear to women – as I perceive by your simpering

none of you hates them – that between you and the women the play may please.

(*As You Like It*, Epilogue, ll. 10–16)

Similar addresses to the women in the audience can be found in the prologues and epilogues of many other plays of the period.[18] Did women, then, comprise a significant proportion of the Elizabethan theatre audience? And if so, what influence (if any) did their presence have on the plays of the period?

The mechanicals' play at the end of *A Midsummer Night's Dream* is watched by a more or less equally mixed audience of men and women; so is the Pageant of the Nine Worthies which is performed by Holofernes and company in *Love's Labours Lost.* But it is far more difficult to estimate the gender balance in a typical real-life Elizabethan public playhouse, or to draw conclusions about the kind of women who attended. One myth of the period held that only lewd or debauched women would be present at a playhouse.

> As at the first, so now, theatres are snares to fair women. And as I told you long ago in my 'School of Abuse', our theatres and playhouses in London are as full of secret adultery as they were in Rome.[19]

Time and again contemporary pamphlets assert that the playhouse was no place for a respectable gentlewoman; they warn against the corrupting influence which the theatre has on women, and they make much of the fact that playhouses were the hunting-grounds of professional prostitutes seeking customers. Many of these writings were by anti-theatrical propagandists who held that no respectable citizen, whether woman or man, should be seen at a playhouse. Nonetheless, it is probable that these contained some truth; and indeed, any large gathering of people – especially of people out for a good time – was a likely place for a working prostitute to solicit custom.

For at least some of the men in the audience, then, the pleasures of the playhouse may well have been a prelude to the pleasures of the brothel: a consideration which reinforces the sense that the theatre was a predominantly male domain. To set against this, however, is the fact that the presence of respectable women theatre-goers is well-documented in the period. Patterns of play-going among women seem to have altered during the period (as they did among male play-goers), but the overall trend seems to have been for an increasing number of women to attend the public theatres; for them to have done so largely in the company of husbands, male servants or other male escorts, or more infrequently in small groups unaccompanied by any man. For example, a Venetian traveller, Orazio Busino, recorded in 1617 that '[English] theatres are frequented by a number of respectable and handsome ladies, who come freely and seat themselves among the men without the slightest hesitation'.[20] Charges of immorality against female play-goers also became less frequent and less virulent after 1600, although there was still a tacit assumption that an unaccompanied woman at a playhouse was a working prostitute (which did not, of course, mean that she might not also have been enjoying the play!). In his study of late-sixteenth- and early-seventeenth-century theatre audiences, Andrew Gurr makes the distinction between, on the one hand, the middle-class women, citizens' wives and the like, whom he describes as having been 'regular playgoers throughout the period' between 1567 and 1642; and on the other hand, 'ladies', who 'went relatively rarely to the common playhouses before 1600, but were in numbers at the Globe from 1599 to 1614, and became a major section at the indoor theatres by Caroline times'.[21] Although precise figures are impossible to come by, Gurr's conclusion, that women comprised a significant proportion of the Elizabethan audiences, has been widely accepted.

But what difference does it make whether the audience in the Renaissance theatre was all-male or mixed male-female? Nick Bottom and his friends are quite clear that the presence of 'ladies' in the audience has a determining effect on what can be presented on the stage:

> *Bottom* There are things in this comedy of Pyramus and Thisbe that will never please. First, Pyramus must draw a sword to kill himself, which the ladies cannot abide. How answer you that? . . .
>
> *Snout* Will not the ladies be afeard of the lion?
>
> *Starveling* I fear it, I promise you.
>
> *Bottom* Masters, you ought to consider with yourself, to bring in – God shield us – a lion among ladies is a most dreadful thing.
>
> (*A Midsummer Night's Dream*, III, i, ll. 8–11, 25–9)

It is unlikely that the professional theatre had such a naïve sense of what was or was not suitable to be played in front of the 'ladies'. Yet, as Richard Levin has argued, it may still be the case that 'during the Renaissance women were regarded as a significant component of the theatre audience, and that their interests and feelings seem to have been taken into account by at least some of the playwrights of the period . . . While women were not represented at the production end of this industry they certainly were at the consumption end, and so probably had some effect upon its products'.[22]

It is not entirely clear, though, what that effect might be. Levin documents several references to women spectators being especially susceptible to tears, and thus perhaps having 'a special preference for pathetic plots and situations'.[23] Such gender-stereotyping (which is only ever documented from a male point of view) might possibly have had an effect on Elizabethan theatre programming, in the same way that the twentieth-century film and television industries have explicitly marketed certain of their products as 'women's films' or 'women's programmes'. The poem by William Turner, quoted earlier in this chapter, about the manly plays staged at the Bull, as opposed to the 'idle tricks of love' to be seen at the Globe and the Swan, may reflect something of this sort. Yet women seem always to have constituted a minority among Elizabethan play-goers, albeit perhaps a significant one; there is nothing to suggest that they attended in sufficient numbers to constitute a targetable audience along the lines of their twentieth-century cinema-going counterparts. Women's tastes may have played a part in the creation of the Renaissance theatrical repertoire, but it is unlikely that it was a particularly large one.

It is more realistic to think of the mixed-gender theatre audience as having a balancing rather than a controlling effect. To put it another way: the important thing is that the audience was *not* entirely and exclusively male. Insofar as women made up a significant part of the audience, they too had to be addressed by the play: their feelings and interests could be (and perhaps had to be) taken into account by the writers and actors. There are plenty of stereotyped women on the Renaissance stage but perhaps fewer, and less simplistically portrayed, than there might have been had the audiences been exclusively male.

The reception of the performance, too, might well have been affected by the presence of a mixed-gender audience. Women spectators, for example, might be expected to exhibit a certain gender-loyalty in their experience of the play. The whole issue of audience 'identification' with characters is a complex one, and depends upon more than just concerns of gender: even so it is likely that the women in a mixed-gender audience might have seen things from the woman's point of view and have taken the part of the female characters more readily than a male spectator would. In plays which deal with conflict between the sexes (as Shakespeare's comedies repeatedly do) this becomes a significant factor in the experience of the play.

As a brief illustration of this point, let us look at Orsino's lines in *Twelfth Night*, in which he makes a comparison between women's and men's capacities to love:

> There is no woman's sides
> Can bide the beating of so strong a passion
> As love doth give my heart; no woman's heart
> So big, to hold so much. They lack retention.
> Alas, their love may be called appetite,
> No motion of the liver, but the palate,
> That suffer surfeit, cloyment and revolt.
> But mine is all as hungry as the sea,
> And can digest as much. Make no compare
> Between that love a woman can bear me
> And that I owe Olivia.
>
> (*Twelfth Night*, II, iv, ll. 92–102)

Taken baldly this is a variation on a common theme of Renaissance misogyny: that women are essentially inferior to men in their spiritual, moral and emotional capacities. The idea can be found frequently enough in homiletic writings: it was certainly part of the cultural baggage of the period, and many people, on one level or another, believed it. Orsino, speaking here, believes it too; and it is possible to read the speech as a simple restatement of what the 'audience' already 'knows' as an article of faith, that women are inferior.

Possible – but not easy. For one thing, there are many factors within the play itself which militate against it. The speech is counteracted and ironized by the events which happen around it in the narrative, which effectively disprove its thesis. But its simple misogyny is also significantly complicated, and undercut, by the nature of the audience which is being addressed. If it is an all-male audience, the speech may well invite simple collusion and agreement from the spectators. But spoken to an audience composed of both men and women, this gender-solidarity is less easily available, and the speech immediately becomes more contentious, more deliberately provocative. It offers the possibility not only of agreement but also of dissent.

The point is, I think, an important one. I have argued throughout this chapter that the Elizabethan stage was, inevitably, intensely aware of the audience which confronted, surrounded and sometimes invaded it; I have stressed the fact that the barriers which existed between audience and stage were permeable, and that the audience was a visible and audible and sometimes participatory part of the dramatic proceedings. If this is indeed the case, it means that the dramatic language of the Elizabethans should be seen as one half of an implied dialectic between stage and audience, a dialectic whose nature is affected by the women in that audience.

We should not make too much of this: the theatre was still a predominantly male domain. Women attended only under certain conditions, and there is no suggestion that any audiences at the Elizabethan public playhouses ever comprised a majority of women. Male playwrights wrote about women from a male point of view, and their creations were personified by young male actors. Nonetheless the presence of women in the playhouse audiences should not be forgotten: in the collaboration between stage and audience which made for the performance, they were expected to play a part as well. And who knows what percentage of the audience at the first performances of *The Taming of the Shrew* might have been cheering (secretly or otherwise) for the unreconstructed Kate?

'A Christmas gambol or a tumbling trick?'

Christopher Sly, the butt of the young lord's joke in *The Taming of the Shrew,* becomes an on-stage audience to the comedy of Petruchio and Kate. He has a vague idea what a comedy is, and certain expectations about what he is to see. When a messenger tells him that 'your honour's players . . . Are come to play a pleasant comedy?', he asks 'Is not a comonty a Christmas gambol, or a tumbling trick?' (*Shrew,* Induction, II, ll. 125–6, 133–4). Bartholomew corrects him: 'No, my good lord, it is more pleasing stuff . . . It is a kind of history' (Ibid., ll. 135, 137).

Sly, the drunken tinker, is not, perhaps, an average Elizabethan play-goer; but what can we discover about what those play-goers might have expected from a comedy? In this section I shall explore further this key aspect of audience formation, by considering some of the stated Elizabethan beliefs about what comedy is, and what it does. What follows, then, is an examination of some of the generic assumptions about the form and functions of comedy which were held in the Elizabethan period.

In his expectation of a 'Christmas gambol, or a tumbling trick', Christopher Sly is perhaps a little out of date, but his instinct is good. In his mind there is an intrinsic link between plays and festivals; what he is thinking of is similar to the festive events which George Puttenham describes sardonically in *The Arte of English Poesie.* These include:

> stories of old time, as the tale of Sir Topas, the reports of Bevis of Southampton, Guy of Warwick and Clymme of the Clough & such other old romances or historical rhymes, made purposely

> for recreation of the common people at Christmas dinners and bride-ales, and in taverns & alehouses and such other places of base resort; also they be used in carols and rounds and such light or lascivious poems, which are commonly more commodiously uttered by these buffoons or vices in plays than by any other person.[24]

The various activities which went to make up the celebration of Elizabethan seasonal festivals involved both participation and performance. The staging of plays took its place alongside other kinds of gambols: drinking, music-making, morris dancing, displays of strength and skill, sports and games, mock 'combats', parodies of rituals and licensed rioting. François Laroque describes the performances at seasonal festivities:

> The various forms of folk plays that survived in late-sixteenth-century England, the Sword Dance, the Hero Combat play and the Wooing play, all incorporate a number of recurrent elements and stereotyped themes, though these may be combined in different ways depending on the region, season of the year or period in which they were performed. The complexity of the various plays depended on the length or richness of the dialogue, the type closest to mimed drama being the sword dance of northern England. But most of them were genuine popular spectacles performed by amateurs in the context of seasonal celebrations rather than for profit.[25]

In many of these cases the boundary between performance and participation was by no means a rigid one: the spectator might easily also be present as a performer.

But Sly's hopes of this kind of folk-entertainment are quickly dashed. He is being offered, not a 'Christmas gambol' but 'a kind of history'. While he expects something suited to a social festival, what Bartholomew has in mind is a more formal and polished artefact, a product of the increasingly literate and literary nature of Elizabethan culture. Moreover this literary artefact, according to Bartholomew, has a therapeutic function; it is designed to do Sly (or at least, the lord Sly now believes himself to be) good. The messenger who announces it explains that

> . . . your doctors hold it very meet
> Seeing too much sadness hath congealed your blood,
> And melancholy is the nurse of frenzy
> Therefore they thought it good you hear a play
> And frame your mind to mirth and merriment,
> Which bars a thousand harms and lengthens life.
> (*Shrew*, Induction, II, ll. 127–32)

This notion, that laughter is good for you, is commonly found today, and not only in popular publications such as *Readers' Digest*, which has a regular feature called 'Laughter – The Best Medicine'. An American hospital patient who took this idea to heart, Norman Cousins, became a *cause célèbre* in the 1980s after claiming to have cured himself of the 'incurable' condition of ankylosing spondylitis by laughter therapy. Moving out of his hospital bed, he checked into a hotel, hired dozens of Marx Brothers movies and other comedy films, and proceeded to watch them. In his own account of his cure (which was first described in the prestigious and very serious *New England Journal of Medicine*) Cousins wrote:

> We took sedimentation rate readings just before as well as several hours after the laughter episodes. Each time there was a drop of at least five points. Each by itself was not substantial, but it held and was cumulative. I was greatly elated by the discovery that there is a physiological basis for the ancient theory that laughter is good medicine.[26]

Even within the dwindling British National Health Service there now exists what the press describe as a 'Laughter Therapy Clinic',[27] and even if there is no unequivocal 'hard evidence' concerning the beneficial medical effects of mirth, our culture subscribes to a general feeling that laughter is indeed good for you. As we can see, this idea was shared by at least some sixteenth-century writers on the subject: the lord's servants in the Induction to *The Taming of the Shrew* suggest as much, although they are actually playing a joke on Sly and not to be trusted anyway. The same idea can also be found elsewhere, though, as in the Prologue to his Terentian comedy *Ralph Roister Doister* (*c.* 1566), Nicholas Udall affirms that there is

> . . . nothing more commendable for a man's recreation
> Than mirth which is used in an honest fashion.
> For mirth prolongeth life, and causeth health,
> Mirth recreates our spirits, and voideth pensiveness,
> Mirth increaseth amity, not hindering our wealth
> Mirth is to be used both of more and less,
> Being mixed with virtue in decent comeliness—
> As we trust no good nature can gainsay the same.
> Which mirth we intend to use, avoiding all blame.[28]

Udall asserts that his comedy is good for an audience's physical health, but he is also careful to reassure his listeners that it is not harmful to their moral health. The mirth which he proposes will be 'mixed with virtue . . . avoiding all blame'. For, to set against the idea of the therapeutic value of mirth was the more contentious argument about comedy which was to be found in the writings of Elizabethan literary theorists: the question of whether it was ethically acceptable.

Among the literary theorists of the English Renaissance there was no agreed test of opinions or principles from which general laws about laughter and comedy could be drawn; it is possible, however, to highlight some of the terms in which the issues surrounding the subject of comedy were debated. Renaissance literary theory derived from debate and disagreement – often disagreement about the basics of political, ethical and theological thought. Much of what is quoted as literary theory appeared in contexts which were themselves not primarily literary; what has come down to us tends to be fragmentary, unsystematic and often derivative; it is a patchwork of arguments, contradictions and quotations. Sometimes concerned with prescribing rules and principles for writers, the literary theorists of the Renaissance are often forced also to engage in literary 'apologetics' – to spring to the defence of literature's moral and social utility, often in the face of Puritan attacks. It is from this latter area of Renaissance literary theory that we can learn most about how writers of the time viewed comedy. However, a warning should be issued: precisely *because* these writers were defending literature in general and the stage in particular from attacks which were frequently made on moral or religious grounds, the tones in which their arguments are couched are themselves often moralistic and solemn. Renaissance literary theorists are rarely heard to suggest, like Udall, that comedy might be worthwhile primarily because it gives the audience a good laugh. They need to establish its value on grounds other than this, and they have a harder time making this argument for comedy than they do for tragedy or lyric poetry. The terms in which they attempt to do so is instructive, since much of their energy is spent in dealing with the question of laughter, and its effects on the spectator.

Ben Jonson not only theorized about comedy but also wrote comedies. Indeed, his plays, such as *The Alchemist, Volpone* and *Bartholomew Fair,* were more directly influential in the subsequent development of an English comic tradition than were Shakespeare's. They were also very different in tone from Shakespeare's comedies, and some of the reasons for those differences may be seen in the way that Jonson describes the comic playwright's art.

> The parts of a Comedie are the same with a *Tragedie,* and the end is partly the same. For, they both delight, and teach . . . Nor, is the moving of laughter alwaies the end of *Comedy,* that

> is rather a fowling for the peoples delight, or their fooling. For, as Aristotle saies rightly, the moving of laughter is a fault in Comedie, a kind of turpitude, that depraves some part of a man's nature without a disease. As a wry face without paine moves laughter, or a deformed vizard, or a rude Clowne, drest in a Ladies habit, and using her actions, wee dislike, and scorne such representations; which made the ancient Philosophers ever thinke laughter unfitting in a wise man . . . So that, what either in the words, or Sense of an Author, or in the language, or Actions of men, is awry, or depraved, doth strangely stir meane affections, and provoke for the most part to laughter.[29]

There are some arguments being made here which we may find surprising in a comic playwright. First of all there is the approving reference to Aristotle's dictum that 'laughter is a fault in Comedie'. Laughter is, according to Jonson and the sources he invokes, 'unfitting in a wise man'; it is provoked by things which are 'awry, or depraved' and is linked with 'meane affections'. A comedy whose aim is to 'move laughter' is therefore ethically suspect: it 'depraves some parts of a man's nature' by bringing out the worst in him. The laughter which Jonson is referring to here is of a kind which we have come across before in Chapter 1, the dark and cruel laughter of ridicule, which seems to be the only kind of laughter that Elizabethan literary theorists recognize. Even so, it is surprising to find the satirical Jonson repudiating laughter so completely, and suggesting in effect that comedy needs to be protected from its mean-spirited effects.

To what extent is Jonson articulating a common Renaissance belief about the relationship between comedy and laughter, and to what extent is he expressing his own idiosyncratic vision? His references to Aristotle and the 'ancient Philosophers' would suggest that he is not alone, and when we turn to Sir Philip Sidney's *Apology for Poetry*, one of the key texts of English Renaissance literary criticism, we see virtually the same case being made. Sidney begins his section on comedy by drawing a strict distinction between delight (which is proper to a comedy) and laughter (which is not), in terms very similar to Jonson's:

> But our comedians think there is no delight without laughter; which is very wrong, for though laughter may come with delight, yet cometh it not of delight, as though delight should be the cause of laughter; but well may one thing breed both together. Nay, rather in themselves they have as it were a kind of contrariety: for delight we scarcely do but in things that have a conveniency to ourselves or to the general nature; laugh-

ter almost ever cometh of things more disproportioned to ourselves and nature. Delight hath a joy in it, either permanent or present. Laughter hath only a scornful tickling. For example, we are ravished with delight to see a fair woman, and yet are far from being moved to laughter. We laugh at deformed creatures wherein certainly we cannot delight. We delight in good chances, we laugh at mischances; we delight to hear the happiness of our friends and country, at which he were worthy to be laughed at that would laugh.[30]

Even in this short space Sidney's argument travels a long way. In playing these two terms, 'delight' and 'laughter', against each other, his first strategy is to deny any inherent link between them. His initial target is the commonplace view that pleasure, or 'delight' as he calls it, necessarily leads to laughter. At the beginning of the argument he seems to accept that 'delight' and 'laughter' may be related ('well may one thing breed both together'), but his point is that they are quite separate symptoms deriving from a common cause. As he gets into his stride, however, he begins to change his mind and argue a more extreme case: 'delight' and 'laughter' are not similar, he now maintains, but are quite opposed to each other and indeed are mutually exclusive – 'they have . . . a kind of contrariety'. He goes on to develop a binary opposition, in which 'delight' accrues a series of positive attributes, and 'laughter' a series of negative ones:

Delight	*Laughter*
'a conveniency to ourselves'	'disproportioned to ourselves'
'a joy'	'a scornful tickling'
'[at] a fair woman'	'at deformed creatures'
'good chances, happiness'	'mischances'

Like Jonson's, Sidney's definition of laughter brackets it with all the crueller impulses of human nature. Having made this distinction, however, between the benevolence of 'delight' and the cruelty of 'laughter', Sidney then goes on to realign his two terms:

Yet I deny not but that they may go well together: for as in Alexander's picture well set out we delight without laughter, and in twenty mad antics we laugh without delight; so in Hercules, painted with his great beard and furious countenance, in woman's attire, spinning at Omphale's commandment, it breeds both delight and laughter. For the representing of so strange a power in love procureth delight: and the scornfulness of the action stirreth laughter.[31]

In his first attempt to affect a *rapprochement* of laughter and delight Sidney chooses a revealing example. In the Greek myth, Hercules in a fit of madness murdered the brother of the woman he loved; as punishment the oracle required him to be sold into slavery to Omphale, Queen of Lydia, who dressed him in women's clothing and set him to women's work. Jonson had used a similar instance for a different purpose: he referred to 'a rude clown dressed in a lady's habit, and using her actions' as an example of precisely that kind of humour which 'wee dislike, and scorne'. Male-to-female cross-dressing, it seems, is a common source of laughter. Jonson chooses a simple version of it, Sidney a more complex one. Jonson's is performed by a 'rude clown', presumably simply as a parody of women's behaviour; Sidney's is performed by a mythical hero and provokes in Sidney a more complex reaction, exciting 'both delight and laughter'. That both these writers choose the image of cross-dressing as a laughter-provoking example is particularly fitting in our present context, given the great play which Shakespearean comedy makes of cross-dressing. From Falstaff disguised as the old woman of Braintree in *The Merry Wives of Windsor* through to the multiple complexities of Rosalind's impostures in *As You Like It*, the image of a male dressed as a female recurs in Shakespeare's plays as an occasion for jokes and laughter.

Sidney goes on, however, to suggest a more appropriate way in which laughter and delight may be combined, and to defend an ideal of comedy in the following terms.

> But I speak to this purpose, that all the end of the comical part be not upon such scornful matters as stir laughter only, but, mixed with it that delightful teaching which is the end of Poesy. And the great fault even in that point of laughter, and forbidden plainly by Aristotle, is that they stir laughter in sinful things, which are rather execrable than ridiculous; or in miserable, which are rather to be pitied than scorned. For what is it to make folks gape at a wretched beggar or a beggarly clown; or against law of hospitality to jest at strangers because they speak not English as well as we do? What do we learn? . . . But rather a busy loving courtier; a heartless threatening Thraso; a self-wise-seeming schoolmaster; an awry-transformed traveler: these if we saw walk in stage names, which we play naturally, therein were delightful laughter, and teaching delightfulness.[32]

Here Sidney reaffirms for comedy that value which he ascribes to all literature – its capacity for 'delightful teaching'. Sidney's essential defence of poetry (and it is echoed by Jonson) is a didactic one: that through the experience of literature we may learn about life. Thus for him the proper subjects of comedy lie not in society's victims but in people who might know better: affected or pretentious characters, the insincere, the bullying, the arrogant. Thus Sidney's vision of comedy comes to represent something akin to satire: a form which puts the baser human instinct of laughter at the service of the higher one of 'delightful teaching'. When, in *Every Man in His Humour,* Jonson cautiously admits that laughter *may,* after all, be allowable in a comedy, he does so in similar terms.

> And persons, such as Comedy would choose,
> When she would show an image of the times,
> And sport with human follies, not with crimes.
> Except, we make 'em such by loving still
> Our popular errors, when we know th'are ill.
> I mean such errors, as you'll all confess
> By laughing at them, they deserve no less.[33]

Sidney and Jonson are both talking about the connections between laughter and comedy: whether to deny that they should go together at all, or to explore the complexities of their interrelationships. Both of them seem at one point to deny any connection whatsoever; both of them elsewhere cautiously allow the possibility of a relationship between them. It is significant that for many writers and theorists of the Renaissance, one of the most problematic things about comedies is that they might make audiences laugh!

What all Elizabethan and Jacobean writers seem to agree on is that the function of comedy is to improve its audience. Thomas Heywood, another successful playwright of the period, describes the 'Use of Comedy' as follows:

> . . . it is pleasantly contrived with merry accidents, and intermixed with apt and witty jests . . . And what is then the subject of this harmless mirth? Either in the shape of a clown, to show others their slovenly and unhandsome behaviour, that they may reform that simplicity in themselves . . . else it intreats of love, deriding foolish inamorates, who spend their ages, their spirits, nay themselves, in the servile and ridiculous imployments of their mistresses.[34]

This continual insistence on comedy as being morally improving may seem over-solemn and strangely limiting, especially coming from the playwrights themselves. It seems that Elizabethan comedy is heir to two distinct and opposing traditions: on the one hand there is this rather solemn, learned and neoclassical line of thought which treats comedy as a branch of moral philosophy. On the other hand there is the tradition which is based in popular culture, in the laughter of holidays, of street entertainments and 'Christmas gambols'. And those apologists of the first tradition write as though they believed that comedy's sole function was simply to provide a gallery of examples of bad behaviour, like a medieval preacher, in order to exhort the congregation not to act likewise. They appear blind to any of the other pleasures of comedy. Did audiences of the period really go to the theatres to be reformed? Did the writers really believe that they did?

It must be remembered that many of the writings which claim a morally improving quality for comedy were published in defence of the stage, and as an attempt to rebut the tide of anti-theatrical pamphlets which continually charged the stage with immorality. Sidney's *Apology for Poetry*, for example, has a specific context: it was almost certainly occasioned by the publication of one of the most virulent Elizabethan attacks on the stage, in Stephen Gosson's pamphlet *The School of Abuse*.[35] Gosson had made the mistake of taking Sidney for a kindred spirit on this issue, and had dedicated his volume to him, hoping for the nobleman's approval and possibly preferment. Instead Gosson was, according to Edmund Spenser, 'for his labour scorned'[36] and his work only prompted Sidney to write the *Apology* in refutation of its arguments. Heywood (as the title of his *Apology for Actors* suggests) is operating in the same tradition as Sidney. He is mounting a defence (which is a contemporary meaning of the word 'apology') of the stage in the face of a series of charges which have been made against it. This is why Elizabethan comic theory makes so much of the moral issue: because it is fighting an ideological battle, on ground which has already been decided by its opponents, concerning the allegedly immoral effects of the theatre.

Heywood, as it happens, has another line to his argument as well. The moral lessons of comedy, he explains,

> are mingled with sportful accidents, to recreate such as of themselves are wholly devoted to melancholy, which corrupts the blood: or to refresh such weary spirits as are tired with labour, or study, to moderate the cares and heaviness of the mind, that they may return to their trades and faculties with more zeal and earnestness, after some small soft and pleasant retirement.[37]

Comedy, according to this, need not merely provide moral instruction; it can also offer entertainment and relaxation. This, too, has a beneficial effect. By allowing the weary to be refreshed and to 'return to their trades and faculties with more zeal and earnestness', Heywood argues, comedies benefit society overall. It is an argument which takes us back, more or less, to where this section started: with Bartholomew recommending a comedy for its therapeutic effect.

These, then, are some of the contradictions inherent in Elizabethan thinking about comedy, even on the part of its defenders. Linked initially with 'Christmas gambols' and other seasonal folk-entertainments, comedy develops into a literary form with its own paradoxes. On the one hand it evokes mirth, which can be therapeutic to the individual; on the other hand it may move spectators to laughter, which could be 'depraved'. Laughter, then, may well be a fault in comedy; however, it could also be put to good use in reforming morals. And besides, comedy may meet a more general social need for relaxation. It is impossible, of course, to know what the relationship was between such ideas and the experience of the majority of Elizabethan theatre-goers. The moral and philosophical arguments about the nature of comedy which permeate the literary theory of the period may have had little effect on the everyday experience of audiences. Even so, these theories of comedy (if read carefully, and with a sense of their polemic context) show some of the ways in which writers in the period thought comedy could work on an audience.

Notes

1. Andrew Gurr, *Playgoing in Shakespeare's London* (Cambridge: Cambridge University Press, 1987) is the best book on this subject. As well as evaluating previous research and proposing his own revised model of play-going patterns, Gurr provides as an appendix an invaluable collection of documents about play-going in the period. In the following notes I have indicated where quoted material is reproduced in that appendix.
2. William Turner, *A Dish of Lenten Stuff* (London, 1613), reproduced in Gurr, *Playgoing in Shakespeare's London*, p. 226.
3. Thomas Norton, 'An Exhortation or Rule Whereby the Lord Mayor of London is to Order Himself and the City' (London, 1574), reproduced in Gurr, *Playgoing in Shakespeare's London*, p. 205.
4. Letter to Lord Burghley, 3 November 1594, reproduced in Gurr, *Playgoing in Shakespeare's London*, p. 210.
5. John Northbrook, *A Treatise wherein Dicing, Dancing, Vain Plays or Interludes, with other Idle Pastimes etc. Commonly Used on the Sabbath Day, are Reproved by the Authorities of the Word of God and the Ancient Writers* (London, 1577), p. 92; reproduced in Gurr, *Playgoing in Shakespeare's London*, p. 205.

6. Anthony Munday, *A Second and Third Blast of Retreat from Plays and Theatres* (London, 1580), p. 106.
7. Petition to the Privy Council (1596), reproduced in Gurr, *Playgoing in Shakespeare's London*, p. 210.
8. Thomas Dekker, *The Gull's Horn-Book* (London, 1609), pp. 27–30.
9. Thomas Dekker and Thomas Middleton, *The Roaring Girl*, I, ii, ll. 14–32, in Fredson Bowers, ed., *The Dramatic Works of Thomas Dekker* (Cambridge: Cambridge University Press, 1958).
10. Thomas Kyd, *The Spanish Tragedy* in F. S. Boas, ed., *The Works of Thomas Kyd* (Oxford: Clarendon Press, 1901; revised edn 1955).
11. Henry Medwall, *Fulgens and Lucrece*, I, ll. 44–56, in F. S. Boas, ed., *Five Pre-Shakespearean Comedies* (Oxford: Oxford University Press, 1934; reissued 1970).
12. Medwall, *Fulgens and Lucrece*, I, ll. 854–9.
13. Ben Jonson, *Bartholomew Fair*, Induction, ll. 66–84, in Michael Jamieson, ed., *Ben Jonson. Three Comedies* (Harmondsworth: Penguin, 1966).
14. Thomas Beaumont and John Fletcher, *The Knight of the Burning Pestle*, Induction, l. 25, in Fredson Bowers, ed., *The Dramatic Works in the Beaumont and Fletcher Canon* (Cambridge: Cambridge University Press, 1966).
15. Edward Gayton, *Pleasant Notes Upon Don Quixote* (London, 1654), pp. 271–2.
16. Jonson, *Bartholomew Fair*, V, v, ll. 31–106.
17. See James Stokes, 'Women and mimesis in medieval and Renaissance Somerset (and beyond)', *Comparative Drama* 27, ii (1993), pp. 176–96.
18. See, for example, the Epilogues to Shakespeare's *Henry IV Part 2* and *Henry VIII* and to Richard Brome's *The Court Beggar* (London, 1639); and the Prologues to John Fletcher's *Love's Pilgrimage* (London, 1616) and James Shirley, *The Coronation* (London, 1635).
19. Stephen Gosson, *Plays Confuted in Five Actions* (London, 1582), sig. F1v.
20. Quoted in Gurr, *Playgoing in Shakespeare's London*, p. 231.
21. Gurr, *Playgoing in Shakespeare's London*, p. 63.
22. Richard Levin, 'Women in the Renaissance theatre audience', *Shakespeare Quarterly* 40 (1989), p. 174.
23. Levin, 'Women in the Renaissance theatre audience', p. 171.
24. George Puttenham, *The Art of English Poesie* (1598) (Menston: Scolar Press, 1968), vol. 2, p. 69.
25. François Laroque, *Shakespeare's Festive World: Elizabethan Seasonal Entertainment and the Professional Stage*, trans. Janet Lloyd (Cambridge: Cambridge University Press, 1991), p. 55.
26. Liz Hodgkinson, *Smile Therapy* (London: Macdonald, 1987), pp. 86–7.
27. This was established by the West Birmingham Area Health Authority.

It is described in Thomas Quirke, 'The Best Medicine', *The Observer*, 6 December 1992, pp. 58–9.

28. Nicholas Udall, *Ralph Roister Doister*, Prologue, ll. 6–14, in Boas, *Five Pre-Shakespearean Comedies.*
29. Ben Jonson, *Timber, or Discoveries*, in C. H. Herford, P. and E. Simpson, eds, *Ben Jonson* (Oxford: Clarendon Press, 1925–52), vol. 8, pp. 643–4.
30. Sir Philip Sidney, *An Apology For Poetry or The Defence of Poesy*, ed. Geoffrey Shepherd (Manchester: Manchester University Press, 1965), p. 136.
31. Sidney, *An Apology For Poetry*, p. 136.
32. Ibid., pp. 136–7.
33. Ben Jonson, *Every Man in His Humour*, Prologue, ll. 22–8, in G. A. Wilkes, ed., *The Complete Plays* (Oxford: Clarendon Press, 1981), vol. 1, pp. 183–4.
34. Thomas Heywood, *An Apology for Actors* (London, 1612), sigs. F3v–F4.
35. Stephen Gosson, *The School of Abuse* (London, 1579).
36. Edmund Spenser, letter to Gabriel Harvey, dated from Leicester House, October 1579.
37. Heywood, *An Apology for Actors*, sig. F4.

4 Twentieth-century readings of comedy

The previous chapter looked at some of the ideas about comedy held by Shakespeare's contemporaries. Before turning to the comedies themselves I now want to look at some key ideas concerning comedy which have been held in the twentieth century. I want to provide a map of some of our own assumptions about comedy which have been inherited from the recent past, and to examine the extent to which twentieth-century expectations of comedy have differed from those of the Elizabethans.

'Recognizing the ridiculous': neo-classical approaches

The arguments which Jonson and Sidney make about the moral value of comedy both refer and belong to a neo-classical tradition with a long and venerable history. It goes back to Aristotle, in whose *Poetics* is to be found one of the earliest definitions of comedy, the definition to which Jonson referred.

> Comedy aims at representing men as worse, Tragedy as better than in actual life . . . Comedy is, as we have said, an imitation of characters of a lower type, – not, however, in the full sense of the word bad, the Ludicrous being merely a subdivision of the ugly. It consists in some defect or ugliness which is not painful or destructive. To take an obvious example, the comic mask is ugly and distorted, but does not imply pain.[1]

The Aristotelean definition of comedy was endlessly echoed and elaborated upon by writers of the Middle Ages and the Renaissance. It holds that comedy is a mode which represents lower types, which caricatures the faults and deformities of men and women, and which aims to teach an audience virtue by means of negative example. It is a tradition which is not completely absent from some versions of twentieth-century criticism. Critics such as R. S. Crane and Elder Olson, who are avowed Aristoteleans, have continued to write on comedy as if its essential function were to offer a form of moral instruction. Elder Olsen, for example, asserts that:

> . . . it is evident that as imitations tragedy and comedy offer us likenesses of the tragic and ridiculous which we recognize as

> such, and in their universal aspect, although manifested through particulars; and that it is upon such recognition that our emotional responses are contingent. Thus imitation affords the pleasure both of learning – through recognising the ridiculous thing precisely as ridiculous, for example – and of emotional satisfaction; though the latter is clearly contingent upon the former. In their proper nature, therefore, the arts offer us proper moral perceptions.[2]

While Crane and Olsen's writings are often afforded a classic status, and are frequently reprinted in collections of criticism on the subject of comedy, they are in a decided minority: twentieth-century writers on comedy have not, on the whole, found the Aristotelean approach particularly illuminating. Umberto Eco's medieval mystery novel *The Name of the Rose* (which it is now virtually compulsory to cite in any book on comedy) bases its utterly fictional plot on the premiss that some killjoy monks in the Middle Ages first suppressed and then destroyed a mythical 'lost' treatise on comedy by Aristotle, in which the Greek philosopher retracted the solemn moralizing of *The Poetics*, replacing it with a vision of comedy which is celebratory and life-enhancing. Such a benevolent vision has been far more typical of twentieth-century approaches to the comic form.

Actually, even to speak about 'the comic form' as if it were a single phenomenon is misleading. Under the vague heading of comedy come a variety of sub-headings and related modes: comedy of humours, comedy of manners, comedy of intrigue, comedy of morals, comedy of situation, high comedy, new comedy, old comedy, sentimental comedy, courtly comedy, romantic comedy, citizen comedy, *commedia dell'arte*, realistic comedy and others, not to mention farces, satires, interludes, burlesques and the theatre of the absurd. It is clearly impossible to deal with all of these in a book of this scope, nor is there any point in attempting to do so. Nor do I want to offer here a complete taxonomy of the various theories which have been generated at various points in time to try to accommodate all the diversities of the comic mode. I do, however, want to look at a few selected ideas about the larger issues of comedy which have been particularly influential in shaping the ways in which scholars and critics, directors and audiences, have responded to these plays of Shakespeare's during the last hundred years or so. I would suggest that we can approach the complex issue of twentieth-century approaches to comedy by thinking more or less chronologically. Until fairly recently, approaches to comedy tended to fall into one of three main camps; they would either (a) define comedy generically, in terms of its literary form, or (b) look for its essence in relation to social-anthropological theories, or (c) discuss its meaning in terms which are broadly theological.

'Turbulenta prima, tranquilla ultima': generic approaches

The first of these, the generic or formalist approach, can be most clearly seen in the dictionary definition of the term. Moelwyn Merchant, in his book on *Comedy*, quotes the Oxford English Dictionary's definition of comedy as 'A stage play of a light and amusing character with a happy conclusion to the plot',[3] and then traces that definition back to Middle English literature, citing *The Chronicle of Troy* (1430):

> A comedy hath in his beginning
> A prime face, a manner complaining
> And afterward endeth in gladnesse.[4]

This minimal definition describes a plot structure which it is not hard to apply to Shakespeare's comedies: the movement from a troubled beginning to a happy ending seems an uncontroversial enough way of thinking about most of these plays. (The medieval formula even solves one of the potential problems of the Oxford English Dictionary's definition, with its implication that we ought to find the narratives 'amusing'!) John Dover Wilson wrote a book entitled *Shakespeare's Happy Comedies*, in which he tells us that 'the quality the first ten ten comedies have in common is happiness, a serene happiness, liable to develop into merriment in the conclusion'.[5] The keynote of this approach to comedy is that it focuses upon the narrative's trajectory towards a particular kind of closure: the design and meaning of the genre is seen in terms of its happy ending. Comedy differs from tragedy in that the narrative structures of the two forms describe opposite arcs. This definition of comedy is one which the twentieth century shares with the sixteenth and seventeenth centuries: in his *Apology for Actors* Thomas Heywood draws this essential difference between comedy and tragedy, that 'In Comedies, *turbulenta prima, tranquilla ultima*, in Tragedies *tranquille prima, turbulenta ultima.* Comedies begin in trouble and end in peace; Tragedies begin in calms and end in tempest'.[6]

Thus the stories of Macbeth, Lear and Othello all begin with the central characters at or near the height of their powers: we see them first as successful warriors, powerful kings, favoured generals; their tragedies then chart their descent into misery. In a comedy like *A Midsummer Night's Dream*, on the other hand, the lovers start out threatened with death but end up happily paired.

Similarly, Rosalind and Orlando in *As You Like It* run away from peril and oppression and are brought to happiness by the end of the play. *Twelfth Night* begins with Viola's despair after the apparent loss of her brother, and concludes with their reunion and a double wedding. The repeated stories of loss and restoration of the late comedies, *The Winter's Tale, The Tempest* and *Pericles,* echo the pattern. In *Much Ado About Nothing* and *All's Well That Ends Well* the threatened unhappiness is located nearer the end of the play, yet again the same narrative seems to be at work: troubles threaten, but they are overcome, and the play ends in happiness.

Yet even this most basic definition can cause problems. For concepts like 'happy ending' are not value-free: 'happy for whom?' one may ask – and on the answer may depend a reading of the play. *The Merchant of Venice,* for instance, sees Antonio getting into trouble early on, but then he is saved by Portia's 'pound of flesh' ruling; his friends and companions Bassanio, Lorenzo, Jessica, Graziano and Nerissa all get their hearts' desires too, and the comic narrative closes itself up happily. But there is also Shylock. The events have anything *but* a happy ending for him. This does not matter in the least, of course, if we simply consign him to the rôle of villain. In that case his happiness is irrelevant, we can align ourselves unproblematically with the point of view of the Christians in the play, and the comic pattern is undisturbed. In ages less troubled than our own by issues of anti-Semitism, this may have been easy enough, but the play is rarely staged nowadays without some attempt to rehabilitate Shylock. Since the Second World War few critics or directors have been comfortable with the idea that Shakespeare might have been blatantly anti-Semitic, and so Shylock's status as villain has been repeatedly problematized. This has led to a constant tension in stagings of the play: for while the pattern of comedy, the drive towards the happy ending, actually *encourages* us to cast Shylock in an uncompromisingly villainous rôle precisely in order to leave its upbeat narrative intact, the more pressing cultural need to absolve Shakespeare (and ourselves?) of racist bigotry seeks to undermine the simple demonizing of 'the Jew'. Whether we see this complication as a good or a bad thing may depend upon how wedded we are to the generic definition of comedy as depending on a happy ending.

The Taming of the Shrew is another case in point. Here the question is not so much 'happy for whom?', as 'happy according to whom?' If we allow the definition of comedy to determine our reading of the play, then we must see Kate's journey as being from misery to joy. She starts out as 'froward', 'curst', 'shrewish'

– and unhappy in her aggressive rejection of love, marriage and men. Then the right man, Petruchio, comes along and, by a series of stratagems, brings her to realize that her true happiness lies with him: she immediately turns into the perfectly subservient wife, and her story 'endeth in gladness'. But a culture which no longer shares Elizabethan assumptions about gender rôles may see in Kate's journey not a happy progression but a miserable diminution. Again, readings and stagings develop which resist – or attempt to negotiate – the interpretation of events which the comic pattern seems to demand. Some of these will be examined more closely in a later chapter.

The Merchant of Venice and *The Taming of the Shrew* are simply two of the most obvious examples of the way in which this seemingly innocuous definition of comedy, as a form concerned with happy endings, can coerce readings with which we may *not* be entirely happy. At the end of *Measure for Measure* the Duke, who has finally restored a kind of justice to the city of Vienna, turns to the much-victimized Isabella and proposes marriage to her. She has no lines with which to respond (the Duke immediately invites everyone back to his palace for the celebration) and it is a problem for every actress who plays the part to decide how she is to react. Again, the 'happy-ending' model of comedy implies that there is no real problem about it. This *is* the promised happy ending and Isabella's just reward: the prize for her virtue and the compensation for all the dangers she has endured. Another kind of logic, though, might whisper that she is simply being victimized again: far from wanting to marry the Duke, the only desire she has shown throughout the play is that of entering a convent. Why should she – or we – think of marriage to the Duke as a happy ending? In *All's Well That Ends Well*, too, marriage to the appalling Bertram seems more like a punishment than a reward for the ever-forgiving Helena.

Yet the sense that comedy is a tale which 'endeth in gladnesse' is deeply ingrained in critical assumptions. Nor is there any need, necessarily, to reject this view out of hand: a happy ending may be a legitimate pleasure in a fiction. It is important, though, that we recognize the way in which the *assumption* of the happy ending can sometimes affect our readings of these plays – coaxing us, at times, to accept values which we might otherwise find unacceptable. It is the grain against which we must occasionally work if we want to argue for different readings of the comedies.

'The triumph of life': rituals of the green world

A different, if related, tradition starts with an argument which sounds as if it was already old by the time Aristotle was writing. Aristotle tells it as a tale of provincial pride in Ancient Greece concerning rival claims of the inhabitants of different regions, the Dorians, Megarians and Athenians, to the invention of comedy and tragedy:

> ... the Dorians claim the invention both of Tragedy and Comedy... In each case they appeal to the evidence of language. Villages, they say, are by them called χωμαι, by the Athenians δημοι: and they assume that Comedians were so named not from χωμαζειν, 'to revel', but because they wandered from village to village (χατα χωμας), being excluded contemptuously from the city.[7]

The rights and wrongs of the various regional claims do not concern us here. But note that involved in their arguments are two alternative linguistic – and social – models for the earliest forms of comedy. One picture shows it deriving from χωμάζειν, 'to revel'; the other from the Dorian word for village – which was the domain of the comedians who were 'excluded from the city'.

It is the former of these, the idea of comedy as a form of revelry, which has been so influential in twentieth-century scholarship. The so-called Cambridge school of anthropologists, writing largely at the beginning of this century, traced the roots of western theatre in general, and the forms of tragedy and comedy in particular, back beyond the annual rites of the ancient Greek Festival of Dionysos. Greek theatre, they argued, was both in origin and in essence ritualistic. According to Jane Harrison:

> The Dithyramb [an early choric hymn, precursor of the drama] was, to begin with, a spring ritual; and when Aristotle tells us tragedy arose out of the Dithyramb, he gives us, though perhaps half unconsciously, a clear instance of a splendid art that arose from the simplest of rites; he plants our theory of the connection of art with ritual firmly with its feet on historical ground.[8]

Deeply ingrained in the thinking of the Cambridge anthropologists (amongst whom was Sir James Frazer, whose massive treatise *The Golden Bough* had so much influence on writers and thinkers of the early twentieth century) is the idea that all the documented folk-rituals of early Europe derive from a single, undocumented, Primal Ritual. This Primal Ritual predates either the drama or the Dionysian rituals of the later Greek religion, and was linked with the death/rebirth myths of the vegetation gods of early Mediterranean civilizations, from the Egyptian Osiris to the Greek Dionysos. These represent the cyclic death and rebirth of the earth and the world, and are hence also seen as foreshadowing the Christian myths of death and rebirth. If the Primal Ritual theory has been most influential with regard to tragedy, comedy has not been ignored. Francis Cornford's 1914 classic *The Origin of Attic Comedy* traced a tradition from the Primal Ritual through phallic dances to the comedy of the Greeks. He asserts, with characteristic confidence:

> That Comedy sprang up and took shape in connection with Dionysiac or Phallic ritual has never been doubted . . . We shall argue that Attic Comedy, as we know it from Aristophanes, is constructed in the framework of what was already a drama, a folk play; and that behind this folk play lay a still earlier phase, in which its action was dramatically presented in religious ritual . . . The forms taken by the rudimentary drama of the fertility ritual can be ranged under several heads . . . All the varieties that we shall pass in review symbolise the same natural fact, which, in their primitive natural intention, they were designed to bring about and further by the familiar means of sympathetic or mimetic representation – the death of the old year and the birth or accession of the new, the decay and suspension of life in the frosts of winter and its release and *renouveau* in spring. Hence, in their essential core, they involve . . . two aspects . . . [of] phallic ritual: the expulsion of death, the induction of life. The ritual ceremonies may be classed according to the modes in which these two powers and the conflict between them [are] symbolised.[9]

Cornford goes on to describe varieties of these ritual ceremonies, listing and naming types of folk-ceremonies: the carrying out of death, the fight of summer and winter, the struggle between the young and old king, and death-and-resurrection ceremonies. There are clear links between this ritual model and the happy-ending model of comedy, since both stress an optimistic pattern which celebrates the triumph of life. Indeed, the happy-ending narrative model can easily be assimilated to this ritual model: it can be argued that comedies end in happiness, celebration, reconciliation, integration with society precisely because they contain within them the folk-memory echoes of this ritual celebration of the 'induction of life'.

We must be clear what is being claimed by this model of

comedy. Cornford was writing about the Greek theatre of the fourth and fifth centuries BC, when writers such as Aristophanes might plausibly have been directly affected by such folk-rituals. But how can that apply to a later writer such as Shakespeare? It is not that when he sits down to write a play he is supposed consciously to have thought 'I'll do this one in the comic tradition, incorporating echoes of Greek phallic dances and seasonal rituals'. Such an idea is patently absurd. The 'ritualistic model' of comedy claims rather that plays get written for a variety of reasons, but that some of them (which we call comedies) unconsciously engage in an activity which in earlier ages took a different form: there is, it suggests, a deep human need to honour the pattern of death and rebirth, and at certain cultural moments this finds expression in certain kinds of theatre. In primitive Greek society this need was originally met by ritual ceremonies. These ritual ceremonies continued, but gave rise also to other, later ways of engaging with the same energies: Greek comedy and, much later, the Renaissance comedies of Shakespeare and his contemporaries. Moreover, these twentieth-century scholars could have quoted Elizabethan and Jacobean sources to support their views. Thomas Heywood affirms that 'Tragedies and Comedies, saith Donatus, had their beginning *a rebus divinis*, from divine sacrifices'.[10] Renaissance writers shared the Cambridge anthropologists' belief in the ritual origins of comedy.

Their view is supported, too, by the scholarship which has gone into examining the equivalent folk-rituals and ceremonies of Shakespeare's time. Christopher Sly's question about whether a comedy is a 'Christmas gambol' is by no means wide of the mark, as the work of several scholars, most notably C. L. Barber, has shown.[11] Barber's close study of sixteenth-century English seasonal rituals such as May-games, maypoles, sword-dances, morris dances, mummers' plays, plough plays, ceremonies of the summer lord, Valentines, Easter and Shrovetide revels, established various relationships between them and the drama of the time. In a similar vein, E. K. Chambers, in his classic work *The English Folk Play*,[12] follows a line which we may recognize as deriving quite directly from Cornford and the Cambridge anthropologists. Folk-ceremonies gave rise to folk-dramas (often performed as part of the ritual itself) which retained the ritual dimension by which they were designed to ensure the renewal of plant life in springtime and thence of good harvests. In an economy such as that of Elizabethan England, which had barely raised itself above the subsistence level, whatever powers controlled the cycle of the seasons were worth propitiating.

The fact that such ceremonies, dances, plays and revels were under attack from both religious and civil authorities in the late sixteenth century has had a double effect on our understanding of their relation to dramatic traditions. Firstly, since the more extreme preachers repeatedly denounced the folk-customs for their paganism, it has encouraged scholars to make links between these folk-rituals and pre-Christian ceremonies. Secondly, it has strengthened the argument which links the folk-rituals with the developing Elizabethan professional theatre: under increasing threat of suppression in their original ceremonial form, the seasonal celebrations were displaced into the new dramatic forms of the burgeoning professional theatre. The fool detaches himself from the morris dance, and turns up on the stage as Feste or Touchstone.

Perhaps the most influential twentieth-century exponent of the 'ritual' school of criticism is the Canadian Northrop Frye, whose attempts to provide literary criticism with a 'scientific' rationale were most fully articulated in his *Anatomy of Criticism* (1957). Here he expounded his theory of modes, symbols, myths and genres. This was an attempt to draw a comprehensive map of literary experience relating to 'archetypal' human symbolic structures: the seasons of the year, the periods of life, processes of death and rebirth and so on. In this map, comedy is allied to the 'Mythos of Spring', and Shakespeare's comedies are linked firmly with seasonal rituals. In his analysis of the workings of this kind of comedy Frye coined the term 'the green world':

> Shakespeare's type of comedy follows a tradition established by Peele and developed by Green and Lyly, which has affinities with the medieval tradition of the seasonal ritual-play. We may call it the drama of the green world, its plot being assimilated to the ritual theme of the triumph of life and love over the waste land. In *The Two Gentlemen of Verona* the hero Valentine becomes captain of a band of outlaws in a forest, and all the other characters are gathered into this forest and converted. Thus the action of the comedy begins in a world represented as a normal world, moves into the green world, goes into a metamorphosis there in which the comic resolution is achieved, and returns to the normal world.[13]

This pattern, it is suggested, is repeated in all but the most ironic of the comedies. Lovers move from the dangerous everyday world to a place of safety but also of change, and then return to the real world again. The green world is usually a wild or rural environment, but need not be: in *The Merchant of Venice* Portia's house in Belmont takes over some of the functions of a green world. Frye specifically links this repeated pattern in Shakespeare's plays with wider patterns of death and rebirth: the drama of the green world, he argues, has its roots in seasonal rituals, and its theme

> is once again the triumph of life over the waste land, the death and revival of the year impersonated by figures still human, and once divine as well . . . The green world charges the comedies with a symbolism in which the comic resolution contains a suggestion of the old ritual pattern of the victory of summer over winter.[14]

A brief comparison between *As You Like It* and *A Midsummer Night's Dream* shows how well Frye's model works as a structural description of a certain kind of Shakespearean comedy. The prototype of *Two Gentlemen of Verona* seems to have been followed faithfully in both these plays. Both plays start with a pair of lovers (or potential lovers) at the court of a Duke. That court becomes a place of threat, and its ruler a potential enemy. As a result the lovers run off to the green world, the forest, which offers the promise of sanctuary for them. Both 'green worlds' are already inhabited, and both sets of lovers find themselves caught up in the doings of those inhabitants. The lovers of *A Midsummer Night's Dream* end up enmeshed unknowingly in the stratagems of Oberon and Puck; those of *As You Like It* join the court-in-exile of the banished Duke Senior in the Forest of Arden. In these respective woods strange things happen. Identities and affections are thrown into doubt; transformations, magical and otherwise, take place. Despite temporary confusions, these transformations tend to act benevolently; the characters who have been through them, having lost themselves for a while, find themselves again, and are able to return to the court once more and take their places in the society from which they came, with their proper partners. Although we are not shown the return to the court in the later play there is no doubt that it is being offered as the fitting resolution to the narrative. At the end of *A Midsummer Night's Dream* after the play-within-the-play, the natural/supernatural forces of the wood join with the humans in celebrating the marriages of the protagonists; in *As You Like It* the Masque of Hymen invokes a supernatural order and performs a wedding ceremony. From an antagonism between the court and the green world the play moves to the staging of a reconciliation between the court and the green world.

Frye's pattern is extremely useful – up to a point. It points out fruitful similarities between various plays and suggests a reason for these similarities. The trouble with this kind of reading, however, is that it tends to produce a sameness of response: it stresses the similarities between the plays at the expense of the differences between them. It also privileges certain of the comedies at the expense of others: it works extremely well for *As You Like It* and *A Midsummer Night's Dream*, but much less so for *Much Ado About Nothing, Measure for Measure, Twelfth Night* or *All's Well That Ends Well.* Moreover, in its insistence on the redemptive scheme of the comedies it leads once more towards a prescriptive and rather conservative version of what the plays might 'mean'. Frye's insight that the comedies celebrate the 'victory of summer over winter' needs to be tempered with reminders that their attitude to this victory is not always straightforward. We will see, for example, in the chapter on *A Midsummer Night's Dream*, how the basic pattern of green world drama may be simultaneously stated and interrogated: there the final act of the play, which dislodges the lovers from the centre of our attention and our sympathies, is more complex and contradictory in its treatment of this 'victory' than Frye allows for.

The deeper problem is that the anthropological model to which Frye was indebted was itself flawed. The Cambridge anthropologists succeeded in ensuring that the connections between theatre and ritual, including the possible derivation of the one from the other, have become a central element in twentieth-century understandings of theatre history. However, their own work has not stood up well to the test of time nor to the development of a more sophisticated scholarly discipline of anthropology. The methodology of Frazer, Cornford, Murray and Harrison is now discredited as conjectural and speculative; the Primal Ritual on which many of their theories are posited has never been discovered; the various links which they claimed existed between primitive ritual, dithyramb and Greek theatre are either dubious or unprovable. Nonetheless, their influence has been strong and echoes of it remain. For example, in 1993 Macmillan published a volume of collected essays entitled *New Directions in Theatre* in a series which is explicitly aimed at addressing the issues of 'a period of transition and debate out of which the theory and practice of theatre cannot but emerge in a new form'.[15] This volume contains an essay by Heinz Fischer entitled 'Audience: Osiris, Catharsis and the Feast of Fools', which cites Frazer quite uncritically, and develops a theory of audience response which takes as its starting point the assumptions of the Cambridge school of anthropology.[16]

In fact the comedy/ritual connection has survived the discrediting of the Cambridge anthropologists' fieldwork (or lack of fieldwork). While the rather mystical notion of the Primal Ritual has now faded from the critical horizon, it has been replaced by a new and more materialist understanding of folk-rituals and festivals which locate them firmly in the collective life and institutions of the people. The political dimension of festivity has become more of a concern to critics and scholars. But the point here is not to prove or to disprove the work of earlier scholars, nor to provide an alternative explanation of the relationship between theatre and ritual. What we are doing now is looking at ways in which certain scholarly assumptions about the origins of theatre have determined twentieth-century approaches to Shakespeare's comedies.

Much scholarly work has gone into looking for ritualistic traces in Shakespearean comedy, and the findings are frequently persuasive. Take, for example, an early comedy and a very late one. In tone *Love's Labour's Lost* might appear as far away as possible from the world of folk-rituals and country festivals. Set in the palace of the young King of Navarre, the play is courtly, sophisticated and elegant. It is often thought of as being *over*-sophisticated, in fact – full of difficult verbal witticisms, rather overstuffed with its own learning, an ivory-tower play with none of the earthy liveliness which makes plays like *A Midsummer Night's Dream* so popular. Bookish, artificial, and shot through with supposed topical allusions to local court affairs, the play looks like an unlikely candidate for elucidation through reference to seasonal ritual. Yet the play ends with an explicit ritual confrontation between winter and spring which conforms uncannily to the Cornford model.

> *Armado* Holla, approach!
> (*Enter Holofernes, Nathaniel, Costard, Mote, Dull, Jaquenetta and others*)
> This side is Hiems, winter,
> This Ver, the spring, the one maintained by the owl,
> The other by the cuckoo. Ver, begin.
>
> *Spring* (*sings*)
> When daisies pied and violets blue
> And lady-smocks, all silver-white,
> And cuckoo-buds of yellow hue
> Do paint the meadow with delight
> The cuckoo then on every tree
> Mocks married men, for thus sings he:
> Cuckoo!
> Cuckoo, cuckoo – O word of fear,
> Unpleasing to a married ear . . .

Winter (*sings*)
When icicles hang by the wall,
And Dick the shepherd blows his nail,
And Tom bears logs into the hall,
And milk comes frozen home in pail;
When blood is nipped and ways be foul,
Then nightly sings the staring owl
Tu-whit, tu-whoo! – a merry note
While greasy Joan doth keel the pot.
(*Love's Labour's Lost*, V, ii, ll. 880–8, 898–905)

What seems initially to be a somewhat inconsequential song with which to end the play turns out to be central to the comic function. Moreover the Spring/Winter opposition can then be seen to refer back thematically to the play as a whole: the Lords of Navarre had initially refused love in favour of a life of the intellect. But their self-imposed winter is to be challenged by the spring of love: outside the gates of the palace are camped the Princess of France and her ladies. Will love enter the ivory tower of the King of Navarre, will winter give way to spring? (The play answers with a modified 'yes': in this case the happy ending is deferred.)

As for the late comedy *The Winter's Tale*, ritual interpretations of it are almost unavoidable. In the first part of the play the jealous Leontes chases away his friend Polixenes and causes the death of his own son and, it seems, his wife Hermione and their baby daughter. Yet the child is saved, grows up unaware of her own identity in Polixenes's country, and eventually returns to reunite her father with his old friend. More miraculously Hermione is not dead after all, but 'comes to life' again. There are shepherds' dances and pastoral celebrations within the play itself; flower imagery is rife, the structure, setting and mood of the play moves from winter to spring, and the story of Proserpina, the maiden who represents the seasonal absence and return of the earth's fertility in Greek myth, is never far below the surface. Ernest Schanzer articulates a common response to the play:

> As we watch, twice over in the play's symbolic pattern, the progression from summer to winter, with the return of spring and summer at the end, the affinity between human affairs and the cycle of the seasons, which is close to the imaginative core of *The Winter's Tale*, is born in upon us.[17]

More recent anthropologists and theatre historians have looked in new ways at the relationship between ritual and theatre: the work of Victor Turner, Clifford Geertz and Richard Schechner has been particularly influential.[18] But their work serves to remind us that origins are not the same as essences; and that theatre begins where ritual ends. As with the happy-ending model, we need to ensure that assumptions about the ritual origins of comedy do not determine our understandings of Shakespeare's comedies, nor blind us to the other possible dimensions and readings of the plays. *The Tempest*, for example, is overtly ritualistic both in its structure and content. Like *The Winter's Tale*, with which it is often linked, it tells a story of loss and redemption, and its central character, Prospero, is a magician. He enacts his own rituals on the stage, controls spirits, and conjures up fertility goddesses to bless the marriage of Ferdinand and Miranda. Yet *The Tempest* is also a deeply political play, embedded in current events of the early 1600s. Conservative and radical scholars alike agree that its subject matter derives in part from contemporary accounts of attempts to establish an English colony in Virginia: it is, to some extent, a play about colonialism. The question then arises how this relates to the 'ritual' dimension of the play, and a variety of different relationships can be suggested, each offering a different reading of the play's politics.

These two 'big ideas' about comedy are the ones which have been most influential in twentieth-century criticism up until comparatively recently. Assumptions which derive from them have underlain much traditional and mainstream Shakespearean scholarship and criticism. Both, as I have suggested, have their uses, but both should be treated with care. Both derive from an attempt to define plays in terms of the 'rules' of their genres, the ways in which meanings inhere in the forms themselves. Much of the criticism which has been published in the last few years has sought either to redefine the terms in which we think about genre, or has looked at ways in which the tyranny of generically determined meanings can be undermined or resisted.

Recent approaches

The face of both literary and performance criticism has changed particularly rapidly over the last quarter of a century, and any discussion of Shakespeare's comedy today immediately becomes embroiled in a series of arguments, questions, assumptions and methods derived from recent literary theory. Thus, while the influence of critics and scholars of the earlier part of this century such as Frye and Barber remains strong, much of what they wrote has been overtaken both by ideas and by history. This is not simply a matter of trends, of literary and critical fashion, though doubtless these too have their part to play in the history of criticism and theory. More importantly, though, it is a result of the extraordinary speed of the changes which are taking place in the intellectual and the material world of western civilization. Changing assumptions about class, race, gender, and religion are only the most obvious; as we move from a historical era in which culture is dominated by typographic means of communication (that is to say, the culture of the printed word) into one which is increasingly dominated by electronic means (from broadcast sound to interactive CDs and virtual reality machines), so our ways of perceiving the world also evolve in accordance with these changes. The world of the late twentieth century is radically different from that of the mid-twentieth century and that difference imprints itself on our brains, on the ways in which we make sense of the world.

Things are further complicated by the fact that we are talking not only about comedy but also about Shakespeare – with all the added baggage the Bard brings with him: 'national' poet, cultural icon, writer of canonical texts, examplar of 'good written English', symbol of a lost England, and so on. And so, while much has changed, there are also continuities. By some kind of fluke, and despite some expectations to the contrary, it seems that reading and seeing plays written by a man living four hundred years ago is still deemed to be a valuable experience on an educational, cultural, and even occasionally a personal level. In this computer age we still read and see, for example, *A Midsummer Night's Dream*, just as some of our parents' or grandparents' generation read it and saw it in the 1960s in the shadow of the Cold War, or as their parents or grandparents might have read it and seen it in the 1940s or the 1920s or in the reign of Victoria or George III, or . . . What we read and see is both the same and different from what our forebears read and saw. And each of their successive generations underwent their own version of this interplay between sameness and difference. These differences arose not merely because of changing editing and staging practices (although, again, they have had an effect) but because the world in which the text is read or staged has changed – sometimes subtly, sometimes radically. The play continually impacts at a moment in history which has points of contact with the past but which is also different from the past.

Nor does it stop there: even at a single historical moment a play like *A Midsummer Night's Dream* lives a multiplicity of simultaneous lives, both on the stage and on the page. On a single night it may exist as, for example, a production by the Royal Shakespeare Company at Stratford-upon-Avon, a school play, a local repertory production, an underfunded small-scale tour, a Theatre-in-Education show, an outdoor staging in a stately home, the centrepiece of a theatrical or literary festival, or an amateur production in a village hall. It may be read by an undergraduate working towards a degree in English, by an actor preparing to play a part, or by a retired civil servant who reads to beguile his leisure hours; by a man or a woman, a radical or a conservative. It may be read in England or America, India or South Africa, Poland or Jamaica, in a school or a hospital, a hotel room or a prison cell. Is it the 'same' text that is read in all these cases? There can only ever be a paradoxical answer to this question, for if one version of 'common-sense' replies that yes, the text is more or less the same whatever the conditions of its reception, another version of common-sense immediately replies that in each of the cases of the above the experience of the text will be different, sometimes radically so.

It may appear that this is leading towards a point of complete relativism, to the point at which we throw up our hands in horror, admit that everybody's own experience of a text is unique, and take refuge in weak formulations about it 'all being a matter of opinion'. It is true that, reading published opinion about Shakespeare, this is how it sometimes seems. To take a single instance, the diverse and frequently contradictory terms by which Shakespeare's continuing cultural importance is justified often seem to suggest that not all his champions have read the same body of work. Some claim that he is a radical social critic; others praise his solid conservatism. Some see his works as universal, transcending class, gender and race; others as being of primarily historical importance, articulating a vision which belongs to a particular place, a particular time and a particular position (sometimes supportive, sometimes subversive) within a political and social hierarchy. For some the interest lies not in what Shakespeare himself thought he was articulating at all, but in the personal and cultural 'unconscious' which is to be deduced from, or read into, the text. Some value his language, others his mastery of narrative; some his clarity of moral vision, others his skill as a theatrical innovator. Most combine two or more of the above positions. Many other people, it must be added, do not like him at all, and frequently for just the same reasons.

Yet there *are* patterns in contemporary Shakespeare criticism. There is order in the variety, and there are recognizable schools of criticism, each with its own characteristic agenda of questions and answers, concerns and methodologies. Feminism, psychoanalysis, structuralism, poststructuralism, cultural anthropology, queer theory, semiotics, new historicism, cultural materialism, reception theory, stage-centred criticism, discourse analysis, linguistic theory, the writings of Freud, Bakhtin, Lacan, Derrida, Kristeva and Foucault – all of these have impacted on modern readings of the comedies. The whole gamut of contemporary critical approaches, fuelled by the developments in literary theory of the last twenty-odd years, has been brought to bear on Shakespeare's plays. Indeed, it is partly because of the 'canonical' status of his plays that Shakespeare studies have become such an important arena for this debating of a variety of contemporary cultural concerns.

This sounds as if it is the cue for a comprehensive survey of contemporary literary theory and criticism as it relates to Shakespeare's comedies. It is not – and for several reasons. The task is too big for this present volume; it is not yet clear which of these various approaches and disciplines will have made lasting contributions to the subject and which will turn out to be only of passing interest; and there are various other publications which already cover this ground.[19] In the remainder of this chapter I simply want to make it clear where my own prejudices lie, and to outline some of the main questions which will be addressed in the chapters on individual plays.

In the first four chapters of this book I have attempted to suggest a social and theatrical context in which the comedies may be viewed. Questions about the functions of laughter, the rôle of the fool and the clown, and the nature of the stage-audience relationship will continue to be asked in the following chapters. In addition I shall be concentrating on issues relating to staging, to gender, and to power. I shall be looking at different ways in which some of the comedies have been understood at different historical times, and at some of the intertextual networks to which they belong. In the light of all this I shall be paying particular attention to the ways in which the plays end, and the problems of closure which they negotiate.

There is significant overlap between these categories. Questions raised by a stage-centred criticism concern matters of theatre history; the stage-audience relationship and the play as performance rather than as literary text. Traditional answers to such questions had to be revised when, in the early 1970s, feminist criticism first put gender issues on the critical agenda, generating questions not only about the relationship of the plays to the prevailing patriarchal structures and their portrayal of gender rôles, family structures and courtship patterns within the plays; but also about issues which are themselves concerned with staging – issues of male and female spectatorship; of the significance of the boy actor in the female rôle; and of the representation of erotic desire on the stage. A debate which quickly developed within feminist criticism was: do the comedies effectively collude in the structures of patriarchy, or are they able to dramatize oppositional positions, not merely reproducing the commonplaces of the time, but offering a critique of them? This question echoes a similar one which is repeatedly asked about the plays' relationship to state power and ideology: the new historicist position that the plays' meanings are constrained by the dominant power structures of the period is opposed by the cultural materialist response that the plays seek to find ways to undermine, challenge or subvert these dominant assumptions. In both the feminist and the cultural materialist/new historicist debates a third possibility emerges, which focuses on the contradictions which these opposing pressures generate in the plays.

If one wanted to choose a single word which best characterized the experience of Shakespeare's comedies for readers and audiences in the middle years of the twentieth century, one might well choose 'celebration', or 'reconciliation'. In the years following one or two world wars this comes as no surprise. But the late twentieth century needs another word, and it is surely this: 'contradiction'. The plays dramatize contradictions, and they are themselves contradictory. 'How shall we find a concord of this discord?' asks Theseus in *A Midsummer Night's Dream* when confronted with the 'very tragical mirth' of the mechanicals' play. How indeed?

Notes

1. Aristotle, *Poetics,* in Bernard F. Dukore, ed., *Dramatic Theory and Criticism, Greeks to Grotowski* (New York: Holt, Rhinehart and Winston, 1974), pp. 33, 35.
2. Elder Olsen, *The Theory of Comedy* (Bloomington: Indiana University Press, 1968), pp. 38–9.
3. Moelwyn Merchant, *The Critical Idiom: Comedy* (London: Methuen, 1972), p. 4.
4. Ibid., p. 5.
5. John Dover Wilson, *Shakespeare's Happy Comedies* (Cambridge: Cambridge University Press, 1938), p. 36.
6. Thomas Heywood, *An Apology for Actors* (London, 1612), sig. F1v.
7. Aristotle, *Poetics,* p. 33.
8. Jane Harrison, *Ancient Art and Ritual* (New York: Henry Holt, 1913), p. 76.
9. F. M. Cornford, *The Origin of Attic Comedy* (London: Edward Arnold, 1914), pp. 3–4, 53–4.
10. Heywood, *An Apology for Actors,* sig. F3v.

11. C. L. Barber, *Shakespeare's Festive Comedy* (Princeton, NJ: Princeton University Press, 1959).
12. E. K. Chambers, *The English Folk Play* (Oxford: Oxford University Press, 1933).
13. Northrop Frye, *Anatomy of Criticism, Four Essays* (Princeton, NJ: Princeton University Press, 1957).
14. Northrop Frye, 'The argument of comedy', *English Institute Essays, 1948*, reprinted in D. J. Palmer, *Comedy: Developments in Criticism* (London and Basingstoke: Macmillan, 1984), pp. 74–84.
15. Julian Hilton, ed., *New Directions in Theatre* (London and Basingstoke: Macmillan, 1993), p. vi.
16. Heinz Fischer, 'Audience: Osiris, Catharsis and the Feast of Fools', in Hilton, *New Directions in Theatre*, pp. 72–86.
17. Ernest Schanzer, 'The structural pattern of *The Winter's Tale*', in Kenneth Muir, ed., '*The Winter's Tale*': *A Selection of Critical Essays* (London: Macmillan, 1969), p. 97.
18. See, for example, Victor Turner, *From Ritual to Theater* (New York: Performing Arts Journal Press, 1982); Clifford Geertz, *The Interpretation of Cultures* (New York: Basic Books, 1973); Richard Schechner, *Performance Theory*, revised edn (New York and London: Routledge, 1988). A useful overview of the subject is to be found in the entry on 'Ritual' by A. E. Green in Martin Banham, ed., *The Cambridge Guide to World Theatre* (Cambridge: Cambridge University Press, 1988).
19. A good survey of critical issues and approaches is provided in Gary Waller, ed., *Shakespeare's Comedies* (Harlow: Longman, 1991), pp. 1–28.

Part Two
Critical Analysis

Shakespeare's early comedies (1588–94)

A Midsummer Night's Dream (*c.* 1595)

Much Ado About Nothing (1598–9)

As You Like It (*c.* 1599)

Twelfth Night (*c.* 1601)

5 Shakespeare's early comedies

Traditional scholarship divides Shakespeare's comedies into chronological groupings. There are first of all, according to this scheme, the early comedies: *The Comedy of Errors*, *The Two Gentlemen of Verona*, *The Taming of the Shrew* and *Love's Labour's Lost.* These are often viewed as Shakespeare's immature work: while they contain the blueprints of his future greatness, they are nonetheless technically less well-constructed than his best plays, remaining too close to his original source material, and lacking the complexity of characterization and breadth of scope to be found in his later work. They were written in the years between Shakespeare's arrival in London (*c.* 1585) and his joining the Lord Chamberlain's Men as a sharer in 1594. During this period Shakespeare was still making a living as a freelance actor and developing into a significant playwright. These early plays were staged by various companies and at various theatres; however, since the public theatres were effectively closed down between 1592 and 1594 by the threat of plague, most of the plays were probably written and first performed during the period 1588–92. One exception to this may be *Love's Labour's Lost*, which may not originally have been written for the public theatre.

After this enforced absence from the London stage, during which he concentrated on writing and publishing narrative poems such as *Venus and Adonis* and *The Rape of Lucrece*, Shakespeare joined the newly-formed Lord Chamberlain's Men in 1594. Initially they were without a permanent and exclusive base of their own, and performed at the Theatre, the Curtain and the Swan until the building of the Globe in 1599. It is to this period of his association with the Lord Chamberlain's Men that Shakespeare's so-called middle comedies belong. The period coincides with the last years of Elizabeth's reign; after her death in 1603, the Lord Chamberlain's Men became members of the royal household, and were re-christened the King's Men.

The middle comedies comprise: *A Midsummer Night's Dream*, *The Merchant of Venice*, *Much Ado About Nothing*, *As You Like It* and *Twelfth Night.* These show Shakespeare, it is said, at the height of his comic powers. By now he has found his own dramatic voice and dramatic vision. His comedies are stories of love, at first frustrated but eventually fulfilled. Lovers face obstacles such as intransigent parents or tyrannous rulers or calculating enemies, but the universe is essentially benevolent, and things work out so that 'Jack shall have Jill/Naught shall go ill' (*Dream* III, iii, ll. 45–6).

These two categories ought, logically, to be followed by a final one called the 'late comedies'. In fact, however, things get a little more complicated now. The early years of the seventeenth century saw most of Shakespeare's output taken up with the great tragedies; during the same period, however, he also produced a couple of plays which seem to belong in some ways with the middle comedies but which contain a new and darker tone and are shot through with unresolved ambiguities. At the end of the nineteenth century the scholar F. S. Boas suggested that *All's Well That Ends Well* and *Measure for Measure* should be seen as belonging to a separate sub-genre, along with *Troilus and Cressida.* Referring to the perplexing, unsatisfying ways in which they failed to fulfil traditional comic expectations and to the tonal difficulties which they present, as well as to the moral problems which they address, he labelled these three 'problem plays', and the name has stuck.[1] *All's Well* and *Measure* are sometimes referred to by themselves as 'problem comedies'.

There *is*, of course, a group of plays known as the late plays. Written between 1608 and 1611, *Cymbeline, Pericles, The Winter's Tale* and *The Tempest* are also sometimes called the 'Romances' – although this is a slightly imprecise use of a generic term. Sometimes, as in Stanley Wells's *Shakespeare: A Bibliographical Guide,* they are termed the 'late comedies'. They date from the period when the King's Men had finally acquired a licence to play at the indoors Blackfriars Theatre, a space which demanded a very different kind of staging and offered opportunities for a new kind of dramaturgy. These plays are the stuff of fairytales, peopled by legendary knights and kings and magicians and telling stories of wrongs forgiven, and of joy snatched miraculously out of the jaws of sorrow. The figure of Prospero in *The Tempest,* the enchanter who forgives his enemies and then renounces his own magic, has been famously identified with Shakespeare himself.

This kind of chronological description of the development of Shakespeare's comedies needs to be treated with care. For one thing, although the rough groupings suggested above are generally agreed, the exact dates of many of the individual plays are uncertain. Then again, the chronology is sometimes taken to imply a master-narrative, a map of the playwright's own development: Shakespeare, experimenting with forms and genres in the early years, eventually develops a comic style capable of tackling the largest themes of love and personal identity. During his tragic period, the sunny resolutions of these middle comedies no long seem adequate to express his darkening vision of the human condition: the comic vision becomes problematized. Then, in his later years, he himself moves into a period of tranquil acceptance, which is articulated in the late plays with their tales of atonement, forgiveness and regeneration.

Such a master-narrative is at best a half-truth: a writer's 'development' is never the straightforward linear process which would be so convenient for the literary historian. This way of thinking of the plays also irons out some of the details both of the plays themselves and of the relationships between them, and enforces certain ways of reading the texts, at the expense of other, potentially equally valid ways. For example, if we approach *The Tempest* with the fixed belief that it is a play about atonement and forgiveness, we may miss the fact that it is also a play about politics, government, and the ruling of a 'commonwealth'. If we approach *Measure for Measure* with the phrase 'problem play' ringing in our ears, we may ignore the possibility that many of the problems may belong to the generation of the nineteenth-century critic who first coined the term, rather than to Shakespeare's contemporaries – or our own!

Yet, treated with appropriate caution, the chronological map is a useful way of exploring some of the relationships between the plays. In the chapters which follow I will be adopting, broadly speaking, a chronological approach. I shall be looking at plays from Shakespeare's early, freelance years, and at a group of the comedies which he wrote for the Lord Chamberlain's Men, both before and after their move to the Globe. The main focus of the analysis will be on four of Shakespeare's best-known comedies: *A Midsummer Night's Dream, Much Ado About Nothing, As You Like It* and *Twelfth Night.* As well as belonging to a specific phase of Shakespeare's professional career, these cohere as a group in that they share a variety of plot-devices and themes: their narratives concern repressed or forbidden desires which are eventually liberated or fulfilled by means of tricks, disguises and strategies. I shall be arguing that these comedies – often known collectively as 'festive comedies' – present problems of tone and of closure which are just as great as those found in the so-called 'problem plays'. First of all, however, I want to look at some of the early comedies, for it is here that the comedic agenda is being established.

The Two Gentlemen of Verona

It is hard not to see *The Two Gentlemen of Verona* simply as an apprentice piece, prefiguring some of the later and more successful comedies. Despite its comparatively small cast and a plot which is easily understood, it is still the least theatrically successful of Shakespeare's comedies, and the one least frequently revived. Yet it contains so many of the ingredients of the later plays.

The four main lovers in the play ought, clearly, to pair off neatly: Proteus with Julia, Valentine with Sylvia – but desire does not always follow neat patterns, and Proteus falls in love with Sylvia as well, leaving the faithful Julia to follow after him in disguise. In this basic situation there are the essential narrative and thematic elements of *A Midsummer Night's Dream, As You Like It, Twelfth Night* and *All's Well That Ends Well.*

The disrupted quartet of lovers foreshadows the lovers in *A Midsummer Night's Dream,* who undergo similar confusions before settling down into the expected pairings. In Valentine we are given the character of the honourable man and the faithful lover; in Proteus (whose name means 'changeable') the epitome of the faithless one. Their names match their plot-functions and remind us of the debt which Shakespearean comic characterization owes to medieval dramatic traditions, in which virtues and vices were portrayed emblematically upon the stage. Although later comedies take more care about psychological plausibility than does *The Two Gentlemen of Verona,* characters in the comedies often retain this emblematic quality. Moreover it is often used, as it is here, for purposes of opposition and contrast: a central thematic conflict in this early play is that between true love and faithlessness.

Like the lovers in *A Midsummer Night's Dream,* and like nearly everybody in *As You Like It,* the characters in *The Two Gentlemen of Verona* find shelter and eventual salvation in the forest. Like *As You Like It*'s Duke Senior, Valentine becomes the leader of an outlaw court, living the pastoral life of a contemplative Robin Hood:

> How use doth breed a habit in a man!
> This shadowy desert, unfrequented woods
> I better brook than flourishing peopled towns.
> Here can I sit alone, unseen of any,
> And to the nightingale's complaining notes
> Tune my distresses and record my woes.
>
> (V, iv, ll. 1–6)

Julia, meanwhile, prefigures a variety of Shakespearean heroines. She resembles not only the Helena of *A Midsummer Night's Dream,* trekking into the woods after the uncaring Demetrius, but also the Helena of *All's Well That Ends Well,* bound on her longer journey in search of the faithless Bertram. Like Rosalind in *As You Like It* and Viola in *Twelfth Night,* she disguises herself as a man to achieve her aim (calling herself, incidentally, Sebastian – the same name as Viola's twin brother in the later play).

The Two Gentlemen of Verona also sees Shakespeare experimenting with two different kinds of clown rôle. The clown routines in the play are provided by Speed and Launce, the servants of Valentine and Proteus respectively. Speed, as his name implies, is quick-tongued and witty, always ready to chop logic with his master or anyone else:

> *Speed* You conclude that my master is a shepherd, then, and I a sheep?
> *Proteus* I do . . .
> *Speed* Nay, that I can deny by a circumstance.
> *Proteus* It shall go hard but I'll prove it by another.
> *Speed* The shepherd seeks the sheep, and not the sheep the shepherd, but I seek my master, and my master seeks not me. Therefore I am no sheep.
>
> (I, i, ll. 76–7, 82–6)

The rôle of Speed was originally written for a boy actor to play: Speed is often referred to as 'boy' in the text, and much of the effect of the repartee may have stemmed from its being a duel of wit between adult and child.

The contrasting clown rôle of Launce is a different matter. Launce is easily confused, low-status and not too bright. The part was almost certainly written for Will Kempe, and Clifford Leech, the editor of the Arden edition of the play, has argued that it was written later than the rest of the play in order to make use of Kempe's comic talents when he joined the Lord Chamberlain's company.[2] Speed, in the earlier version, was the main comic part, but he was displaced to make way for Launce, whose routines, as both scholars and audiences have often noticed, have little to do with the main action of the play, and seem to be largely there to provide the opportunity for a good comedian to improvise. The famous speech in which he tries to recreate for the audience the scene of his leaving home, for example, works in visual as much as in verbal terms.

> Nay, I'll show you the manner of it. This shoe is my father. No, this left shoe is my father. No, no, this left shoe is my mother. Nay that cannot be so neither. Yes, it is so, it is so, it hath the worser sole. This sole with the hole in it is my mother, and this is my father. A vengeance on't, there 'tis. Now, sir, this staff is my sister, for, look you, she's as white as a lily and as small as a wand. This hat is Nan our maid. I am the dog. No, the dog

is himself, and I am the dog. O, the dog is me, and I am myself. Ay, so, so.

(II, iii, ll. 13–23)

It adds nothing to the story-line, other than to establish that Launce's dog did not cry when they left home; but modern audiences often experience the routine as the high point of the show. Perhaps, with Kempe in the part, that was true in its original performances as well. Shakespeare's later comedies integrate this kind of clown rôle more fully into the narrative in the figures of Dogberry and Nick Bottom. It is not until Kempe leaves the Lord Chamberlain's Men at the end of the century, and is replaced by Robert Armin, that the type of clown rôle tried out here in the part of Speed really comes into its own, with characters such as Touchstone and Feste and another famous 'boy', Lear's Fool.

The list of ways in which *The Two Gentlemen of Verona* prefigures other comedies could go on. I only want to point to one more feature, however: not a character-type or a stock situation, so much as a problem. It occurs in the much-discussed final scene of the play. Proteus, infatuated with Sylvia, has betrayed his childhood friend Valentine, forcing him to flee to the forest, where he became a bandit leader. Eventually the other lovers end up in the same forest. Julia, still in disguise, is accompanying Proteus as his page, when Proteus rescues Sylvia from some rather inoffensive outlaws (belonging, as it happens, to Valentine's band). Proteus expects her to soften towards him, but she expresses only contempt – to which he responds with violence.

Proteus Nay, if the gentle spirit of moving words
Can no way change you to a milder form
I'll woo you like a soldier, at arm's end,
And love you 'gainst the nature of love: force ye.
Sylvia O heaven!
Proteus (*assailing her*)
I'll force thee yield to my desire.

(V, iv, ll. 55–9)

Valentine, who has overheard all this, steps forward and prevents the rape which Proteus intends, heaping insults upon him for his treachery. Proteus immediately repents:

Proteus My shame and guilt confounds me
Forgive me, Valentine. If hearty sorrow
Be a sufficient ransom for offence

I tender't here. I do as truly suffer
As e'er I did commit.
Valentine Then I am paid,
And once again do receive thee honest.
Who by repentance is not satisfied
Is nor of heaven nor earth. For these are pleased;
By penitence th'Eternal's wrath's appeased.
And that my love may appear plain and free,
All that was mine in Silvia I give thee.
Julia O me unhappy!

(V, iv, ll. 73–83)

It is an extraordinary moment. In the space of less than thirty lines, love turns to rape, which is prevented; the villain repents – and the hero offers Sylvia to the would-be rapist!

It could be – and often is – simply dismissed as a bit of bad writing. David Daniell, for example, talks of the 'absurdity of the last 118 lines, containing a succession of emotional nonsenses from the two heroes . . . The further perfunctory tying-up feels something of a mockery'.[3] Thus, with the end of the play in sight the author is hurrying through everything in order to reach the final curtain; trying to pull together his various thematic and narrative strands (love and friendship, disguise, constancy, forgiveness) in order to provide the expected comedic happy ending, with all the lovers sorted out into their correct pairs. And so, in order to tell his parable of friendship and forgiveness, he jettisons even the sketchy psychological realism to which the play had laid claim up until this point.

In doing so he also exposes an underlying misogyny in the play. The male friendship between Proteus and Valentine is, we now realize, more important than Valentine's feelings for Sylvia. More to the point, it is more important than Sylvia's own feelings about the man she loves solemnly handing her over to the man who has just attempted to rape her! The play finally makes it clear that Sylvia exists, not as a character in her own right, but as a commodity to be transferred between the two men. And with this coming just a few lines from the end of the play, what are we expected to make of the comedic happy ending, with its promise to 'include all jars / With triumphs, mirth and rare solemnity' (V, iv, ll. 158–9)? We might start to notice that Sylvia has no more lines in the play after 'O heaven!', and wonder what to make of her silence.

Frank Kermode once observed that 'the point is that all the comedies are problem comedies'.[4] He meant that all the comedies deal with serious issues, such as love, friendship and justice.

I would like to make the same observation, but with a different meaning. All the comedies are problem comedies because for a twentieth-century audience there is such a distance between their world and ours. At the beginning of this book I made the point that laughter is socially specific, and that 'getting' a joke involves affirming an identity with a social grouping. In the same way the celebratory tone with which a comedy ends invites an audience to endorse the values which the world of the play has propounded; and so, paradoxically, these celebrations can become quite exclusive if an audience feels reservations about those values, or about the implications of the play's narrative. And in Shakespearean comedies there is much to feel reservations about: the justice of the Christians' treatment of Shylock in *The Merchant of Venice*; the desirability of Bertram as a husband for Helena in *All's Well That Ends Well*; the motives of the Duke in *Measure for Measure*. All these can leave a modern audience with the uncomfortable sense of not quite being at the same party as the characters who are celebrating on stage, and the more confident the text (or production) appears that all the problems have been solved, the more uncomfortable that feeling is. In the late twentieth century no Shakespeare play has raised more problems concerning its ending than *The Taming of the Shrew*.

The Taming of the Shrew

The Two Gentlemen of Verona is seldom seen on the commercial stage, and its story is not well-known. Throughout the late 1970s and early 1980s the former could also have been said of *The Taming of the Shrew* – but not the latter. *The Taming of the Shrew* is one of those texts which have a status in a culture's mythology which far outstrips their actual currency; for example, comparatively few people have read *A Christmas Carol*, but 'everybody' knows who Scrooge is and, more or less, what happens to him. There are perhaps a couple of dozen texts like this, known in their outlines by millions who have never read them: *Don Quixote* is about the mad knight who tilted at windmills; *Wuthering Heights* is about passionate romantic love; *Robinson Crusoe* is about the man cast away on a desert island. In the same way, 'everybody knows' that *The Taming of the Shrew* is about the resourceful but loving rogue who tames the scolding bad-tempered wife. Or, to put it another way, that it is about the independent woman who is bullied into submission by a potentially dangerous megalomaniac.

It is only comparatively recently that audiences have begun to feel uncomfortable at the end of *The Taming of the Shrew*, that audiences have booed, not the actors' performance, but the play's implications; or that pressure groups have picketed theatres that staged the play. A generation ago, this would have been unthinkable. In 1960 John Barton directed a production of *The Taming of the Shrew* for the RSC at the Shakespeare Memorial Theatre in Stratford-upon-Avon. It featured Dame Peggy Ashcroft as Katherina and Peter O'Toole as Petruchio. As with all records of past theatre productions, it is impossible for those of us who were not present at the performance to judge the truth of what the critics say. We do not have the information necessary to distinguish between what the critics tell us that they saw and what actually went on on the stage, to compare their reactions with what the actors actually achieved. Nonetheless, the quotations which follow show a fair degree of unanimity, and published interviews with O'Toole and Ashcroft suggest that what the reviewers saw was very much what the production wanted them to see. But in any case, the reviews and criticisms are of interest in their own right, as examples of a way of responding to the play which is no longer unproblematically available to us.

Take, for example, the following remarks from a review of the production in *The Wolverhampton Express and Star*. It starts off with an appreciative estimation of Peter O'Toole's Petruchio, whom it describes as:

> a man intelligent enough not to sit down under fate and human enough to be mightily relieved when his sabre rattling works. His strength makes Katherina surrender; his sensitivity makes her want to . . . When she resists him, a twitch of amusement hovers about her mouth. Her suffering before the submission is therefore nominal and fit to joke about; the submission itself is easily swallowed dramatically, and the whole effect is happier and kinder.[5]

Nowadays Petruchio's 'sensitivity' is seldom an issue in criticism, academic or journalistic; and Katherina's submission is not often 'easily swallowed' by anybody.

Another review of the same production in a national newspaper speaks from an even more uncompromisingly pro-Petruchio standpoint. According to the theatre critic of the (appropriately-named) *Daily Mail*:

> [Dame Peggy Ashcroft's] Kate is a raging hoyden who with every shrug, every pout, every word, suggests that behind the habitual mask of the shrew, there breathes a woman simply dying to be . . . tamed.[6]

The reviewers tend to agreed that Petruchio is a suitably rollicking dominant male; that Kate fancies him from the start; that his humiliation of her is done all for her own good; that what she wants most is for him to master her; that when she submits at the end she does so genuinely and completely; and that this is all good and proper. Not only the anonymous theatre critics of local and national papers, but eminent figures in the Shakespearean critical establishment sound the same note. Gareth Lloyd-Evans, for example:

> Peter O'Toole's Petruchio is a creature of grace, fire and flashes of gentleness . . . The keynote of their interpretation of tamer and tamed is fiery respect growing into immense love. It is as if the challenge thrown down by this vixen lady leads, not so much to cowed captivity, as to a release in the victim of hidden gentleness, and, in the victor, of courteous adoration.[7]

It comes as a bit of a shock to realize that another thing on which these critics largely agree is that this production is a more than usually humane one, and that, as the *Wolverhampton Express and Star* puts it, the overall effect is 'happier and kinder'. (Happier and kinder than what, is not made completely clear. Than straightforward domestic violence, perhaps?)

Nor do these 1960s critics write as if the theatre were a realm of pure aesthetics, hermetically sealed from society and having nothing to do with historical reality. On the contrary, the theatre is expressly seen as political, even if the politics are reactionary. Milton Shulman crows 'There is no doubt that women's suffrage suffers a considerable beating in the completeness of [Kate's] capitulation'[8], while Kenneth Tynan (one of the archetypal 1960s sexual liberationists) records wistfully that:

> Dame Peggy plays the last scene, in which the rival husbands lay bets on their wives' obedience, with an eager, sensible radiance that almost prompts one to regret the triumph of the suffrage movement.[9]

These quotations are late examples of a consensus view of the play which operated fairly recently, but which is now out-dated. This version of *The Taming of the Shrew*, and these comments about it, can be called the 'authorized version'. They are 'authorized' by years of tradition and repetition, by critics and by actors, by directors and audiences, editors and readers, who have agreed to assign (with minor variations) a certain meaning to the play, seeing it as the story of a headstrong woman who meets her match in a strong man who, for her own good, tames her and thus creates the conditions for a potentially ideal relationship.

The last scene, opening as it does with the line 'At last, though long, our jarring notes agree', signals a comedic ending of reconciliation and future happiness, made possible by Kate's acceptance of her true rôle in relation to her husband.

Although I have nominated 1960 as a year which exemplifies a 'late' example of this authorized view of the play, it is not an end point. This way of reading the Kate / Petruchio narrative continues to feature in productions and accounts of the play in the 1970s and 1980s, although during this period the tone in which it is articulated begins to change. In a recently reprinted and popular book entitled *Women in Shakespeare*,[10] Judith Cook presents the results of interviews and conversations with British actresses who have played some of the major Shakespearean women's rôles. In the section dealing with Kate she refers to Dame Peggy Ashcroft's 1960 interpretation, but quotes more extensively from discussions with more recent interpreters of the part, Jane Lapotaire and Janet Suzman. All these actresses agree with Cook's own view, that *The Taming of the Shrew* is a benevolent play, one which tells a story which each of them can feel happy with. Cook cites Dame Peggy Ashcroft's opinion 'that the overriding fact is that Kate actually falls in love with Petruchio at first sight, and everything she does stems from that'.[11] Jane Lapotaire says:

> I feel [Kate] falls in love almost immediately with Petruchio but she must fight him on her own level . . . It is essential to put over a huge sense of fun. We hoped that the audience would realize the true situation from the word go and then go along with it. You must not send up the part. You have to give all your life and energy to the battles in which you join, remembering that both have met their match and therefore fight as equals . . . If you turn it into a sadistic exercise as the last production did at the RSC then it becomes totally unacceptable and makes absolute nonsense of the last speech . . . [12]

Janet Suzman, who played the part in 1967, broadly agrees with this, although she pinpoints a moment when, in her interpretation of the rôle, the quality of this love changed:

> In that scene about the moon and the sun we made a useful discovery; if you can laugh *with* somebody you can't fight them any more. What Petruchio is doing in that scene is teaching a small lesson in humour. We found a particular moment when she realizes what he's up to . . . Their love – combated, spirited, and until this moment, unspoken – can now flourish. Each has

> found an ally. Her pride has been restored. That hyperbolic speech at the end of the play, reviled by feminists, can now become Kate playing, in public, the exact game she has been taught in private. It is a paean to the secretiveness of real passion. And remember – Petruchio *always* stops before anything dangerous happens; no harm ever comes to Kate, does it?[13]

Although both Suzman and Lapotaire put their cases forcefully, there is an unmistakeably defensive tone about what they say. No longer is there that confidence. Now, it seems, the case has to be argued – and what Judith Cook's interviewees are arguing is that it is all right to enjoy the play really. All right because she loves him. All right because it's fun. All right because he stops before anything dangerous happens. All right because actually both have met their match and fight as equals. All right because no harm ever comes to Kate.

Many of these arguments are, as it happens, quite specious. Kate and Petruchio do not meet as 'equals' at all: at their first meeting he announces, despite her protestations to the contrary, that they will marry; on their wedding day he explains that 'I will be master of what is mine own. She is my goods, my chattels' (IV, ii, ll. 101–2); and from there on he deprives her of food, sleep, forces her to go with him against her will, and puts her under continual emotional pressure. What kind of equality is even hinted at in the play? And there is something not only specious but desperate about Janet Suzman's plea that Petruchio always stops short of actual harm. What is being implied here? That if we had seen him actually beat her, break a bone or two, raise the odd bruise, that would have been a bit much, but that since the only cruelty he inflicts on her is mental cruelty, then we can relax?

These are intelligent, even brilliant, actresses who are trying, honestly, to explain their approach to playing a character, to report after the event some of the ways in which they constructed that character in their own minds so as to make it possible for them to play her. So why does what they say seem so strained? The note of defensiveness which characterizes their descriptions of playing Kate is notably absent elsewhere in the book, when the same actresses are discussing how they feel about Viola or Beatrice, for example. It is so noticeable here because they are responding to the changing consensus mentioned above – the growing feeling that we cannot join in with what the play asks an audience to celebrate. By the end of the 1970s, when the interviews were carried out, the play had already turned from a romantic comedy into a problem play. It was not 'the play itself' that had changed, of course. The words on the page were the same. But a shift had taken place in the cultural climate of Western Europe and North America; the social impact of the Women's Movement and the corresponding intellectual impact of feminist thought had created an environment in which Kate's last speech had become a compendium of unacceptable ideas, a blatant statement of a visible patriarchal ideology. 'You must not send up the part', admonished Lapotaire.[14] Yet how was it possible now to take straight a part which contained lines like these?

> *Kate* Thy husband is thy lord, thy life, thy keeper,
> Thy head, thy sovereign, one that cares for thee,
> And for thy maintenance commits his body
> To painful labour both by sea and land,
> To watch the night in storms, the day in cold
> While thou liest warm at home, secure and safe,
> And craves no other tribute at thy hands
> But love, fair looks, and true obedience,
> Too little payment for so great a debt.
> Such duty as the subject owes the prince,
> Even such a woman oweth to her husband
> And when she is forward, peevish, sullen, sour
> And not obedient to his honest will,
> What is she but a foul contending rebel,
> And graceless traitor to her loving lord?
> I am ashamed that women are so simple
> To offer war where they should kneel for peace,
> Or seek for rule, supremacy and sway
> When they are bound to serve, love and obey . . .
> (V, ii, ll. 151–69)

And so on. The speech is uncompromising, relentless and extremely long. It is also pivotal to the comedic 'happy ending' of the Kate/Petruchio plot: the whole logic of the play insists that it is precisely *because* Kate has reached the point where she is willing to speak these lines that a happy ending is able to exist at all. And this crucial speech, this lynch-pin of the play's structure, expresses a world-view and a vision of gender relations which is repulsive to the growing consensus. The actresses quoted by Cook attempt to deal with the problem by implicitly marginalizing the consensus, as if it were simply a minority of feminist extremists who would find the speech offensive. Suzman refers to it as 'that hyperbolic speech at the end of the play reviled by feminists'.[15] Another actress, Sarah Badel, who played Kate in the

BBC TV Shakespeare production of *The Shrew*, is elsewhere quoted as referring to it as 'the speech to make Germaine Greer sick'.[16] (With Greer, by implication, standing for the – very few – humourless ideologues who object to this speech). But this will not do: it is not a narrow-minded few who find this speech problematic, but the majority of the reasonably well-educated middle-class people, both men and women, who attend plays. It is the very audience, in fact, which the mainstream commercial and subsidized theatres are trying to attract, and which recognizes in Kate's final speech one of the most tired clichés of an increasingly discredited patriarchal mind-set.

Worse, since this mind-set is discredited but by no means dispelled, and since debates about gender relations are still very much part of the agenda of cultural struggle, the speech represents a point of view which is worth vigorously rejecting. The very fact that ('elsewhere in society'? 'outside the theatre'?) there might still be ('uncultured'? 'uneducated'? 'unenlightened'?) men who would like to applaud Kate's sentiments, makes it all the more difficult for a contemporary audience to hear this speech, as it seems to be presented, as the triumphant articulation of the play's 'message'.

As a result, *The Taming of the Shrew* became the most problematic of Shakespeare's comedies. The history of recent productions of the play is the history of attempts to solve this central problem, and to find ways of staging the play which will negotiate an acceptable relationship between the attitudes to male-female relationships which were meaningful in the late sixteenth century and those that are meaningful in the late twentieth. These attempts have ranged from direct assault on the 'authorized version' of the play's meaning, through to subtle undercutting of it.

Cook's *Women in Shakespeare* was first published in 1980, and there is a notable omission from its line-up of Kates. Jane Lapotaire refers to 'the last production at the RSC', which she considers turned the play 'into a sadistic exercise . . . [and was] totally unacceptable'. Judith Cook herself mentions the same production earlier in the chapter:

> In 1979 Michael Bogdanov directed a production . . . [in which] Kate was totally beaten into abject submission at the end. The result was not only distasteful, but seemed contrary to the spirit of the play.[17]

The Kate in this production was Paola Dionisotti, and her views on playing the part are not included in *Women in Shakespeare*. This is a shame, since the production (which actually opened in 1978) has attained a historical importance, and, according to

Christopher J. McCullough, 'changed the way many people now think about the play'.[18] However, the director, Michael Bogdanov, has articulated in no uncertain terms the interpretation of the play which underlay the production:

> It was based on a theory that this is, in fact, a play about a male wish-fulfilment dream of revenge upon women. The humiliation to which Kate is subjected is what happens in a world ruled and dominated by men, where any woman who challenges male supremacy has to be smashed down by any means possible, until she is submissive, pliant and occupies her rightful place in the world, which is to warm the slippers, cook the meals and come when called.[19]

Unlike Janet Suzman's argument that the play is all right really because 'no harm ever comes to Kate, does it?', Bogdanov asserts that Kate *is*, very definitely, harmed – 'smashed down by any means possible until she is submissive, pliant'. In Bogdanov's production, 'any means possible' included both the threat and the actuality of physical harm. Jonathan Pryce played Petruchio with an energy which bordered on the psychopathic and which frequently erupted into actual violence. Even more disturbing than these physical outbursts were some of the moments when the possibility of violence was only suggested; it was a terrifying reminder that the power of the abuser lies not only in what he does, but what he might do.

Bogdanov's production was one of many recent ones which has tried to reclaim the play for a contemporary audience by confronting rather than by ameliorating its misogyny. By showing the destructive capacities of a misogynistic culture (which was both Renaissance Padua and our own society) the play was presented not as a celebration of Petruchio's 'taming' of Kate, but as a bitter indictment of it. Speaking at a London symposium addressing the general topic of 'Is Shakespeare Still Our Contemporary?', the Hungarian critic Anna Földes described a production in Budapest which gave the story the same twist:

> The director succeeded in altering the conflict and the conclusion of the play. Even the set was unusual. It was composed of gold chains suggesting the golden prison of marriage. Instead of the normal induction scene, the director opened the play with the closing monologue, as a statement about marriage and about accepting the traditional passive role in marriage, as a lively young girl might do, enthusiastically, hopefully, but also ironically. Later on, as in the text, the monologue was repeated, but the meaning was different. Kate's confession

> sounded like a bitter, hopeless protest song. Kate, as she gave herself up, was lost . . . That was how it ended, with the image of her pale face and grey dress; and beneath them, we felt all the lost illusions . . . [20]

In the same discussion, the Turkish writer Zeynep Oral described an even more radical Turkish production, in which the play was turned unambiguously into a tragedy: as Kate delivered her final speech she stood with her arms covered in a huge shawl. As she reached the end of the speech, the audience discover that she had cut her wrists: the play ended with her death. Some people might find such a radical staging of the play unacceptable in terms of what has traditionally been seen as the play's intended meaning. It is not necessary at this point to go into the whole literary-critical debate about the place and validity of an author's supposed intentions in an interpretation of a text: sufficient to say that the production deliberately went against the grain of expected interpretations. Zeynep Oral, at any rate, accepts that this ending 'may have been the complete opposite of what Shakespeare intended'[21] and she finds nothing wrong with that.

Another kind of solution to the problems of the play was found by Mark Brickman in his 1990 production at the Crucible Theatre, Sheffield. This production made much of the framing device of the Induction and the Christopher Sly plot, in order to create a critical distance from the Kate-narrative. In doing so, it drew on recent trends in editorial scholarship.

Most modern printed editions of *The Taming of the Shrew* tend to derive from the Folio edition of Shakespeare's plays, printed in 1623, seven years after the author's death. There was no edition of the play we know published in Shakespeare's lifetime. There was, however, a play entitled *A Pleasant Conceited Historie, Called The Taming of A Shrew*, published anonymously in 1594, which has survived. Until recently, *The Taming of A Shrew* was not easily available and tended to be read only by specialists of Elizabethan drama, who were more or less unanimous in their condemnation of it as an inferior piece of theatre.

The similarities between *A Shrew* and *The Shrew* are more striking than the differences. *A Shrew* is set in Athens, not in Padua, and the main characters, with the exception of Kate, have different names from their counterparts in *The Shrew*, but the action of both plays is more or less identical, as are many of the speeches. The exact relationship between *A Shrew* and *The Shrew* has never been established, and traditional scholars were split between those who viewed the 1594 play as a pirated version of the 'authentic' Shakespearean text (represented by the Folio version of the play) which had been reconstructed from memory by an unscrupulous literary bootlegger, and those who saw it as a play in its own right, written by an anonymous playwright and then used by Shakespeare as source material for his own play. More recent Renaissance editorial scholarship, however, tends to place less stress on locating any single authoritative original text of a play. It is now more commonly accepted that, even in Shakespeare's own time and in Shakespeare's own company, his plays were likely to have existed in multiple drafts. According to this view, *A Shrew* is as valuable and as valid a text as the 1623 Folio version.[22]

The point about these editorial arguments is that they relate, in this case, to a significant difference which does exist between the two texts, a difference which concerns the Christopher Sly plot. In the 1623 Folio and in most subsequent editions of *The Shrew*, Sly disappears early on in the play: he is there to introduce the main plot which concerns Kate and Petruchio, but having introduced it he is of little further interest. The earlier text, on the other hand, never lets the audience forget his presence: he interrupts the action from time to time to have the plot explained to him, then falls asleep again, only to wake once more to try to interfere in the action. The play ends, not with Kate's big speech at the banquet and Lucentio's chagrin, but back outside the door of the inn from which Sly was so ignominiously ejected at the beginning of the play. There the Tapster finds the sleeping Sly, who, like Bottom awaking from his enchantment, attempts to make sense of the 'dream' he has just had.

> *Sly* Who's this? Tapster, oh Lord sirra, I have had the bravest dream tonight, that ever thou hadst in all thy life.
>
> *Tapster* Ay marry, but you had best get you home, for your wife will curse you for dreaming here tonight.
>
> *Sly* Will she? I know now how to tame a shrew. I dreamed upon it all this night till now, and thou hast wakt me out of the best dream that ever I had in my life. But I'll to my wife presently and tame her too, an if she anger me.[23]

Mark Brickman's 1990 production used this short exchange as a key with which to re-open the seemingly closed ending of the play. During Kate's final speech, which had been played entirely straight, the audience sat in intense and uncomfortable silence, broken by a few hisses towards the end of it. The shift into the Sly scene broke the tension. Sly's claim that 'I know now how to tame a shrew . . . I'll to my wife presently and tame her too, an if she anger me' was played as the empty boasting of a windbag – and the 'Tapster' (played in this production as a woman) responded by chasing Sly out of the auditorium. The focus was shifted away from Kate's speech itself, and onto the question of how it might be read, and of what audiences do with plays. Sly's naïve assumption, that he – or we – have just been treated to an object lesson in how to handle a woman, is abruptly refuted.

I am not suggesting that any one of the productions mentioned above has 'the' answer to *The Taming of the Shrew.* Theatre is by its nature ephemeral; solutions are always partial and contingent and each time they have to be sought anew. The point is that staging *The Taming of the Shrew* involves precisely this: searching for solutions. The same is true of other Shakespeare comedies as well, and there is, perhaps, no way out of this problematic – apart from that advocated by David Thacker in the 'Is Shakespeare Still Our Contemporary?' symposium. Appealing to radicals and conservatives alike, he expressed doubts about attempts to restage Shakespeare in such a way as to highlight contemporary meanings:

> If you think that *The Merchant of Venice* is an antisemitic play, the answer is not to change it, but not to do it at all. The same applies to *The Taming of the Shrew.* If you think it's sexist, don't do it . . . You don't have to alter *The Merchant of Venice* to validate the play, just as you needn't have Katherine slashing her wrists at the end of *The Shrew* to make it less sexist. But if you feel that these plays are sexist or racist, don't do them. There are other plays which you can do instead.[24]

This is true enough. But it is also an opting out of the continual renegotiation of meanings to which all texts – but especially ones with the mythological status of *The Taming of the Shrew* – are subject.

Love's Labour's Lost

Love's Labour's Lost provides an audience with a different kind of problem of accessibility: it seems to be (on one level at least) one big in-joke, written for private performance before a particular audience and containing a wealth of topical allusions which are directed at that audience. For a long time this reputation was sufficient to keep it off the stage: no performance of it is recorded between 1605 and 1829, when it was revived at Covent Garden. In the mid-twentieth century, its topicality gave it an attraction for scholars, who traced allusions to contemporary events and personalities such as Sir Walter Raleigh, the rivalry between pamphleteers Nashe and Harvey, Anglo-Russian relationships, the Queen's progresses, the Earl of Northumberland and the Earl of

Essex, as well as to Shakespeare himself and the Dark Lady of his sonnets. Frances Yates argued that the play was Shakespeare's intervention on the side of Essex in a personal and ideological quarrel between the Earl and Sir Walter Raleigh;[25] Richard David describes it as 'a battle in a private war between court factions'.[26] None of this helped make it a popular stage play, though.

Nor did the play's obsession with some specifically Elizabethan debates about language, which has more recently attracted the attention of critics with an interest in linguistic theory, theory of discourse and semiotics. The play was written at a time when the English language was going through a period of rapid change, and the variety of registers and idiolects which are used in the play bears witness to Shakespeare's interest in this. The play is, in part, *about* language, and the different relationships in which people stand to it: the pomposity of Armado and Holofernes derives in part from the fact that they see words as ends in themselves.

> *Holofernes* The deer was, as you know – *sanguis* – in blood, ripe as the pomewater who now hangeth like a jewel in the ear of *caelo*, the sky, the welkin, the heaven, and anon falleth like a crab on the face of *terra*, the soil, the land, the earth . . .
> (IV, ii, ll, 3–7)

Holofernes's rhetoric, the wordplays of Moth (or 'Mote'),[27] Costard's malapropisms, Armado's magniloquence, the lords' sonneteering and love-speeches, 'honey-tongued' Boyet's smooth courtesies, call into question the relationship between words and things. This was a question particularly pressing at a time when claims were being pressed for a review of the status of the English language as a medium for serious discourse.

More recently, however, it has become more common to play down the specifically Elizabethan and topical dimensions of *Love's Labour's Lost*, and to argue for it more pragmatically, as a play which works well theatrically, no matter what its origins in Elizabethan linguistic theory or factional politics.[28] Yet if the play *does* work theatrically, it does so by breaking some of the most basic rules in the playwright's handbook. A play, according both to common tradition and to Aristotle, is supposed to have a beginning, a middle and an end: *Love's Labour's Lost* manages a little more than one out of three.

A beginning it certainly has. The basic situation of the play is established in the opening moments, and its theme stated clearly. In order to cheat 'cormorant devouring time . . . And make us heirs of all eternity' (I, i, ll. 4, 7), the King of Navarre attempts to set up an alternative world of learning in his court, an ivory tower divorced from the real world.

> *King* Our court shall be a little academe
> Still and contemplative in living art.
> You three – Biron, Dumaine and Longueville –
> Have sworn for three years' term to live with me
> My fellow scholars, and to keep those statutes
> That are recorded in this schedule here.
>
> (I, i, ll. 13–18)

Since one of the 'statutes' involves the injunction 'not to see a woman in that term' (I, i, l. 37), the thematic opposition between love and learning is established. It is then played out in terms as formal as a medieval debate play (such as John Redford's *Wit and Science*) or an allegorical Jacobean masque (such as Ben Jonson's *Pleasure Reconciled To Virtue*). The unexpected arrival of the French Princess and her train disrupts the King's plans: the 'little academe', the ivory tower of the mind, cannot ignore the demands of the body. Desire triumphs over ascetism, and the male world of pure intellect is shown up as an impossible and undesirable fantasy. In later plays this kind of conflict will prove damaging: when desire strikes into the unemotional world of Angelo in *Measure for Measure* the results are disastrous. In *Love's Labour's Lost,* however, the King and his courtiers are persuaded easily enough that their original attempt to separate mind from body, and intellect from passion, was mistaken. Berowne (or Biron),[29] who was never too keen on the idea in the first place, reconciles the two: women's eyes, he explains to the others,

> . . . are the books, the arts, the academes
> That show, contain and nourish all the world . . .
> Let us once lose our oaths to find ourselves,
> Or else we lose ourselves to keep our oaths.
>
> (IV, ii, ll. 328–9, 337–8)

And so ascetism is renounced in favour of courtship, which is the true learning, after all.

But although the thematic level is played out clearly enough, with love being reconciled to intellect, readers and audiences have often felt that not a great deal actually happens in terms of the story, that the play does not have much of a 'middle'. '*Love's Labour's Lost* is more like a . . . revue, or a musical comedy without music, than a play', says one critic. 'It is deficient in plot and in characterisation. There is little story in it. Its situations do not present successive incidents in an ordered plot.'[30] Another complains that '*Love's Labour's Lost* has no known source and almost no action. Some ladies arrive and at the end a messenger arrives'.[31] The plot is not quite as threadbare as this makes it seem: eavesdroppings, disguises, misdirected letters and scenes involving the local villagers contribute to the narrative. Yet a feeling of stasis does pervade the play, as if the King of Navarre's attempt to create a world outside time had had an effect on the plot.

This stasis stems from the fact that the plot is full of things which seems *about* to happen, but which are continually interrupted, frustrated or simply left unfinished. Louis A. Montrose has called *Love's Labour's Lost* a 'scenario for dramatic imitations of games and rituals';[32] but it is better described as a series of failed stratagems. The title of the play is strikingly apt: time after time the labours of the lovers come to nothing. Costard's wooing of Jaquenetta is interrupted, nor does Armado's letter reach her. Berowne's letter to Rosaline is similarly diverted; the King and lords are each interrupted in the middle of their soliloquies about love, and then in their subsequent hypocritical attempts to claim the moral high ground regarding their oaths. Their courtship of their chosen ladies is equally disastrous: the impersonation of the Russian ambassadors is a miserable failure which fools nobody, and each man ends up talking to the wrong woman. The play-within-the-play, the Pageant of the Nine Worthies, is interrupted almost continually by the audience butting in, and then by the arrival of Mercadé with the news for the Princess of her father's death.

None of these interruptions is strange in itself, although perhaps the sheer number of them is. But comedies are frequently structured around interruptions: they are the obstacles which characters have to overcome in order to reach their goals. What is unusual about *Love's Labour's Lost* is that there is so little forward movement in it. Characters do not overcome obstacles: they go back and start again. Moreover, in the last few moments of the play, when it looks as though, finally the various stratagems and flirtations are about to lead up to something, Shakespeare pulls off a strange *coup de théâtre* which caps all the previous interruptions. Mercadé's announcement does not only interrupt the Pageant of the Nine Worthies: it interrupts *Love's Labour's Lost*, too. The promised ending seems all set to materialize, with the ladies about to accept the lords as lovers, when it is all postponed. Just as romantic love had broken into the world of art, so death breaks into the celebrations of romantic love.

Thus the play ends with deferral. The happy ending lies twelve months beyond the play, during which time both the King and Berowne are to undergo further trials. The King must

> . . . go with speed
> To some forlorn and naked hermitage
> Remote from all the pleasures of the world.
> There stay until the twelve celestial signs
> Have brought about the annual reckoning.
> If this austere, insociable life
> Change not your offer made in heat of blood . . .
> I will be thine.
>
> (V, ii, ll. 787–93, 800)

Rosaline, meanwhile, instructs Berowne that:

> to win me, if you please,
> Without the which I am not to be won,
> You shall this twelvemonth term from day to day
> Visit the speechless sick and still converse
> With groaning wretches, and your task shall be
> With all the fierce endeavour of your wit
> To enforce the pained impotent to smile.
>
> (V, ii, ll. 835–41)

The appropriateness of the men's tasks has often been remarked upon: Berowne is a creature of wit and language, and Rosaline's injunction that he should 'jest a twelvemonth in a hospital' (V, ii, l. 858) offers him a chance to put his talents to altruistic use. The changeable King is given a year to think about things: a prudent move on the part of the Princess. But the tasks also imply a change on the part of the King and lords: they will at the end of this time be more suited for marriage than they are now. Thus the comedy locates its primary agency for character development outside the play itself: it is what takes place in the next twelve months that will make the difference, not what we have seen in the play.

The final moments of *Love's Labour's Lost* also contain an element of circularity. The King and Berowne are both enjoined to remove themselves from the world for a period of time: which is what the King wanted to do at the very start of the play. Not only does *Love's Labour's Lost* leave its characters to develop beyond the narrative bounds of the play, it suggests (especially in the task imposed on the King) that the debate between the values of the ivory tower and the world outside is not finally settled after all.

It may be that the deferred happy ending of *Love's Labour's Lost* was constructed for a specific and very practical purpose: that of allowing room for a sequel. What we have may be the first play of a two-parter which was planned – or even written. In

Francis Meres's *Palladis Tamia* (1598),[33] there is a list of contemporary authors and works: *Love's Labour's Lost* is paired with another play, entitled *Love's Labour's Won.* No play of that name is extant, and nobody knows quite what to make of Meres's entry. The existence of a play of that name, however, has been substantiated from other sources: a stationer's stock-list for August 1603 mentions it. Could it be that *Love's Labour's Won* refers to a lost Shakespeare play – perhaps one which took up the story of *Love's Labour's Lost* and brought it to a conclusion?

Love's Labour's Won remains an enigma, and anything to do with it is sheer speculation. My own preference is for the alternative popular hypothesis: that what we see is what we get, and that the 'lost' play never existed, but that the title refers to one of Shakespeare's known plays under a different name (*The Taming of the Shrew, All's Well That Ends Well* and *Much Ado About Nothing* have all been proposed). *Love's Labour's Lost* ends the way it does, not because a sequel was expected, nor because Shakespeare was too young and inexperienced to do any better, but because he was discovering something essential about the kinds of comedies he wanted to write: that the conventional comedic happy ending constituted a problem rather than a solution. To disrupt the ending as he did in *Love's Labour's Lost,* to defer the gratification to a fictional point twelve months hence, was an ingenious solution – but one which could work only once. From this point onwards he needed to find other ways of coming to terms with the problem of closure.

Notes

1. F. S. Boas, *Shakespeare and his Predecessors* (Murray, 1896).
2. William Shakespeare, *The Two Gentlemen of Verona,* ed. Clifford Leech (London: Methuen, 1969), pp. xxiv–xxviii.
3. David Daniell, 'Shakespeare and the traditions of comedy', in Stanley Wells, ed., *The Cambridge Companion to Shakespeare Studies* (Cambridge: Cambridge University Press, 1986), pp. 104–5.
4. Malcolm Bradbury and David Palmer, eds, *Stratford-Upon-Avon Studies, 14: Early Shakespeare* (London: Edward Arnold, 1972), p. 220.
5. Quoted in Graham Holderness, *Shakespeare in Performance: The Taming of the Shrew* (Manchester: Manchester University Press, 1989), p. 40.
6. Quoted in ibid., p. 41.
7. Quoted in ibid., pp. 40–1.
8. Quoted in ibid., p. 46.
9. Quoted in ibid., p. 41.
10. Judith Cook, *Women in Shakespeare* (1980, reprinted London: W. H. Allen & Co., 1990).

11. Ibid., p. 28.
12. Ibid., pp. 28–9.
13. Ibid., p. 29.
14. Ibid., p. 28.
15. Ibid., p. 29.
16. Quoted in Holderness, *Shakespeare in Performance*, p. 117.
17. Cook, *Women in Shakespeare*, pp. 27–8.
18. Christopher J. McCullough, interview with Michael Bogdanov in Graham Holderness, ed., *The Shakespeare Myth* (Manchester: Manchester University Press), p. 89.
19. Michael Bogdanov, quoted in John Elsom, ed., *Is Shakespeare Still Our Contemporary*? (London: Routledge, 1989), pp. 69–70.
20. Anna Földes, quoted in Elsom, *Is Shakespeare Still Our Contemporary*?, pp. 73–4.
21. Zeynep Oral, quoted in Elsom, *Is Shakespeare Still Our Contemporary*?, p. 75.
22. See William Shakespeare (?), *The Taming of A Shrew*, ed. Graham Holderness and Bryan Loughrey (Brighton: Harvester Wheatsheaf, 1992), pp. 13–40.
23. Ibid., p. 89.
24. David Thacker, quoted in Elsom, *Is Shakespeare Still Our Contemporary*?, p. 179.
25. Frances Yates, *A Study of Love's Labour's Lost* (Cambridge: Cambridge University Press, 1936).
26. William Shakespeare, *Love's Labour's Lost*, ed. Richard David (London: Methuen, 1956), p. 1.
27. Stanley Wells and Gary Taylor, the editors of the Oxford *Complete Works* of Shakespeare, the edition referred to throughout this volume, are occasionally idiosyncratic about the versions of characters' names which they chose to employ, frequently using a variant which is at odds with accepted usage. Most editors, for example, call Armado's boy 'Moth' and the Lord of Navarre 'Berowne'; the Oxford editors prefer 'Mote' and 'Biron'. These variants have their advantages ('Mote', for example, draws attention to the character's small size) but they are not necessarily more 'correct' than traditional usage: in both the first Quarto and the first Folio editions of the play, 'Moth/Mote' is generally referred to in the speech-tags as 'Boy', whereas 'Biron' as a variant of 'Berowne' first appeared in the second Folio. To avoid confusion on the part of readers familiar with traditional versions of the names I have signalled where a variant is used by the Oxford editors, but have tended to revert in the text to conventional usage.
28. William Shakespeare, *The Complete Works*, eds Stanley Wells and Gary Taylor (Oxford: Oxford University Press, 1986–7), p. 315; Daniell, 'Shakespeare and the traditions of comedy', p. 107.

Plate 1: Engravings in The Sport and Pastimes of the People of England *by Joseph Strutt, 1810. Reproduced with kind permission of the Bodleian Library (shelfm. Douce S 803).*

Plate 2: Miniature in the fourteenth century Li Romans du boim roi Alixandre. *Reproduced with kind permission of the Bodleian Library (shelfm. 264, fol. 181 v lower border left.)*

Plate 3: British Library, Harley MS 3885 fol. 19.

Plate 4: From the title page of Kempe's Nine Day's Wonder, *1600. Reproduced with kind permission of the Bodleian Library (shelfm. 4 L 62 Art (12)). (left)*

Plate 5: From the title page of Robert Armin's Two Maids of More-Clacke, *1609. Reproduced with kind permission of the Bodleian Library (shelfm. Mal 201(2)).*

Plate 6: Woodcut, pre-1600. From the collection of EJ Burford. Previously published in Of Bridles and Burnings: The Punishment of Women, *by EJ Burford and Sandra Schulman (New York: St Martin's Press, 1992), page 80.*

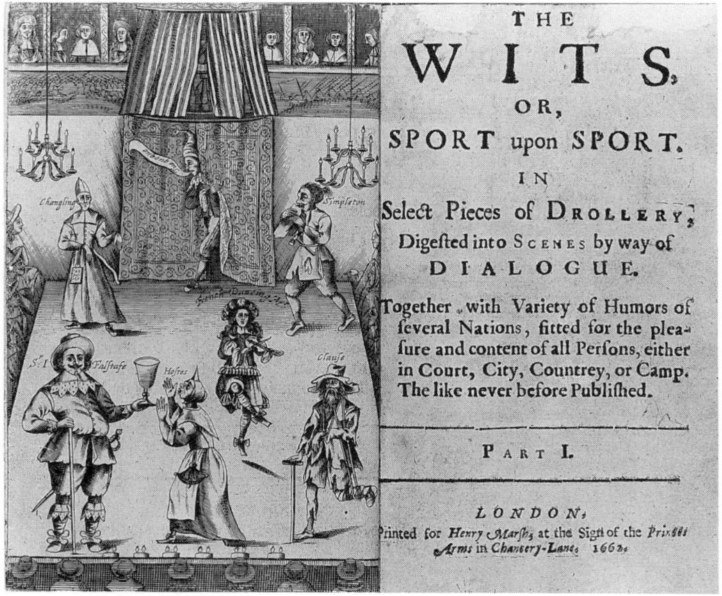

Plate 7: Title page of Robin Goodfellow: His Mad Pranks and Merry Jests, *London 1639. Reproduced with kind permission of Folger Shakespeare Library.*

Plate 8: Title page and illustration from The Wits: Or Sport Upon Sport, *London 1662. Reproduced with kind permission of Folger Shakespeare Library.*

Plate 9: Manuscript music by William Byrd, from the private collection of Lord Petre. Reproduced with kind permission of the Essex Record Office.

Plate 10: 'The Fight Between Carnival and Lent' by Pieter Bruegel, 1560. Reproduced with kind permission of the Kunsthistorisches Museum, Vienna.

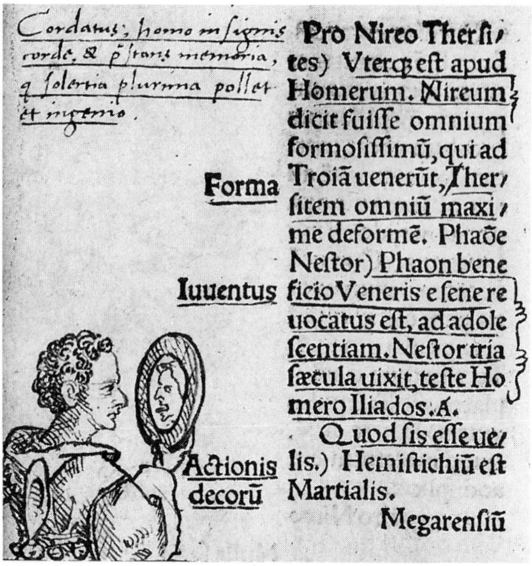

Cordatus; homo insignis corde, & p̃stans memoria, q solertia plurima pollet et ingenio.
Pro Nireo Thersi/
tes) Vterq3 est apud
Homerum. Nireum
dicit fuisse omnium
formosissimũ, qui ad
Forma
Troiã uenerũt, Ther/
sitem omniũ maxi/
me deformẽ. Phaõe
Nestor) Phaon bene
Iuuentus
ficio Veneris e sene re
uocatus est, ad adole
scentiam. Nestor tria
sæcula uixit, teste Ho
mero Iliados. A.
Quod sis esse ue/
Actionis decorũ
lis.) Hemistichiũ est
Martialis.
Megarensiũ

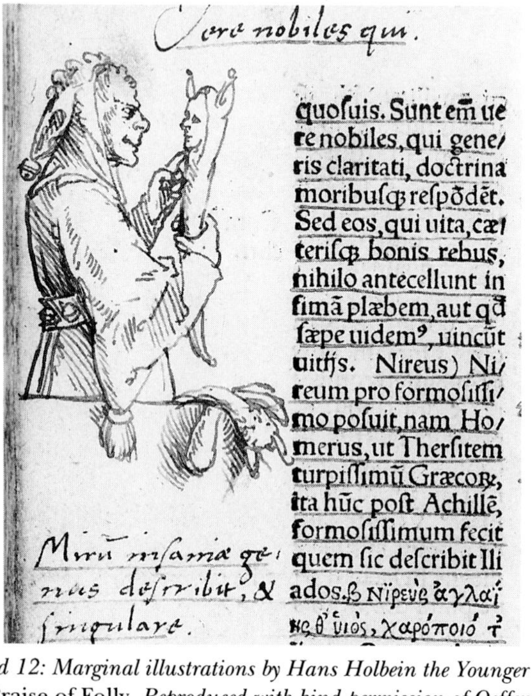

Vere nobiles qui.
quosuis. Sunt em̃ ue
re nobiles, qui gene/
ris claritati, doctrina

Sed eos, qui uita, cæ/

nihilo antecellunt in

uitijs. Nireus) Ni/

mo posuit, nam Ho/

quem sic describit Ili

Plate 11 and 12: Marginal illustrations by Hans Holbein the Younger in Erasmus's Praise of Folly. *Reproduced with kind permission of Oeffentliche Kunstsammlung, Basel.*

29. See note 27 above.
30. H. B. Charlton, *Shakespearian Comedy* (London: Methuen, 1939), p. 270.
31. Daniell, 'Shakespeare and the traditions of comedy', p. 106.
32. Louis A. Montrose, ' "Sport by Sport O'erthrown": *Love's Labour's Lost* and the politics of play', in Gary Waller, ed., *Shakespeare's Comedies* (Harlow: Longman, 1991), p. 32.
33. Francis Meres, *Palladis Tamia* (London, 1598).

6 A Midsummer Night's Dream

'A league without the town'

A Midsummer Night's Dream tells the story of an escape:

> *Lysander* I have a widow aunt, a dowager
> Of great revenue, and she hath no child,
> And she respects me as her only son.
> From Athens is her house remote seven leagues.
> There, gentle Hermia, may I marry thee,
> And to that place the sharp Athenian law
> Cannot pursue us. If thou lov'st me then
> Steal forth thy father's house tomorrow night,
> And in the wood, a league without the town,
> Where I did meet thee once with Helena
> To do observance to a morn of May,
> There will I stay for thee.
>
> (I, i, ll. 157–68)

Faced with an impossible choice, between marriage to a man she does not love, or death, or a lifetime's vow of chastity, Hermia flees with Lysander, away from the court of Athens towards the safety of his dowager aunt's house. Of course they never get there: the journey takes them no farther than that part of 'the wood, a league without the town' where the action of the central three acts is set. From the very start the setting is imbued with significance: Lysander reminds Hermia that it is the place where they once met with Helena to celebrate May Day. In Tudor times May Day was one the main festivals of the year, and was associated both with erotic licence and with magic. And now they plan to meet there again on Midsummer's Night, another similar festival. François Laroque gives the following description of the Midsummer celebrations:

> In England, as in most of the countries of mainland Europe, the advent of summer and the triumph of light over darkness was greeted with a show of bonfires. These bonfires were the focus for all kinds of revelries which perpetuated the memory of superstitions and quite a few magic rites, all of which were associated in popular culture with the particular powers of this, the shortest night of the year. The magical fascination of fire was supplemented by the burning of certain herbs to the accompaniment of incantations. In London and other large

> towns the Midsummer festival was also an occasion for grand parades . . . [containing figures such as the] giants who were no doubt the equivalent of those who paraded at Carnival time on the Continent. As many of these figures also appeared in the May game, a certain confusion arose between the rites of May and those of Midsummer's Eve . . . At all events, Midsummer was a season which became synonymous with confusion and even mental aberration. Midsummer's Eve was traditionally a night of mistakes and wandering wits.[1]

On such a night of mistakes and wandering wits the lovers meet in the wood outside the city. When they return to the court they, like Nick Bottom, have undergone a kind of transformation: Jack has Jill and the affections of all the young people have been realigned in ways which allow their reintegration into the society which seemed, at the beginning of the play, intent on punishing them.

It is a typical pattern of Shakespearean comedy: an opposition between on the one hand an authoritative (even authoritarian) structure and on the other something subversive, something which will reject or oppose and potentially undermine that authority. In this case the oppositions are between law and love: the law which Egeus invokes, and the love between Hermia and Lysander which is not socially sanctioned but which is, we are in no doubt, 'true love'. These binary oppositions of Shakespearean comedy are frequently linked, as they are here, to symbolically contrasting places: in *A Midsummer Night's Dream* the court is opposed to the country as it is in *As You Like It* and *The Winter's Tale.* In each of these cases the pattern is similar: the court represents a harsh or threatening environment, the countryside a place of escape, which may contain its own dangers but which allows the protagonists a temporary haven before their eventual return to the court.

And so *A Midsummer Night's Dream* starts in the court of Duke Theseus. This, for all its preparation for the wedding night celebrations, is a place which is portrayed in this early part of the play as harsh, uncompromising, and unsympathetic to the claims of the young lovers. Egeus treats it not only as a court of princes but also as a court in that other sense of the word, a court of law. Bringing Hermia before it for judgement, he claims that 'As she is mine, I may dispose of her' (I, i, l. 42). In this Egeus is stating an Elizabethan commonplace. The importance of the patriarchal family was central to sixteenth-century concepts of order: it was the foundation of a hierarchical concept of society which linked monarch and subject. The authority of the male head of the household was analogous to that of the head of state; and the fact that the monarch, throughout the later part of the sixteenth century, was biologically female had little effect on this way of thinking. As Sir Robert Filmer explained: 'As the father over one family, so the King, as father over many families, extends his care to preserve, feed, clothe, instruct and defend the whole commonwealth'.[2] Thomas Beard developed the idea in his *Theatre of God's Judgement*: 'As it is a thing required by law and reason that children bear the honour and reverence to their natural parents which is commanded, so it is necessary . . . that all subjects perform that duty of honour and obedience to their Lords, Princes and Kings'.[3] Thus the Elizabethan father's authority derived from the same source as the ruler's, and to challenge one was tantamount to challenging the whole societal hierarchy.

Small wonder, then, that Egeus approaches Theseus's court confident of its unqualified support; nor that he receives it. Theseus upholds Egeus's complaint and warns Hermia that:

> To you your father should be as a god,
> One that composed your beauties, yea, and one
> To whom you are but as a form in wax,
> By him imprinted, and within his power
> To leave the figure or disfigure it.
>
> (I, i, ll. 47–51)

Even by the standards of sixteenth-century English attitudes towards parental authority this sounds a little extreme – as are the legal reprisals which Hermia faces should she choose to disobey the combined power of her father and her prince.

> *Hermia* But I beseech your grace that I may know
> The worst that may befall me in this case
> If I refuse to wed Demetrius.
> *Theseus* Either to die the death, or to abjure
> For ever the society of men . . .
> Take time to pause, and by the next new moon –
> The sealing day betwixt my love and me
> For everlasting bond of fellowship –
> Upon that day either prepare to die
> For disobedience to your father's will,
> Or else to wed Demetrius, as he would,
> Or on Diana's altar to protest
> For aye austerity and single life.
>
> (I, i, ll. 62–6, 83–90)

The court of Duke Theseus represents, among other things, a

particularly harsh version of patriarchal authority. It is an authority which the action of the comedy's next few acts goes on to oppose.

And so Hermia and Lysander, pursued by Demetrius and Helena, run away from that world of law, reason and society, into the 'wood, a league without the town' (I, i, l. 165). The wood is all that lies outside Theseus's rational world. The old English word 'wood' also meant 'mad', and this meaning – almost obsolete by the end of the sixteenth century – is mobilized again by Shakespeare. Demetrius, searching for Hermia and attempting to shake off Helena, makes the pun explicit. Describing his own frenzied state of mind, he says:

> Thou told'st me they were stolen unto this wood
> And here am I, and wood within this wood
> Because I cannot meet my Hermia.
>
> (II, i, ll. 190–2)

The court versus country opposition thus takes on another dimension: that of the opposition between a kind of reason and a kind of madness. But the 'reason' which Athens represents at the beginning of the play is, as we have seen, repressive and authoritarian. It is precisely to escape from the court and its endorsement of parental authority that the lovers run off through the woods. They seek a refuge, the house of Lysander's aunt. They are running away from the male environment towards a female place of safety, but in order to reach that destination they must pass through the 'wood', the place of liberating 'madness', of healing chaos. The wood in which they lose themselves appears to be the very antithesis of Theseus's court: the domain of the subconscious, perhaps, as opposed to the conscious, rational and repressive world of the court.

The lovers seek different things in the wood. Hermia and Lysander seek a refuge, a place where they can be free to love. Demetrius seeks Hermia, and Helena Demetrius. In terms of the play's psychodynamic structure it appears that the magic of the wood, and of the creative order-in-chaos of nature which they encounter there, acts to heal the wounds of a society in which parental authority seeks to trample over the desires of young lovers. The wood, it seems, will be the place of healing in which the lovers find fulfilment – and each other.

Not that this happens without peril. The lovers encounter there more than they bargain for, and are continually subject to the whims of the *genii loci*, the spirits of the place, in the persons of Oberon, Puck and the other fairies. These act upon them in ways they do not expect; nor do the lovers ever become conscious of them. For some time it appears that their night of 'dreaming' is going to make things worse rather than better, as affections are magically and chaotically transferred from person to person.

There is, then, something dangerous about this wood; and although the powers which inhabit it act, in the end, benevolently towards the Athenian lovers, they do so only as a by-product of their own continuing 'brawls', which have already seeded natural disorders and disasters, so that

> . . . the winds, piping to us in vain
> As in revenge have sucked up from the sea
> Contagious fogs, which, falling in the land,
> Hath every pelting river made so proud
> That they have overborne their continents.
> The ox hath therefore stretched his yoke in vain,
> The ploughman lost his sweat, and the green corn
> Hath rotted ere his youth attained a beard.
> The fold stands empty in the drowned field,
> And crows are fatted with the murrain flock.
> (II, i, ll. 88–97)

That picture of agricultural desolation is one which would have been grimly familiar to Shakespeare's audiences, who in the years 1594–97 experienced four successive years of disastrous harvests. The repeated cycle of famine which was a feature of sixteenth-century English life was particularly intense as Shakespeare wrote *A Midsummer Night's Dream.* London's own economy was wealthy enough and flexible enough to supplement its home produce with imported grain from the Balkans, and thus ensure that Londoners did not die in large numbers for want of food, as they had during earlier famines of Elizabeth's reign. Nonetheless there were rural populations in the northern and western counties who *were* starving to death, and even closer to the capital the intensity of the resulting social distress led to petitions, disturbances and riots.[4] And Shakespeare annexes the real-life famine as part of his own fictional world. The forest spirits who act so benevolently towards the Athenian lovers are also, on an allegorical level, the 'parents and original' of the famine that stalked the land, and representatives of a more savage aspect of nature which was well-known to the Elizabethean peasantry.

Yet the play is a comedy, and the comic trajectory ensures that although the protagonists may be surrounded by potential disasters, they will survive to celebrate an ending where 'Jack shall have Jill, Naught shall go ill, The man shall have his mare again, and all shall be well' (III, iii, ll. 45–8). Despite its dangers, the place they have arrived in is one which works benevolently upon them – even though they themselves know little about it. Unlike the heroes and heroines of romance or epic, who have to struggle to prove themselves, pass tests, overcome great obstacles, these comic heroes and heroines are simply there. They are virtually passive as enchantments are worked upon them, and the happy ending to their muddles is brought about by placing a spell on Demetrius from which he never emerges. The Athenian lovers have almost nothing to do – except lie down, fall asleep and dream.

'It seems that yet we sleep, we dream'

The title of the play signals the importance of dream and its associated modes of knowing: fantasy, imagination, magic. Both for an Elizabethan audience and – even more so – for a twentieth-century one, dreams can be seen to represent a kind of truth. A modern audience can bring to the play the great body of Freudian and post-Freudian thought which stresses the importance of dreams in the makeup of the human psyche, and their ability to function as what Freud called, in *Five Lectures on Psychoanalysis*, the 'royal road to a knowledge of the unconscious'.[5] Modern art-forms have relied heavily on dream imagery as a source of meaning, and it has become a commonplace of a certain kind of psychoanalytic criticism that Shakespeare intuitively shared this belief in the meaningfulness of dreams.[6] We have learned to see important links between the creativity of the artist and that of the dreamer, and *A Midsummer Night's Dream* makes constant play with these associations.

Freud and the twentieth-century psychoanalytic tradition provide one well-developed framework for the interpretation of dreams, but the significance and importance of the language of dreams is well established in both classical Greek and Roman, and also in the Judaeo-Christian hermeneutic traditions to which Elizabethan culture was heir. There are obvious examples in those Biblical stories which proclaim the significance of dreams, which forewarn the dreamer of danger, or act as a medium through which God speaks to the dreamer. Prominent among these is the story in the book of *Genesis*, in which the imprisoned Joseph interprets the dreams of the baker and the butler, and then of Pharoah. Medieval scholars debated the relationships between dreaming and waking, and Chaucer's *Nun's Priest's Tale* both summarizes and parodies several of the scholastic arguments.[7] Meanwhile the dream was an essential structuring device for Chaucer and other Middle English poets, giving rise to a great variety of narrative and visionary poems, from *Piers Plowman* to *Pearl*, from *The Parliament of Fowls* to *The Dream of the Rood*.

Even in these early texts, which focus primarily on dreams as prophecy, there is a clear awareness of the ways in which dream-meanings are encoded in symbols, condensed narratives and displaced images. It is possible to see both the similarity and the difference between medieval and twentieth-century traditions of dream exegesis by looking at Hermia's dreams in Act II Scene ii of *A Midsummer Night's Dream*. Waking in panic, she calls out:

> Help me, Lysander, help me! Do thy best
> To pluck this crawling serpent from my breast!
> Ay me, for pity. What a dream was here?
> Lysander, look how I do quake with fear.
> Methought a serpent ate my heart away,
> And you sat smiling at his cruel prey.
> Lysander – what, removed?
>
> (II, ii, ll. 151–7)

Medieval dream interpretation reads this as a warning to Hermia – a vision which tells her what the audience already knows, that Lysander no longer cares for her. The dream is telling her a truth about what is going on around her.

A classical psychoanalytic interpretation shows a greater interest in the subconscious of the dreamer than in the dream's representations of events in waking life: in this interpretative frame, the function of the dream is to tell the dreamer about his/her own inner life. Such an analytic interpretation might thus stress the dual way in which Lysander is represented in Hermia's subconscious: on the one hand he is the phallic serpent, emblem of a threatening sexuality which attacks and harms her (just as Lysander had wanted to lie closer to her than she had been comfortable with); on the other, there is his cold, removed aspect, sitting smiling by while she is tortured.[8] That kind of character-based psychoanalytic criticism might well conclude that the dream conceals/reveals Hermia's hidden ambivalence towards Lysander, feelings perhaps related to those she has for her sinister father-figure Egeus, who holds the power of life or death over Hermia in his attempts to dispose of her sexuality as he sees fit.

Inherent in this interpretive strategy is an assumption that a literary dream such as Hermia's is essentially like the dreams of real-life patients in analysis. Not everybody would agree with such an assumption, including many psychoanalytically-influenced literary critics. Even so, however we approach this particular dream, it does seem that, one way or another, dreams offer themselves up to be read, to be interpreted. And throughout *A Midsummer*

Night's Dream the truth-value of dreams is insisted upon. Linked with this is the reiterated idea that what appears to be a dream may sometimes be literally true. There is a repeated motif in the play, in which a character assumes that they have been dreaming when in fact they have not. Thus Bottom wakes from a charmed sleep and proclaims

> I have had a most rare vision. I have had a dream past the wit of men to say what dream it was . . . I will get Peter Quince to write a ballad of this dream. It shall be called 'Bottom's Dream' because it hath no bottom . . .
>
> (IV, i, ll. 202–4, 211–3)

The audience, however, knows that this was not a dream but reality. Similarly, the lovers, waking from *their* charmed sleep a moment or two earlier, have been confused about their state. Reassuring themselves that they are now awake, they return to Athens, recounting the 'dreams' of the past night – which again the audience have witnessed as truth. Earlier still, Titania has woken from *her* charmed sleep; she too assumes that she has been dreaming: 'What visions I have seen! / Methought I was enamoured of an ass' (IV, i, ll. 75–6). Oberon shows her the still-sleeping Bottom and she accepts her dream as reality.

And so throughout the middle scenes of the play we are repeatedly shown characters falling asleep and waking up. While they sleep on the stage, things happen around them, to them, in spite of them or oblivious to them. In most plays by Shakespeare – and indeed by most playwrights – characters not directly involved in the action are usually left off-stage; in *A Midsummer Night's Dream* they are just as likely to lie down on stage in full view of the audience and fall asleep. This has the double effect of removing characters from the action while keeping them in the eye of the audience: they are both there and not there. (This is perfectly clear in performance, yet it is easy to lose sight – literally or figuratively – of these sleepers when reading the text.) Thus in Act II, Scene ii, Titania falls asleep to the tune of her fairies' song, and lies unconscious while Oberon anoints her eyes with his magic juices; Lysander and Hermia fall asleep exhausted, and Helena wanders onto the scene talking to herself until she stumbles over the sleeping Lysander and wakes him up. Hermia sleeps on while Lysander steals away with Helena, then wakes in terror, frightened by her nightmare. In later scenes all four Athenian lovers sleep on-stage unnoticed by Titania and her fairies, and remain asleep while the massed huntsmen of Theseus's court gather round them; Bottom, on another part of the stage, dozes through both this and the disenchanting of Titania.

People sleep, people dream, and at the end of the night, magically, everything is sorted out. The descent into the wood, the place of the unconscious, the place of dreams, is itself a therapeutic process. Even without the benefit of psychoanalysis (for 'Man is but an ass if he go about t'expound this dream' (IV, i, l. 204)) characters find that their desires can be accommodated to social reality. Hermia and Lysander find that the obstacle to their love has been removed; Demetrius, much to his surprise, finds that he loves Helena better than Hermia after all; 'And the country proverb known, / That "every man should take his own", / In [their] waking shall be shown' (III, iii, ll. 42–4).

And as characters sleep and wake, the play's narrative and imagery itself takes on the logic of a dream: fairies, spirits, magic, animal transformations, inexplicably changed affections. Hermia's nightmare about the snake attacking her is less dream-like than what 'actually' happened: that a fairy put a magic potion on Lysander's eyelids so that when Helena passed by he woke up and immediately fell in love with her. Perhaps *all* the events in the wood are a dream after all? But if so, whose? Not one of the characters', surely, for none of them has a sufficiently broad perspective to encompass all the events in the wood. In which case perhaps the dream is ours, the audience's?

As the play continues, this conceit is developed: the world of dreams and the world of theatrical representation are analogous to each other. All the world is a stage and life is a dream:[9] these two famous Renaissance conceits feed off each other. The audience is invited to participate in a fiction which is itself dream-like, and to consider the similarities between theatrical illusion and the experience of dreaming. In *The Taming of A Shrew* Christopher Sly saw a play and thought afterwards that he had been dreaming. And here, in the play which is commonly called 'the *Dream*', the same issue is raised. In Puck's final Epilogue the audience's experience of the play they have just seen as a whole is explicitly likened to that of a dream:

> If we shadows have offended,
> Think but this, and all is mended:
> That you have but slumbered here,
> While these visions did appear;
> And this weak and idle theme,
> No more yielding but a dream . . .
>
> *Epilogue*, ll. 1–6)

Puck's apparent dismissal of dreams as 'weak and idle', and

yielding nothing, is ironic; throughout the play the audience has been shown repeatedly the 'truth' which resides in dreams. Now, by extension, the same truth-value is attributed to the stage. 'Bottom's Dream' is also ours, and it has been made not into a ballad by Peter Quince but into a play by William Shakespeare. The play which continually argues for the truth of dreams argues also for the truth of the stage.

'Man is but an ass if he go about t'expound this dream'

But what is this 'truth of the stage'? Not, presumably, a truth divorced from historical conditions, or from the conditions of performance. There is a well-established tradition that *A Midsummer Night's Dream* was written to be first performed at the celebrations of an aristocratic wedding. There is no consensus as to which wedding it might have been, although many have been proposed. The editor of the Arden edition, Harold F. Brooks, tells us that 'most scholars are agreed that the *Dream* was designed to grace a wedding in a noble household',[10] and he believes it to have been the marriage of Elizabeth Carey and Thomas, son of Henry Lord Berkeley. The wedding of Mary Countess of Southampton and Thomas Heneage has also been proposed, and more recently, a strong argument has been made that the occasion was that of the marriage between William, the Sixth Earl of Derby, and Elizabeth deVere.[11]

While the hypothesis of the play's being written for such an event remains unproven it is certainly a sufficiently plausible one. The custom of having such dramatic entertainments at aristocratic weddings is well-documented historically, and it is also testified to in the *Dream* itself. In the last act, the Peter Quince Players perform for Duke Theseus's celebrations – just as, we might imagine, the Lord Chamberlain's Men were performing for the household of the Berkeleys, Southamptons or Derbys. *A Midsummer Night's Dream* is already a strikingly self-reflexive play, staging as it does the staging of a play; but if the original conditions of performance were at a royal wedding, it takes on yet another dimension of reflexivity. A real-life English aristocratic audience at a wedding celebration watches a play which contains a fictional Athenian aristocratic audience at a wedding watching a play.

For those twentieth-century readers and audiences who enjoy texts and performances which draw attention to their own fictionality, which foreground and problematize the relationship between the performance-as-narrative and the performance-as-event, this hypothesis of the wedding performance may add an extra level of pleasure. But for others, I suspect, the hypothesis will rather diminish the play and its effects. The notion of the play's being written for a particular family, for a particular and extremely exclusive gathering of a powerful clan, runs counter to a common image that we have about the Elizabethan theatre and about Shakespeare in particular: an image that they are essentially democratic rather than aristocratic, written for performance at the Theatre, the Rose, or the Globe, for the London populace at large. Nor is this merely a sentimental myth. There has been much scholarly debate concerning the social composition of Shakespeare's audience, and recent research suggests that in fact it was less inclusive in its range than was once supposed.[12] Nonetheless, it is an important aspect of Shakespeare's place in cultural history that he was writing plays for a public and commercial theatre which was, in principle at least, accessible to a broad spectrum of the populace.

Recent elaborations of this point of view have argued that the commercial theatre of Elizabethan London was a place of licensed carnival.[13] Situated in the appropriately-named Liberties, outside the jurisdiction of the civic authorities, the stage was a place which was beginning to take over, on a year-round basis, some of the functions which had previously been attributed to specific festive occasions in the Elizabethan calendar – in particular the function of articulating an oppositional and sometimes subversive vision of social reality, one which escaped from and sometimes challenged the authorized truths of sixteenth-century cultural life. If the official world-view of Elizabethan culture was articulated in the pulpit, in the law courts and in books of moral and political instruction, the theatre's particular appeal lay in its ability to state realities alternative to those of the authorized version. Part of its necessary function was to explore those areas which lay outside the permitted cultural norms, to debate moral and social definitions, and to enact imagined possibilities which could range from the frivolous to the deadly serious and from the conventional to the subversive. The reading of the play which I have been pursuing is in broad agreement with this belief about the Elizabethan theatre. It suggests that the sympathies of *A Midsummer Night's Dream* lie outside the established order; that the play stages a festive misrule which challenges and subverts the hierarchies of official culture as represented by Duke Theseus.

Not all scholars and critics agree, however, with this model of the Elizabethan theatre-as-carnival. In direct contrast to this is a view of the drama of the period which sees the theatre in general, and Shakespeare in particular, as being completely subservient to the interests of the state, and so functioning as little more than a mouthpiece for official ideology. It is argued that in his cycle of history plays, for example, Shakespeare acts as a public relations man for the Tudor monarchy; and in his comedies and tragedies he is a propagandist for feudal, nationalist or patriarchal values. The old image of Shakespeare as a writer who transcends the specifics of time, place, or ideology has been replaced – in some accounts at least – with a picture of a writer who is the fawning servant of ruling-class interests, dependent for his livelihood on aristocratic patronage and in consequence desperately eager to please. Barbara Freedman describes the play as:

> ... openly celebrating the shaping vision of an aristocratic ideology. The harmless question 'What hempen homespuns have we swagg'ring here, / So near the cradle of the Fairy Queen' (3.1.77–78) is also a question of the precise and limited conditions under which the different classes of poets and patrons can meet. And *A Midsummer Night's Dream* promptly answers that question through its fawning collaboration with state ideology. The terms governing the prince-poet relationship in *A Midsummer Night's Dream,* like those governing the husband-wife relationship in *The Taming of the Shrew,* are nostalgically tailored along the lines of an idealized pact between feudal lord and gratefully submissive servant. The play fashions itself as a mediator between court and poet as if charged with legislating their proper interaction; it genially mocks offensive playwrights while humbly requesting that they be pardoned. At the same time the play panders to an aristocratic ideology by wreaking comic punishment on all those who defy the prince's legislation of desire. Finally the play sets out a self-serving and conciliatory relationship between poet and prince with its gestures of flattery, apology and self-abasement.[14]

According to this reading of the play, the 'celebration' which *A Midsummer Night's Dream* stages is a servile one, whose 'gestures of flattery, apology and self-abasement' do little more than 'pander to an aristocratic ideology'. The hypothesis that *A Midsummer Night's Dream* might have been written for an aristocratic wedding thus becomes bound up with debates about how the play should be understood. One way of putting it is that it becomes a question of who owns the meanings of a play. If a play is – as *A Midsummer Night's Dream* may well have been – written for an aristocratic audience at a particular occasion such as a wedding, to what extent does the meaning of the play become bound up with that event, that audience? And does it therefore add up to little more than a graceful and self-serving compliment to the aristocracy?

'A play there is, my lord . . .'

The question needs to be taken seriously since the play itself addresses it so directly. Interwoven with the lovers' story is the story of people attempting to put on a play, a story in which the nature of drama, and the contract which exists between the stage and the audience, are debated. Debates in Shakespeare's plays are rarely straightforward, however, and this one in *A Midsummer Night's Dream* is particularly complex, since we are presented not only with some ideas about the theatrical contract, but also with a parody of those ideas and an illustration of the breakdown of those ideas: the whole argument is shot through with uncertainty and irony. We can see examples of this in, on the one hand, the rehearsals and performances of 'Pyramus and Thisbe' by Peter Quince's Men; and on the other, Duke Theseus's theories of drama and perception.

Looked at in one way, the 'mechanicals' sub-plot seems to support the idea that *A Midsummer Night's Dream* does indeed embrace the values and aesthetics of the aristocracy. The 'common' people in the play – the weaver, the carpenter, the bellows-mender, the joiner, the tinker and the tailor – are, it seems, brought in to be laughed at both by the on-stage audience and by the aristocrats in the play. The 'hempen homespuns . . . swagg'ring here' (III, i, l. 71) are made fun of in a very class-conscious way. The mechanicals' play is a parody of inept dramaturgy, staged by a group of amateurs who are trying, and often failing, to get to grips with the basic principles of theatrical representation – the aesthetic contract between stage and audience. Their problems begin in rehearsal:

> *Quince* . . . but there is two hard things: that is, to bring the moonlight into a chamber – for you know Pyramus and Thisbe meet by moonlight.
>
> *Snout* Doth the moon shine that night we play our play?
>
> *Bottom* A calendar, a calendar – look in the almanac, find out moonshine, find out moonshine.
>
> [(*Enter Robin Goodfellow the puck, invisible*)]
>
> *Quince* (*with a book*) Yes, it doth shine that night.
>
> *Bottom* Why, then you may leave a casement of the great chamber window where we play open, and the moon may shine in at the casement.
>
> *Quince* Ay, or else one must come in with a bush of thorns and a lantern and say he comes to disfigure, or to present, the person of Moonshine.
>
> (III, i, ll. 43–56)

As it happens, the issue of theatricalization which they are debating here is the same one which faced Shakespeare in the middle acts of *A Midsummer Night's Dream*: that of staging the night-time. Peter Quince and Nick Bottom actually come up with diametrically opposed solutions to the problem of moonlight. Bottom plumps for a literal and naturalistic answer: leaving the casement open so that actual moonshine shines into the room. Peter Quince favours a more symbolic approach: an actor to represent the moonshine. In performance we find that symbolism has triumphed over naturalism: Starveling is there with his lantern, dog and bush of thorn to represent the moon in person. It is, of course, a mistake: the amateur thespians have spent an unnecessary amount of energy solving a problem which did not exist. Conventions of Elizabethan staging allowed a playwright to create darkness, moonshine, sunlight or clouds through language; a character simply announces that that is the case, and the writer expects the spectators to adjust their mental picture of the stage accordingly.

Many of Bottom and Quince's dramaturgical problems stem from the fact that they do not trust their audience to be able to 'read' stage images. Bottom's assumption that his audience is dramatically illiterate, that it lacks sufficient knowledge of dramatic conventions to make sense of the theatrical experience, continues even in performance. Overhearing a comment from Duke Theseus to one of his cronies, Bottom pauses to 'correct' the spectator and explain the theatrical process:

> *Theseus* The wall, methinks, being sensible, should curse again.
> *Bottom* (*to Theseus*) No, in truth, sir, he should not. 'Deceiving me' is Thisbe's cue. She is to enter now, and I am to spy her through the wall. You shall see, it will fall pat as I told you.
> (V, i, ll. 182–5)

Because they know so little about them, the mechanicals open up for inspection the conventions of stage representation, the tacit agreements which govern the drama, and which make possible the imaginative collaborations between stage and audience on which the Elizabethan theatre so clearly depended. The debate starts with aesthetics, but it soon becomes a matter of more than just that: underlying the concerns about theatrical misunderstanding is a concern about power. The mechanicals are playing for high stakes. If their play is preferred, if it is successful, they hope to profit financially. If Flute's estimate that Bottom's Pyramus would have earned him 'sixpence a day during his life' (IV, ii, ll. 18–19) is anything near realistic, then they would all indeed have been, as Snug the joiner puts it 'made men' (IV, ii,

l. 17). But if their expectations of the rewards of success are high, so are their fears of the penalty of failure:

> *Bottom* Let me play the lion too . . .
> *Quince* An you should do it too terribly you would fright the Duchess and the ladies that they would shriek, and that were enough to hang us all.
> *All the rest* That would hang us, every mother's son.
> *Bottom* I grant you friends, if you should fright the ladies out of their wits they would have no more discretion but to hang us . . .
>
> (I, ii, ll. 66, 70–6)

We may not believe that Bottom's lion would be so terrifying as to frighten the warrior Queen of the Amazons, nor that the death penalty would actually be incurred if by chance it did. Yet the actors' fears may not have sounded totally misplaced to an Elizabethan audience, who would have been aware that theatrical licence had its limitations, and that plays on the London stage which caused offence to those in power would call down upon dramatists and actors the wrath of the Privy Council, who might question, imprison or otherwise punish those concerned. Hence the repeated concern which Peter Quince's Men express about misjudging their performance.

> *Bottom* There are things in this comedy of Pyramus and Thisbe that will never please. First, Pyramus must draw a sword to kill himself, which the ladies cannot abide. How answer you that?
> *Snout* By'r la'kin, a parlous fear.
> *Starveling* I believe we must leave the killing out, when all is done.
> *Bottom* Not a whit. I have a device to make all well. Write me a prologue, and let the prologue seem to say we will do no harm with our swords, and that Pyramus is not killed indeed; and for the more better assurance, tell them that I, Pyramus, am not Pyramus, but Bottom the weaver. This will put them out of fear.
>
> (III, i, ll. 8–20)

Their continual worry is that their audience (especially the 'ladies' in the audience, of whose understanding the mechanicals seem to have a particularly low opinion) will mistake playing for reality. Their solution is to insist on the illusory nature of the stage, and thus to destroy any possibility of illusion.

Bottom Nay, you must name his name, and half his face must be seen through the lion's neck, and he himself must speak through, saying thus or to the same defect: 'Ladies', or 'fair ladies, I would wish you' or 'I would request you' or 'I would entreat you not to fear, not to tremble. My life for yours. If you think I come hither as a lion, it were pity of my life. No, I am no such thing. I am a man, as other men are' – and let him tell them plainly he is Snug the joiner.

(III, i, ll. 33–42)

Perhaps this concern about what might be the price of theatrical failure explains the nervous self-abasement of Peter Quince's garbled prologue:

> If we offend, it is with our good will.
> That you should think: we come not to offend
> But with good will. To show our simple skill,
> That is the true beginning of our end.

(V, i, ll. 108–11)

If Peter Quince's men represent the Lord Chamberlain's Men, if Peter Quince's prologue represents Shakespeare's vision of the relationship between the Elizabethan stage and the power of the nobility, then perhaps we do have a play which represents the relationship between prince and poet as being the same as those 'between feudal lord and gratefully submissive servant' (Freedman). But there are too many ifs here. Let us look at the other side of the equation: the aristocratic vision of Duke Theseus.

'Theseus, our renowned Duke'

The mechanicals are far from ideal actors. But what about the audience to whom they play? It is sometimes assumed that Theseus, in the final act at least, stands as spokesman for the values which the play endorses. Such an assumption contributes to those readings of the play which condemn it for 'pandering to an aristocratic ideology' (Freedman). But is this really the case?

Certainly, in the final act of the play, Theseus puts forward a model of stage-audience relationships which seems on first sight to be unexceptionable. Asked to choose his wedding-night entertainment, he rejects a scholarly satire on learning, the eunuch's song about the battle of the centaurs, and a version of *The Bacchae.* (We do not know who the supposed performers of these were – although the 'Athenian eunuch' was probably a professional entertainer, and the other two entertainments sound like Elizabethan University drama.) Theseus, against the advice of his Master of the Revels, opts for the local am-dram group, performing 'A tedious brief scene of young Pyramus and his love Thisbe: very tragical mirth'.

> *Theseus* I will hear that play
> For never anything can be amiss
> When simpleness and duty tender it.
> Go bring them in; and take your places, ladies.
> *Hippolyta* I love not to see wretchedness o'ercharged,
> And duty in his service perishing.
> *Theseus* Why gentle sweet, you shall see no such thing.
> *Hippolyta* He says they can do nothing in this kind.
> *Theseus* The kinder we, to give them thanks for nothing.
> Our sport shall be, to take what they mistake,
> And what poor duty cannot do
> Noble respect takes it in might, not merit.
>
> (V, i, ll. 81–92)

What Theseus has to say here sounds very much like a textbook account of the Elizabethan stage. It echoes the ideas of theatre expressed in the Prologue to *Henry V*, which insist that dramatic meaning is created through a dynamic and creative interplay between stage and audience.

> Can this cockpit hold
> The vast fields of France? Or may we cram
> Within this wooden O the very casques
> That did affright the air at Agincourt? . . .
> Piece out our imperfections with your thoughts:
> Into a thousand parts divide one man,
> And make imaginary puissance.
> Think, when we talk of horses, that you see them,
> Printing their proud hoofs i'th'receiving earth;
> For 'tis your thoughts that now must deck our kings . . .
>
> (*Henry V*, prologue, ll. 11–14, 23–28)

In these terms Theseus seems to be the ideal spectator – precisely the sort of spectator which the Prologue to *Henry V* asks for: someone who is willing to 'take what they mistake', or, as the Prologue puts it, to 'piece out [their] imperfections with [his] thoughts'.

As he goes on to elaborate his dramatic theory, however, Theseus rather spoils the effect:

> Where I have come, great clerks have purposèd
> To greet me with premeditated welcomes,

> Where I have seen them shiver and look pale,
> Make periods in the midst of sentences,
> Throttle their practised accent in their fears,
> And in conclusion dumbly have broke off,
> Not paying me a welcome. Trust me, sweet,
> Out of this silence yet I picked a welcome,
> And in the modesty of fearful duty
> I read as much as from the rattling tongue
> Of saucy and audacious eloquence.
>
> (V, i, ll. 93–103)

If Theseus's initial remarks about the drama seem well-intentioned, his choice of illustration sounds a more sinister note. The analogy of the inept performer and the civic functionary, terrified to the point of speechlessness before the warrior lord, might not be as reassuring to the Amazon Queen as he might have expected. By reminiscing at this point about the terror he inspires in others, making even 'great clerks . . . shiver and look pale', Theseus emphasizes the power of life or death which he holds in actuality over those who speak in his company. We may remember Hermia at the start of the play, facing the possibility of a death sentence; or the mechanicals' nervousness at the prospect of misjudging their performance and being too frightening. Even Theseus' new bride was gained by conquest in battle, as he himself had earlier reminded her: 'I wooed thee with my sword, And won thy love doing thee injuries' (I, i, ll. 16–17).

Theseus's aesthetic is an aesthetic of power. Although apparently resembling the Prologue in *Henry V*, it differs from it in emphasis. Listening to the clerks, Theseus 'hears' the welcome which they are too frightened to speak; listening to the play, he intends to 'take what they mistake'. In both cases Theseus remains in control: *he* decides what meanings he wants to hear.

And if we suspect that Theseus's judgement of the things of the imagination might not, after all, be perfect, we have only to look at the speech with which he began the scene, the famous statement of his world-view. Here he speaks as a rational, no-nonsense pragmatist, the sort of man for whom dreams and fairytales are nothing more than make-believe:

> *Hippolyta* 'Tis strange, my Theseus, that these lovers
> speak of.
> *Theseus* More strange than true. I never may believe
> These antique fables, nor these fairy toys.
> Lovers and madmen have such seething brains,
> Such shaping fantasies, that apprehend
> More than cool reason ever comprehends.

The lunatic, the lover and the poet
Are of imagination all compact:
One sees more devils than vast hell can hold;
That is the madman: the lover, all as frantic,
Sees Helen's beauty in a brow of Egypt:
The poet's eye, in a fine frenzy rolling,
Doth glance from heaven to earth, from earth to
  heaven;
And as imagination bodies forth
The forms of things unknown, the poet's pen
Turns them to shapes and gives to airy nothing
A local habitation and a name.
Such tricks hath strong imagination,
That if it would but apprehend some joy,
It comprehends some bringer of that joy:
Or, in the night, imagining some fear,
How easy is a bush supposed a bear!

(V, i, ll. 1–22)

Theseus's speech links 'lovers and madmen', performing in a phrase what the middle of the play itself enacts in its setting and structure. But he links them only to dismiss them both. Theseus sees his task as being to rationalize. His analysis upholds the values of 'cool reason' over those of 'shaping fantasies', and his confident eloquence seems at first to prevail. Hippolyta, however, is unconvinced:

Hippolyta But all the story of the night told over
  And all their minds transfigured so together
  More witnesseth than fancy's images,
  And grows to something of great constancy.

(V, i, ll. 23–6)

And in all sorts of ways, even as he speaks, Theseus's position is undercut. Firstly, of course, there is the basic joke that Theseus, himself the creation of a 'poet's pen', is here denying the very creative act that gave him breath to speak. That irony is compounded by the fact that the character whom Shakespeare chooses to represent Athenian logic is not Plato, Socrates or Aristotle – not, that is, one of the philosophers of ancient history – but Theseus, a creature himself of myth and legend. The ironic undercutting of his speech, moreover, is clear enough, for we, the audience, *know* that he is wrong. We have seen Acts II, III and IV of the play, and we know that whatever account the lovers gave of it, the 'truth' is more outlandish than Theseus's well-ordered world can conceive of. In Theseus's limited world-view there is room only for the truth of everyday, common-sense experience: all that lies beyond that is 'antique fable', and that which is 'strange' is almost certainly not also 'true'. We know better.

Theseus's aesthetic is not to be taken seriously. He hardly takes it very seriously himself. When the performance of 'Pyramus and Thisbe' starts the actors are accorded none of the 'noble respect' which he talks about to Hippolyta; Theseus and his courtiers continually attempt to take over the performance, repeatedly heckling and interrupting the action with their witticisms and criticisms.

> *Theseus* This fellow does not stand upon points.
> *Lysander* He hath rid his prologue like a rough colt: he knows not the stop . . .
> *Theseus* I wonder if the lion be to speak.
> *Demetrius* No wonder, my lord – one lion may, when many asses do . . .
> *Theseus* Now is the wall down between the two neighbours.
> *Demetrius* No remedy, my lord, when walls are so wilful to hear without warning . . .
> *Lysander* This lion is a very fox for his valour.
> *Theseus* True, and a goose for his discretion.
> *Demetrius* Not so, my lord, for his valour cannot carry his discretion, and the fox carries the goose.
> *Theseus* His discretion, I am sure, cannot carry his valour, for the goose carries not the fox.
> (V, i, ll. 117–9, 151–3, 205–8, 228–33)

These are typical of the aristocrats' interruptions. What the actors mistake, they take and turn into their own form of entertainment. They take over the meanings of the story and read them in their own ways. ' "Merry" *and* "tragical"?' Theseus had earlier asked, '. . . How shall we find the concord of this discord?' (V, i, ll. 58, 60). In fact they do not find concord at all, since the play that the mechanicals stage and the one which the aristocrats witness are two different things. Hippolyta puts it succinctly in answer to Theseus.

> *Theseus* The best in this kind are but shadows, and the worst are no worse if imagination amend them.
> *Hippolyta* It must be your imagination, then, and not theirs.
> (V, i, ll. 212–14)

The mechanicals present a touching tragedy; Duke Theseus and his friends watch a pure farce.

And so do we, of course. We are implicated in the process as well. If the aristocrats sneer at the incompetence of Bottom and his friends, the real-life audience is also invited to feel superior to these bumbling amateurs, and to laugh at their naïve attempts at play-making. Perhaps we would laugh at them even more if it were not for the continual interruptions of Theseus, Demetrius and Lysander. The on-stage audience and the real-world audience ought, in theory, to be in agreement here; they should be similarly 'placed' in relation to the action of the mechanicals' play. But by one of those see-saw effects which is endemic to the theatre, the more the aristocrats sneer at the 'common folk', the less we may want to align ourselves with them. The witty-sophisticated jests of the privileged at the expense of the artisan classes wear thin rather quickly, with the result that the real-world audience is confronted with two alternative possible responses, neither of which is completely satisfactory in itself. Simply to laugh at the mechanicals and to align oneself with the sneering courtiers and their ungenerous reactions is uncomfortable; yet the invitation to join in with that laughter is unmistakeably there.

And perhaps this is the point: that Theseus once more is wrong. Wrong because the mechanicals' play somehow survives the superior jibings of the wedding party. The mechanicals have conquered their qualms about misjudging the tone of the piece, and present their play with some confidence. The irrepressible Nick Bottom gives the performance of his life, and dances the bergomask at the end. Even Robin Starveling, playing the part of Moon, battles on through the audience's chattering to deliver his lines. The real-world audience are offered a glimpse of something beyond the surface of the bad performance: the Pyramus and Thisbe story is a burlesque, of course, of *Romeo and Juliet*, but it is also a comment on the stories of the lovers in the *Dream* itself, some of whom were also initially separated by parental jealousy. The lovers, if only they could see it, are watching what might have happened to them: 'Pyramus and Thisbe' is a reminder of the tragic potentials within the story which we have seen turn out happily. Perhaps a glimmer of this does eventually get through to the cynical on-stage audience of aristocrats. As Bottom/Pyramus bewails the supposed death of Flute/Thisbe, Hippolyta says 'Beshrew my heart, but I pity the man' (V, i, ll. 285) – and it is even possible that she is not being ironic here.

Such a reading of Hippolyta's line would be consistent with the mood of *A Midsummer Night's Dream* as a whole: it would resonate with the sense which permeates the play that meanings above and beyond those of Theseus's rational world can be glimpsed at unexpected moments. Bottom's 'dream' speech typifies this.

> *Bottom* . . . I have had a most rare vision. I have had a dream past the wit of man to say what dream it was. Man is but an ass if he go about t'expound this dream. Methought I was – there is no man can tell what. Methought I was, and methought I had – but man is but a patched fool if he will offer to say what methought I had. The eye of man hath not heard, the ear of man hath not seen, man's hand is not able to taste, his tongue to conceive, nor his heart to report what my dream was. I will get Peter Quince to write a ballad of this dream. It shall be called 'Bottom's Dream', because it hath no bottom, and I will sing it in the latter end of a play, before the Duke.
>
> (IV, i, ll. 198–214)

The memory is there, yet Bottom's language cannot quite deal with it. Time and again words fail him, and the language of the senses collapses into nonsense ('The eye of man hath not heard . . .'). But this is not just a jibe at an under-educated artisan. As meaning slips away from him, Bottom backs away from his attempts to articulate his experience. We can never describe our dreams quite as they were when we experienced them; as Freud acknowledged, 'we distort dreams in attempting to reproduce them'.[15] Bottom holds out some hope that art may succeed where 'ordinary' language fails, but Peter Quince's ballad never gets written, or at least it is never performed before the Duke. (It may be, of course, that this is the redundant Epilogue which Theseus turns down in favour of the bergomask dance.) Yet in another sense, Bottom's Dream *has* been written down, and we have watched it being staged. Again, we are faced with two apparent opposites: that the dream is unrepresentable, and that we have seen it represented.

'So good night unto you all'

What of the very end of the play? As the story draws to a close the fairies take over the stage space once more, unknown to the mortals. Their presence is ambiguous: haunting the palace they are a reminder of the wilder subconscious energies that lie hidden beneath the civilized surface. They are also there to bless the marriages, and in this, finally, surely we see that celebration of aristocratic ideology?

> To the best bride bed will we
> Which by us shall blessèd be,
> And the issue there create
> Ever shall be fortunate . . .

And the blots of nature's hand
Shall not in their issue stand.
Never mole, harelip, nor scar,
Nor mark prodigious such as are
Despisèd in nativity
Shall upon their children be.

(V, ii, ll. 33–6, 39–44)

The gesture is there, certainly: the fairies, who in English folklore are so rarely benevolent towards human children, bestow their blessings on the offspring of these particular unions. What is striking, though, is how this is contextualized. The blessing of the couples is almost lost in a series of dramatic flourishes in which, in its last few minutes, *A Midsummer Night's Dream* plays games with the conventions of dramatic closure.

The play finishes with a series of false endings; several times it teases the audience with the possibility of an ending, only to come back to life again. The process actually started at the end of Act IV, where the lovers' story seemed all but over. Their statement about returning to the court could have signalled the end of the action (as it does in *As You Like It*), but Bottom, who has slept through their discovery, suddenly wakes up and lets us know that there is more to come. Then, once 'Pyramus and Thisbe' has been performed *A Midsummer Night's Dream* appears about to finish too: 'Will it please you to see the Epilogue, or to hear a Bergomask dance between two of our company?' (V, v, ll. 346–8) asks Bottom. Theseus chooses the bergomask and the play is ended by a dance – a common practice in the Elizabethan playhouse, of course. But the dance ends and the play continues. Theseus steps forward and delivers a speech which clears the stage of all the actors:

The iron tongue of midnight hath told twelve.
Lovers, to bed; 'tis almost fairy time . . .
    Sweet friends, to bed.
A fortnight hold we this solemnity
In nightly revels and new jollity.

(V, i, ll. 349–50, 354–6)

The audience is getting ready to clap by now – but the clearing of the stage is not quite complete: as the mortal characters make their exit, Puck steps forward to deliver an epilogue.

Now the hungry lion roars,
And the wolf behowls the moon . . .
And we fairies, that do run
By the triple Hecate's team

From the presence of the sun,
Following darkness like a dream,
Now are frolic; not a mouse
Shall disturb this hallowed house.
I am sent with broom before
To sweep the dust behind the door.
(V, i, ll. 373–4, 385–92)

This should be an even more definite cue for the action to end, as Puck's last couplet begins to question his own status: is he supernatural being or actor-cum-stage-hand? The Epilogue's traditional task of modulating from the world of the fiction back to the world of the audience's everyday reality seems to have been accomplished. But again the ending is a false one. Oberon and Titania return to the stage for their final number. A speech, then a song and dance. Once more the play seems to have ended – but no, Oberon has yet to bless the marriage beds before the stage empties again. Surely, this must be the end? No, once again, Puck frustrates the potential moment of closure. He stays – or returns – for one final address to the audience, modulating more completely now into the actor who asks for applause rather than the 'serpent's tongue' of the audience's hisses. Even in this speech Shakespeare cannot resist one last twitch of the rope: 'So goodnight unto you all', says Puck, but stays yet another moment for his punchline:

Give me your hands if we be friends
And Robin shall restore amends.
(Epilogue, l. 16)

Now, finally, the play really is over. Like Nick Bottom's Pyramus, it has staved off its own death several times, but finally it relaxes its grip on the spectators and allows them to applaud if they will, and then to leave the theatre, to go back to their homes, their lives. This series of false endings, the continual uncertainty as to whether the play is actually over yet, has placed the audience in a position at the end of the play which is rather like that of the lovers at the end of Act IV Scene ii – unsure which world they inhabit, that of fantasy or of reality, but faced with the claims of both. It is another rebuttal of Theseus's 'cool reason'.

The series of false endings emphasizes the play's own inconclusiveness, or rather the problems which it has – or presents us with – concerning its own closure. Dreams allow for no simple interpretation; nor does the *Dream*. Dreams often seem to mean several things at once, or contradictory things; and so does the *Dream*. Seen in one light it is a play of reconciliation: the lovers escape from the harsh Athenian law and find refuge in the healing energies of the natural world of the wood, which solves their individual problems and allows them to return to, and be reconciled with, their own newly harmonious society, where lovers, rulers, artisans and fairies all coexist peacefully. Seen in another light, the play is a collaboration with ruling-class power, in which the 'subconscious' patterns of the wood merely reiterate and endorse the patriarchal patterns of the civic world, and the Athenian artisans who dare to emulate high culture are mocked out of court by the insensitive male courtiers whose new brides sit dumbly by.

Neither reading of the play seems sufficient: like the problem of laughing at the mechanicals' performance, like the audience caught at the end of a play which refuses to *come* to an end, we are back with the experience of being suspended between conflicting realities. The story of the lovers has both a happy and a sad ending: happy in that it conforms to romantic expectations, but sad in showing the lovers transformed into the unattractive stereotypes which they become in the last act. The mechanicals are both the object of laughter and also the true heroes of the play. How *are* we to find a concord of this discord?

Peter Quince tries and fails. Let us look again at his Prologue to 'Pyramus and Thisbe', his nervous attempt to keep on the right side of his audience:

> If we offend, it is with our good will.
> That you should think: we come not to offend
> But with good will. To show our simple skill,
> That is the true beginning of our end.
> Consider then we come but in despite.
> We do not come as minding to content you,
> Our true intent is. All for your delight
> We are not here. That you should here repent you
> The actors are at hand . . .
>
> (V, i, ll. 108–15)

Peter Quince says the right words, but he delivers the wrong message. Punctuation, and the actor's equivalent, delivery, betray him and the meaning slips away from him. It was intended to 'set out a self-serving and conciliatory relationship between poet and prince with its gestures of flattery, apology and self-abasement'.[16] Yet in the performance it all goes wrong, and humility comes out sounding very much like aggression: 'we come not to offend . . . our true intent is all for your delight' is overtaken by 'We do not come as minding to content you . . . All for your delight we are not here'. The performance generates meanings above and beyond the original text, and the expression of subservience, in the very act of being spoken, modulates into opposition.

Is this a way of thinking about the *Dream*? A play was commissioned by the Derbys, or the deVeres or the Southamptons. *A Midsummer Night's Dream* was written, and the text presented to the equivalent of Egeus or Philostrate, the local household's Master of the Revels, who looked it over and approved it. It seemed an innocuous enough piece of theatre after all, and ended with a wedding celebration and fitting blessings of the newly-weds and their marriage beds. The play was deemed completely suitable. *A Midsummer Night's Dream* was performed at the wedding and the aristocratic audience saw and heard (like Theseus with his clerks) what it wanted to see and hear – a celebration of courtly love and the dignity of the aristocratic household. The writer and company were paid, and everyone went home happy. Back in London, later in the season, when the play was revived for the public stage, the audience at the Theatre in Shoreditch saw something quite different: a play in which nothing is quite as it seems, in which Bottom and his companions come out of it with more dignity than the courtiers, in which Theseus's aesthetic is as palpably wrong as his endorsement of Egeus's parental authority, and whose whole point is to show how meanings can slip away from the control of authorized versions.

I am making this up, of course. It is all too utopian, and besides I do not know that this is how it was. But then, nobody does. Nobody knows if *A Midsummer Night's Dream* ever was 'designed to grace a wedding in a noble household', yet authorities declare that 'most scholars are agreed'[17] that it was. Fair enough. Another thing that most scholars who know anything about the theatre are agreed upon, is that the nature of the audience is a prime determinant in the meaning of the theatrical event. Different audiences conjure different meanings from the same text. An audience can – as that on-stage audience of 'Pyramus and Thisbe' aptly demonstrates – turn a tragedy into a farce. It needs a much less radical re-reading than this to liberate the oppositional and carnival aspects of *A Midsummer Night's Dream*.

Notes

1. François Laroque, *Shakespeare's Festive World: Elizabethan Seasonal Entertainment and the Professional Stage*, trans. Janet Lloyd (Cambridge: Cambridge University Press, 1991), p. 141.
2. Sir Robert Filmer, *Patriarcha and Other Political Works*, ed. Peter Laslett (Oxford: Oxford University Press, 1949), p. 63.

3. Thomas Beard, *The Theatre of God's Judgement* (1597, 4th edn, 1648), p. 160.
4. See D. M. Palliser, *The Age of Elizabeth: England under the later Tudors* (Harlow: Longman, 1983), pp. 189–92.
5. Sigmund Freud, *Five Lectures on Psychoanalysis* (1909), reprinted in James Strachey, ed. and trans., *Two Short Accounts of Psychoanalysis* (Harmondsworth: Pelican Books, 1962), p. 60.
6. See Norman N. Holland, 'Hermia's Dream' in *The Annual of Psychoanalysis*, vol. 7 (1979), reprinted in Gary Waller, ed., *Shakespeare's Comedies* (Harlow: Longman, 1991), p. 83.
7. Geoffrey Chaucer, *The Nun's Priest's Tale*, in F. N. Robinson, ed., *Works* (London: Oxford University Press, 1957), pp. 198–206.
8. See Holland, 'Hermia's Dream', p. 83.
9. Pedro Calderón de la Barca's play *La Vida es Sueño (Life is a Dream)* was first performed in 1635.
10. William Shakespeare, *A Midsummer Night's Dream*, ed. Harold F. Brooks (London: Methuen, 1979), p. liii.
11. John Idris Jones, 'The structure of *Venus and Adonis*, the spirit of *A Midsummer Night's Dream*: the case in favour', *New Welsh Review* 25, pp. 58–65.
12. Jean Howard, *The Privileged Playgoers of Shakespeare's London 1576–1642* (Princeton: Princeton University Press, 1982).
13. Steve Mullaney, *The Place of the Stage: License, Play and Power in Renaissance England* (Chicago: University of Chicago Press, 1988).
14. Barbara Freedman, *Staging the Gaze: Postmodernism, Psychoanalysis and Shakespearian Comedy* (Ithaca: Cornell University Press, 1991), p. 155.
15. Sigmund Freud, *The Interpretation of Dreams* (1900), ed. and trans. James Strachey (Harmondsworth: Pelican Books, 1976), p. 658.
16. Freedman, *Staging the Gaze*, p. 155.
17. See note 10.

7 Much Ado About Nothing

'Huddling jest upon jest'

Much Ado About Nothing picks up on the themes of two of the early comedies examined in Chapter 5: *The Taming of the Shrew* and *Love's Labour's Lost.* The analogies with *The Shrew* have often been remarked upon. Beatrice, like Kate, has words like 'shrewd' and 'curst' associated with her:

> *Leonato* By my troth, niece, thou wilt never get thee a husband if thou be so shrewd of thy tongue.
> *Antonio* In faith, she's too curst.
>
> (II, i, ll. 16–18)

Like *The Shrew, Much Ado About Nothing* is a play which is at least partly based on the theme of a battle of the sexes: the sparring between Beatrice and Benedick recalls some of the sparring between Kate and her suitors, especially Petruchio. But in the years between the two plays something has changed. It is not just that Beatrice repeatedly gets the better of Benedick in their wit-skirmishes, in a way that Kate only rarely does of Petruchio. It is that the character of the independent woman is no longer demonized: in the earlier play Kate's independence was perceived as a threat to male power, and she was therefore seen as an unruly hoyden who had to be, literally, 'tamed'. But in *Much Ado About Nothing* the taming metaphor would be completely inappropriate. The patriarchal authority of a Petruchio is not ascribed to Benedick; his point of view is no more valid than Beatrice's, since he is also a descendant of the love-refusing lords in *Love's Labour's Lost.*

In his commonplace book, published in 1598 as *Palladis Tamia,* the Elizabethan writer Francis Meres mentioned an unknown play by Shakespeare entitled *Love's Labour's Won.* A popular theory is that this is one of Shakespeare's existing plays which was published under another title, and *Much Ado About Nothing* is one of the favourite contenders for this honour. Whether or not this is the case is quite unknown; there is no other evidence to suggest that *Much Ado About Nothing* is a companion piece to the earlier play. Nonetheless, the suggestion points up ways in which themes, ideas and characters from *Love's Labour's Lost* are reworked in *Much Ado About Nothing.* The two plays share a few stock devices – poem scenes, parallel eavesdropping routines and, most notably, the mask scene – but more importantly they share a central situation, in which characters who profess disdain for romantic love end up falling in love; and although this disdain is no longer a purely male prerogative, the character of Berowne has much in common with that of Benedick.

The critic Louis A. Montrose has written plausibly of the 'ludic' quality of *Love's Labour's Lost*: its element of games-playing. He writes,

> The world of Navarre has the appearance of a playground, a special place marked off from the pressures of social reality and the unpleasant implications of a world of fallen nature. Here Shakespeare explores the dimensions of the play faculty, from charming fripperies to serious products of the imagination . . . Every activity in which the male quartet engages takes on the character of play . . . [1]

Something similar is true of *Much Ado About Nothing*: I want to explore the functions of two kinds of 'play', the verbal joke and the practical joke, in this 'play'. In an earlier chapter I looked at various kinds of laughter – the laughter of everyday life, the laughter of festivity and the laughter of scorn and ridicule – and suggested that their social uses ranged from the celebratory to the punitive, in Elizabethan society. If I now suggest that *Much Ado About Nothing* is a play which has much to do with laughter and laughing, it is in the light of that chapter: the laughter in Messina is problematic.

The tone is set by the blokeish camaraderie of the bachelor soldiers returned from the war, whose conversation typically comprises banter and teasing. Don Pedro, for example, teases Benedick for his characteristic pose of misogyny:

> *Don Pedro* Thou wast ever an obstinate heretic in the despite of beauty.
>
> *Claudio* And never could maintain his part but in the force of his will.
>
> *Benedick* That a woman conceived me I thank her; that she brought me up I likewise give her most humble thanks. But that I will have a rechate winded in my forehead, or hang my bugle in an invisible baldrick, all women shall pardon me. Because I will not do them the wrong to mistrust any, I will do myself the right to trust none; and the fine is (for the which I may go the finer), I will live a bachelor.
>
> (I, i, ll. 223–37)

This kind of jokey verbal duelling characterizes the relationship between the men: it is both friendly and aggressive, relaxed and competitive. Benedick has the reputation of being the wittiest of the three, but they all take part in the banter. In the early part of the play, the joking that goes on between Claudio, Don Pedro and Benedick returns repeatedly and almost obsessively to the topic of love. In fact, it is even more limited than that; the basic joke that none of them seem as though they will tire of is Benedick's stance of the professed and committed bachelor. Their attitude towards this is actually quite complex: they laugh at him for it, and they eventually trick him out of it and into a relationship with Beatrice; yet they also encourage him in his misogyny. Their pleasure in his rôle as 'heretic in despite of beauty' is manifest. It is as if Benedick expresses for the whole male group within the play some of the feelings which they all share, but which they cannot always express. Beatrice refers to him at one point as 'the Prince's jester', and while the remark is intended primarily as an insult it has some truth to it. One of a jester's functions is to speak what others are thinking but not saying – or acknowledging.

The play begins, after all, at a moment of change for the younger men. They have returned from the wars, and are having to deal once more with being at peace; the previously shared male solidarity of the military campaign is beginning to fragment. Benedick laments this fragmentation, which he sees happening most clearly in the character of Claudio:

> I have known when there was no music with him, but the drum and fife, and now had he rather hear the tabor and the pipe. I have known when he would have walked ten mile afoot to see good armour, and now will he lie ten nights awake carving the fashion of a new doublet. He was wont to speak plain and to the purpose, like an honest man and a soldier, and now is he turned orthography. His words are a very fantastical banquet, just so many strange dishes.
>
> (II, iii, ll. 12–21)

Benedick sets the worlds of love and of war in opposition to each other, and leaves it in no doubt which he prefers. Claudio, incidentally, confirms Benedick's account of his transformation; he tells Don Pedro about his sudden interest in Hero:

> O my lord,
> When you went onward on this ended action
> I looked upon her with a soldier's eye,
> That liked, but had a rougher task in hand
> Thán to drive liking to the name of love.
> But now I am returned, and that war-thoughts

> Have left their places vacant, in their rooms
> Come thronging soft and delicate desires . . .
>
> (I, ii, ll. 270–86)

While Claudio, then, consciously changes his rôle from that of soldier to that of lover, Benedick continues to express his mistrust of women and his intention to 'live a bachelor', devoting himself to manly pursuits such as drinking. The other men in the play seem to find this rather reassuring.

Benedick's rejection of love and marriage is based on a particularly cynical view of male-female relationships. Love, according to Benedick, is a trap, marriage is a prison, women are deceivers and every husband an eventual cuckold.

> *Benedick* The savage bull may [bear the yoke] but if ever the sensible Benedick bear it, pull off the bull's horns and set them in my forehead, and let me be vilely painted, and in such great letters as they write 'Here is a good horse to hire' let them signify under my sign 'Here may you see Benedick, the married man'.
>
> (I, ii, ll. 245–50)

In his fantasy Benedick directs a charivari against himself, but the 'crime' he imagines committing is that of getting married at all. In 'Benedick the married man' he paints a figure of ridicule who is already wearing the emblem of shame, the cuckold's horns: to be married is to be cuckolded already. In the first part of this book it was argued that the jokes which a society tells are a significant index of that society's concerns and anxieties. The repeated 'cuckold' jokes in *Much Ado About Nothing* point to an underlying anxiety in the society of the play about the relations between men and women, one which is brought to the surface by the developing events within the play.

The presence of Beatrice feeds this anxiety. She is the rule-breaker, the woman who refuses to accept the gender rôle which the social structure provides for her. Like Kate in *The Taming of the Shrew*, she presents her society – and in particular her uncles, with whom she lives – with a problem: she shows no sign of wanting to find a husband who will support her. Leonato, it is true, shows none of the desperation which Baptista does in the earlier play about getting the (financially and legally, if not emotionally) dependent young woman off his hands; family structures in Messina seem more able to accommodate Beatrice than those of Padua were to accommodate Kate. Even so, Leonato does occasionally remind Beatrice what her expected destiny is:

Leonato Well, niece, I hope to see you one day fitted with a husband.
Beatrice Not till God make men of some other mettle than earth. Would it not grieve a woman to be overmastered with a piece of valiant dust? – to make an account of her life to a cloud of wayward marl? No, uncle, I'll none. Adam's sons are my brethren, and truly I hold it a sin to match in my kindred.
(II, i, ll. 53–8)

Beatrice's last remark contains a hidden truth. Spoken by her as a joke, another excuse not to take a husband, it points to her own 'kindred' with the men in the play. Her wit, for example, is as sharp as any of theirs, and of a similar kind. She stands out from the rest of the women in Messina because she is as good as any of the men at the verbal banter which is their characteristic mode of conversation. Thus she threatens them, not only by being as resolutely single as Benedick, but also by annexing an area of discourse which the bachelors of Messina, and Benedick in particular, usually treat as a male preserve: the witty and aggressive wordplay which is used to ward off the prospect of marriage. The other women of Messina can laugh and joke together, and can even – when suitably masked for a ball – hold their own in flirting conversations with Don Pedro, Balthasar and Antonio. But it is only Beatrice who will openly claim her fair share of lines in a conversation with a man, and it is only Beatrice who makes their kind of bantering language completely her own. Moreover, she can do this without seeming merely to be copying the men because she shares Benedick's contempt for love and marriage. One of the things which make Beatrice simultaneously so attractive to an audience and so threatening to Benedick is the fact that she effectively steals all of Benedick's best lines. For Benedick's pose of the confirmed bachelor and reputed libertine depends on a view of society in which women can be seen as somehow predatory, wanting to 'capture' a man and contain him in marriage, only to torture him with subsequent betrayal. Faced with a woman who proclaims herself equally contemptuous of marriage (and for the same reasons), Benedick's rôle is immediately compromised. Beatrice even appears to agree with his most cherished article of faith: the inevitability of a wife betraying a husband:

Beatrice . . . it is said 'God sends a curst cow short horns', but to a cow too curst he sends none.
Leonato So, by being too curst, God will send you no horns.
Beatrice Just, if he sends me no husband.
(II, i, ll. 22–7)

Beatrice, like Benedick, equates a husband with 'horns'; she makes the threat explicit, that any husband of hers would indeed end up as a cuckold.

The cuckold is a familiar figure of fun in many comedies of the Elizabethan period, but there are few plays in which the idea of a wife's betrayal of her husband is so obsessively harped upon as it is in *Much Ado About Nothing*. In Messina there are, it appears, only two possible ways of thinking about love. One is the cynical view of love, marriage and cuckoldry which Benedick expresses. The other is the version of idealistic courtly love which appears at first to be exemplified by Hero and Claudio: romantic attraction (at a distance) followed by a happy-ever-after marriage. Claudio, newly in love with Hero, rejects Benedick's view of love in favour of this, the alternative. The jokes between the two men in the early part of the play arise from the fact that they berate, tease and insult each other about their respective points of view. But the continual jokes about husbands and cuckolds indicate the underlying anxieties about gender rôles, about women's possible sexual licence. And when Borachio's plot to discredit Hero in Claudio's eyes succeeds, the effect is to bring this anxiety into the open: the unspoken fear turns out, they think, to be well-founded, Borachio succeeds in getting Claudio to exchange one view of love – and of Hero – for the other. Thus, unable any longer to see Hero as a chaste and idealized goddess, Claudio immediately reverts to a view even more cynical than Benedick's. He concludes that she is a whore. The flood of vitriolic abuse which is subsequently unleashed on Hero by her fiancé, her father and her Prince is another, and more destructive, manifestation of those anxieties which had previously been the topic of jokes and wordplay.

'Deceivers ever'

The verbal jokes with which the play abounds have a close thematic correspondence to the practical ones which constitute so much of its plot. Practical jokes, of course, are part of the stock-in-trade of Shakespearean comedy in general. In these plays characters laugh at each other, and play elaborate practical jokes upon each other, spying, eavesdropping and gloating at their victims' discomfiture. In *The Taming of the Shrew*, for example, the lord plays an elaborate trick on the tinker Christopher Sly, and Petruchio plays a series of much crueller ones on Kate; in *Twelfth Night* Sir Toby, Maria, Andrew Aguecheek, Feste and Fabian punish Malvolio through the practical joke of a forged letter, while Toby tricks Sir Andrew and 'Cesario' into a supposed duel; another trick duel features in *The Merry Wives of Windsor,* where the main narrative is taken up by the tricks played by Mistress Ford and Mistress Page on the lecherous and opportunistic Falstaff; in *All's Well That Ends Well* the braggart captain Parolles is 'captured' on the battlefield by his own comrades, who pretend to be enemy soldiers, while Helena regains her faithless husband by the bed-trick; in *A Midsummer Night's Dream* the mythical trickster Robin Goodfellow (Puck) aids his master in playing a joke on the sleeping Titania, ensuring that she will fall in love with the first creature she sees on waking. This turns out to be Bottom, who has been transformed into part-man part-ass in another of Puck's practical jokes. At the risk of being reductive, in fact, it might be suggested that the practical joke lies at the root of the plotting of Shakespeare's comedies. These jokes range from the malicious to the benevolent; some are born out of desperate need, others are the whim of a moment; sometimes they are constructed for the benefit of an on-stage audience, sometimes they have no audience but the real-life one in the auditorium and the tricksters themselves.

Sometimes these practical jokes are staged in a light-hearted or inconsequential manner; elsewhere they turn extremely serious, and become the fulcrum on which the happiness or sadness of the characters depends. The priestly disguise which Feste wears in *Twelfth Night* reappears in a very different mood in *Measure for Measure* where the Duke puts on a priest's robes in order to play games of life and death with the other characters. In the late plays such as *The Tempest* and *The Winter's Tale* the practical joke takes on extraordinary new dimensions of magic and illusion. The entire plot of *The Tempest* is, in one sense, a huge practical joke, played by the magician Prospero upon Antonio, Sebastian, Ferdinand and Alonso in order to bring them to recognition of themselves. At the end of *The Winter's Tale* the penitent King Leontes is shown a 'statue' of Hermione, the wife whose death he had caused sixteen years before, and whose loss he has grieved ever since. But the statue comes to life, turning out to be Hermione herself; she has been hidden all this time and is only now restored to him in this fashion. On one level it is a bizarre practical joke, stage-managed by Hermione's lady-in-waiting Paulina and taking sixteen years of preparation. On another level, it is an extraordinary and moving theatrical moment, made all the more resonant for the fact that the audience is as unsure as Leontes about the nature of the reality they are witnessing.

The jokes of Shakespearean comedy frequently repeat themselves in terms of subject matter and action. The subject matter is frequently to do with the victims' own image of themselves; the action works to transform that image. Victims have their 'true' characters revealed, like Parolles, or else they are reconstructed in a new identity by the trick, like Christopher Sly. Sometimes it is ambiguous as to which of these processes is going on. In *Twelfth Night* Malvolio appears in yellow cross-garters: a figure of fun but also an incongruous emblem of 'young love'. The trick transforms his status in the eyes of the other characters, but also reveals his desire for his mistress, which he has previously concealed. Similarly, Nick Bottom undergoes a transformation from weaver into ass; some critics have argued, however, that the spell reveals rather than transforms, merely making visible to audience and characters alike that element of Bottom's character which is in any case asinine.

In *Much Ado About Nothing* tricks and practical jokes are even more central to the action than they are in most other Shakespearean comedies. Like the verbal ones, these practical jokes return repeatedly to the theme of deception in love, and of swearing fidelity to one person and ending up in the arms of another. They take a variety of forms, have a variety of motives behind them, and are carried off with varying degrees of success. Among the most successful and benevolent of them are the parallel practical jokes played on Beatrice and Benedick in order to trick each of them into a relationship with the other. Within Benedick's hearing, the men discuss how enamoured of him Beatrice is:

> *Don Pedro* Come hither, Leonato. What was it you told me of today, that your niece Beatrice was in love with Signor Benedick?
> *Claudio (aside)* O ay, stalk on, stalk on. The fowl sits. – I did never think that lady would have loved any man.
> *Leonato* No, nor I neither. But most wonderful that she should so dote on Signor Benedick, whom she hath in all outward behaviours seemed ever to abhor.
> *Benedick (aside)* Is't possible? Sits the wind in that corner?
> *Leonato* By my troth, my lord, I cannot tell what to think of it. But that she loves him with an enraged affection, it is past the infinite of thought.
>
> (II, iii, ll. 90–101)

It is a benign version of the 'letter' plot against Malvolio from *Twelfth Night.* Benedick's self-esteem is so tickled that a few minutes later he can pluck a hidden sexual invitation out of the most unlikely of Beatrice's words: 'Ha! "Against my will, I am sent to bid you come in to dinner." There's a double meaning in that.' (II, iii, ll. 245–60).

Immediately afterwards, in a parallel scene, Beatrice overhears a similar conversation concerning her:

> *Hero* No, truly, Ursula, she is too disdainful.
> I know her spirits are as coy and wild
> As haggards of the rock.
> *Ursula* But are you sure
> That Benedick loves Beatrice so entirely?
> *Hero* So says the Prince and my new trothèd lord.
> *Ursula* And they did bid you tell her of it, madam?
> *Hero* They did entreat me to acquaint her of it.
> But I persuaded them, if they loved Benedick,
> To wish him wrestle with affection
> And never to let Beatrice know of it.
>
> (III, i, ll. 34–43)

Thus primed, the two become lovers almost immediately – as the audience expected them to all along. Part of the pleasure of the plot is that the stratagem used to catch this witty, intelligent pair is such a simple one. It is a playground trick – the sort of practical joke young adolescents play on each other: 'so-and-so fancies you . . .'. And as such it is appropriate to the not-quite-grown-up world of erotic relationships in Messina. Beatrice and Benedick begin the play by proclaiming images of themselves which are overturned by the stratagems of their friends. Benedick is proud of his 'hard heart' (I, i, ll. 120) and Beatrice of her 'cold blood' (I, i, ll. 124). The practical joke which sends them into each other's arms allows them to discover other aspects of themselves: they are both transformed and revealed.

Different in tone and detail, but similar in purpose and effect, is the trick played by Claudio and Don Pedro, when the disguised Prince woos Hero for his friend. Don Pedro thinks up the plan:

> I know we shall have revelling tonight
> I will assume thy part in some disguise,
> And tell fair Hero I am Claudio.
> And in her bosom I'll unclasp my heart
> And take her hearing prisoner with the force
> And strong encounter of my amorous tale.
> Then after to her father will I break,
> And the conclusion is, she shall be thine.
>
> (I, ii, ll. 303–10)

Again, this trick is a benevolent one: the avowed aim is not to humiliate Hero but to find a way of breaking through some of the barriers of etiquette which might otherwise keep the lovers apart. But the actual mechanism, whereby a woman is deceived into thinking she is being proposed to by one man, when in fact it is another who is speaking, is that of a practical joke. The context in which the proposal takes place makes it impossible for us to ignore this, for Don Pedro's 'wooing' takes place at the masked ball in Act II Scene i, a scene in which nearly everybody plays some sort of joke on somebody else. It is a rather genteel kind of inversionary festival, where the conventions of mask and disguise allow people to play comedic games with their own identities, and in which everyday hierarchies are temporarily suspended, so that the serving-girl can flirt with the governor's brother. We do not actually see the encounter between Don Pedro and Hero – that happens off-stage – but we see most of the other men and women take advantage of the masked ball to pretend to be someone else or to pretend that they do not know who they are talking to. This multiple trickery continues, for the most part, to be light-hearted and benevolent – with one significant exception.

One of the masquers is Don John, who knows Don Pedro's plan and attempts to turn it to his own advantage. He approaches Claudio, pretending to think that Claudio is Benedick, in order to impugn Don Pedro's motives for wooing Hero.

> *Don John* Are not you Signior Benedick?
> *Claudio* You know me well. I am he.
> *Don John* Signior, you are very near my brother in his love. He is enamoured on Hero. I pray you dissuade him from her; she is no equal for his birth. You may do the part of an honest man in it.
>
> (II, i, ll. 151–6)

Like nearly every one else in this scene, Don John is playing a practical joke – albeit a particularly nasty one, and one that only John himself and his henchmen are likely to laugh at. In fact, it is not even a particularly good joke, and is doomed to failure from the start. He goes out of his way to throw suspicion on Don Pedro, implying that the Prince is wooing Hero not for Claudio, but for himself. As it happens, he need hardly have bothered: Leonato and Antonio are already under this misapprehension anyway, as a result of some faulty eavesdropping by one of Antonio's own servants. And although the misunderstanding causes Claudio some momentary pain, the confusion cannot last for long: the truth is bound to come out, as soon as Don Pedro, Hero and Claudio compare notes. And indeed, so it does, a few lines later:

> *Don Pedro* Here, Claudio, I have wooed in thy name, and fair Hero is won. I have broke with her father and his good will obtained. Name the day of marriage, and God give thee joy!
> (II, i, ll. 279–82)

Rather more successful is the second 'practical joke' which Don John and his henchmen play upon Hero and Claudio. This is the balcony plot, which leads Claudio to believe that Hero has been unfaithful to him. Although Don John takes the credit and the blame for this, it actually has very little to do with him; it is thought up, arranged and carried out by his servant Borachio, and all Don John has to do is watch and keep quiet. Don John is actually a rather unsuccessful villain. This trick, however – the most malevolent trick of them all – is an elegant and sinister variation and combination of the practical jokes which have been played before.

> *Borachio* Find me a meet hour to draw Don Pedro and the Count Claudio alone. Tell them that you know that Hero loves me. Intend a kind of zeal both to the Prince and Claudio as in love of your brother's honour who hath made this match, and his friend's reputation who is thus like to be cozened with the semblance of a maid, that you have discovered thus. They will scarcely believe this without trial. Offer them instances, which shall bear no less likelihood than to see me at her chamber window, hear me call Margaret Hero, hear Margaret term me Claudio. And bring them to see this the very night before the intended wedding, for in the mean time I will so fashion that matter that Hero shall be absent, and there shall appear such seeming truth of Hero's disloyalty that jealousy shall be called assurance, and all the preparation overthrown.
> (II, ii, ll. 29–45)

Borachio's plan resembles the original trick by which Don Pedro brought the lovers together, for again it depends on disguise and substitution of one of the lovers: this time, however it is not Claudio who is substituted but Hero. Moreover, it also resembles the jokes which Claudio and his friends played on Beatrice and Benedick: like them Claudio believes himself to be an unsuspected eavesdropper, when in reality the scene is being played out entirely for his benefit. Claudio, in fact, is caught in very much the kind of trap he had previously set for others.

The plot of *Much Ado About Nothing* revolves around these elaborate practical jokes, and it is according to the logic of jokes, rather than the logic of naturalism, that it should be understood.

While *Much Ado* is a 'realistic' comedy in the sense of not being set in a world of fairy woods or pastoral retreats, it is sometimes commented upon that its plot is far-fetched, or illogical. For example, the famous nineteenth-century actress Ellen Terry once received a letter from an equally famous nineteenth-century writer, who complained:

> Why in the world did not Hero (or at any rate Beatrice on her behalf) prove an 'alibi' in answer to the charge? It seems certain that she did *not* sleep in her room that night . . . Borachio says, after promising that Margaret shall speak with him out of Hero's chamber window, 'I will so fashion the matter that Hero shall be absent' (*How* he could possibly manage any such thing is another difficulty, but I pass over that.) Well then, granting that Hero slept in some other room that night, why didn't she say so? . . . She could, of course, prove [it] by the evidence of the housemaids, who must have known that she occupied another room that night.
>
> But even if Hero might be supposed to be so distracted as not to remember where she had slept the night before, or even whether she had slept *anywhere*, surely Beatrice had her wits about her? And when an arrangement was made, by which she was to lose, for one night, her twelvemonths' bedfellow, is it conceivable that she didn't know *where* Hero passed the night? . . . With all these excellent materials for proving an 'alibi', it is incomprehensible that no-one should think of it.[2]

But once you start looking for logical inconsistencies in the plot, it is difficult to stop. The various elements of the narrative seem to vie with each other for the highest level of implausibility. It is pretty implausible, after all, that Hero should be successfully wooed on behalf of Claudio by the disguised Don Pedro. And the way in which the truth is eventually brought to light by the inept Watch (who arrest Conrade and Borachio in an impossible search for an imaginary villain called 'Deformed') is one of the most absurd series of events in Elizabethan drama. The whole thing is topped off by the way in which the happy ending is finally staged: this involves Leonato suddenly inventing a previously unknown 'cousin' of Hero, and Claudio both believing in her and being willing to marry her in order to make up for his previous bad behaviour. The entire plot of *Much Ado About Nothing* is basically absurd.

And this, of course, is part of the point. Comedies do not operate according to the rules of everyday likelihood, and in a play like *Much Ado About Nothing* the very absurdity of the events is part of the enjoyment that the audience is offered. It is ironic, therefore, that the writer quoted above, who so exasperatedly points out the holes in the plot, is none other than Lewis Carroll. The author whose own fictions display such a delight in irregularity and inconsistency, in breaking the rules of naturalism and in playing games with cause, effect, and logical narrative progression, seems almost offended when faced with inconsistencies in Shakespeare's comic narrative. It is not, after all, as if *Much Ado About Nothing* presented itself as a piece of dramatic naturalism. Shakespeare may have talked about the importance of drama holding 'a mirror up to nature', but that mirror is often a distorting one; the comic world of Messina is located somewhere through a looking glass. The Messina of *Much Ado About Nothing* is a world which both generates and obeys its own comic rules, just as the wood outside Athens, or the Forest of Arden, or Carroll's own Wonderland generate and obey theirs.

If the play is brought near to tragedy by means of Borachio's malevolent trickery, it is also through a sequence of tricks that it is led back towards its inevitable happy ending. It may be thought that Friar Francis's plot to hide Hero away and give out that she is dead hardly merits being called a trick or joke since the context at that point is too serious. However it, too, bears structural similarities to earlier tricks in the play: by giving out false information, the Friar intends to release the true emotion of sorrow and repentance in Claudio's breast, and force him into self-recognition – just as Beatrice and Benedick had been fed false information as their friends attempted to trick them into recognizing their true love for each other.

> *Friar Francis* . . . For it so falls out
> That what we have we prize not to the worth
> Whiles we enjoy it; but being lacked and lost,
> Why, then we rack the value, then we find
> The virtue that possession would not show us
> Whiles it was ours. So will it fare with Claudio.
> When he shall hear she died upon his words
> Th'idea of her life shall sweetly creep
> Into his study of imagination
> And every lovely organ of her life
> Shall come appareled in more precious habit,
> More moving, delicate, and full of life
> Into the eye and prospect of the soul
> Than when she lived indeed. Then shall he mourn
> If ever love had interest in his liver . . .
>
> (IV, i, ll. 216–30)

As it happens, the Friar's plot fails, for he has completely under-estimated Claudio's capacity for self-deception and self-justification. Claudio's response to the news is shockingly cold-blooded: he shows no concern at all for the person he earlier claimed to love so dearly, and denies any responsibility for her supposed death.

> *Leonato* . . . I say thou hast belied mine innocent child.
> Thy slander has gone through and through her heart,
> And she lies buried with her ancestors;
> O, in a tomb where never scandal slept,
> Save this of hers, framed by thy villainy!
> *Claudio* My villainy?
> *Leonato* Thine, Claudio; thine I say.
> *Don Pedro* You say not right, old man.
> *Leonato* My lord, my lord,
> I'll prove it on his body if he dare,
> Despite his nice fence and his active practice,
> His May of youth and bloom of lustihood.
> *Claudio* Away! I will not have to do with you.
>
> (V, i, ll. 67–79)

It is not until Hero's innocence is established and the truth about Borachio's plot finally revealed that Claudio accepts any responsibility for what he has done. And, as if to achieve some kind of dramatic expiation of this guilt, a final trick is constructed in order to bring the lovers together after all. This involves a shift in tone whereby the plot is taken into the realms of folk- or fairytale as Leonato invents a previously unknown 'cousin' of Hero, whom Claudio must not only believe in but promise to marry. Once more it is a variation of the 'disguised lover' motif which has featured throughout the play. The difference is that this time the motif appears both as a practical joke and as a test, and what is being tested is the sincerity of Claudio's repentance. By virtue of one of those slightly uncomfortable paradoxes in which Shakespearean comedy abounds, it is only when Claudio renounces his own free will and agrees to marry whomever he is directed, that he finally shows himself to be worthy of Hero.

Thus the verbal witticisms in the play are linked thematically to the play's sequence of practical jokes and tricks. These in turn pass through a cycle which leads from well-meaning trickery to malevolent plotting, and then back finally to the benevolent love-trick out of which the happy ending is forged.

'I cannot woo in festival terms'

Comedies end happily and the happy ending is symbolized by marriage: that, at least, is the conventional view. In *Much Ado About Nothing* there are two sets of couples with, initially, contrasting attitudes towards the comedic happy ending of marriage. Hero and Claudio are the conventional lovers of comedy, for whom the expected wedding day will (supposedly) symbolize the culmination of their desires. This is why the disruption of the ceremony which takes place in Act IV Scene i makes for such a painful moment, not only for Hero but for the audience: the promised ending of the narrative has been snatched away, the comedy has collapsed, and the play teeters on the brink of tragedy. And what makes it so poignant is that Hero and Claudio (but especially Hero) had believed in the message which the structure of romantic comedy implies: that the marriage ceremony offers the perfect ending to the story.

Beatrice and Benedick, on the other hand, reject the assumption that marriage makes for a happy ending. Beatrice sees it as a stage in a process of deterioration, and warns Hero that:

> wooing, wedding and repenting is as a Scotch jig, a measure and a cinquepace. The first suit is hot and hasty, like a Scotch jig – and full as fantastical; the wedding mannerly modest, as a measure, full of state and ancientry. And then comes repentance, and with his bad legs falls into the cinquepace faster and faster till he sink into his grave.
>
> (II, i, ll. 65–72)

They are a comic hero and heroine who, at first at least, reject the logic of comedy: the assumption that marriage will see them live happily ever after.

In other plays by Shakespeare those who turn their backs on the forces of Eros (like the lords of Navarre in *Love's Labour's Lost* or Kate in *The Taming of the Shrew*) are usually treated as proud figures heading for a fall. This is how Beatrice and Benedick's friends see them, and in the early scenes the audience is invited to share this point of view – hence the humour of the parallel tricks which are played upon them: it derives from a comfortable shared awareness that Beatrice and Benedick ought to be brought into the comedic marriage arrangements.

I have talked about the trick which their friends play upon them as being benevolent – designed to do them good. There is another way of looking at it, however, which does not contradict that but which stresses another aspect of the trick. As we saw in the early chapters of this book, laughter can be used as a weapon against those who flout the norms of a society; it can be used to discourage socially deviant behaviour. Beatrice and Benedick's 'deviancy' lies in their professed rejection of the pattern of comedy. The trick which is played upon them is a way of mobilizing the laughter of the audience in order to bring them back into line, and to make them behave according to the expected norms – not so much of their society as of their genre.

As the play progresses, however, the conventional model of romantic love, represented by Hero and Claudio, becomes increasingly compromised. Seen from Claudio's point of view it is compromised by Hero's supposed faithlessness; more importantly, seen from the point of view of the audience (who know the truth of the matter) it is compromised by the ease with which Claudio's adoration collapses into loathing. The audience is made more and more uncomfortably aware that Beatrice and Benedick may be justified in their original suspicions of love and marriage as they exist in Messina. And the more the relationship between Beatrice and Benedick develops, the more the one between Hero and Claudio is brought into question.

Throughout the play, the courtship of Hero and Claudio is compared and contrasted in this way with that of Beatrice and Benedick. In many respects the two courtships are each other's opposite: in one respect, though, they are similar, in that both courtships are initially frustrated by the couples' inability to express love directly. The disguised Don Pedro has to speak for Claudio, taking his place in the courtship ritual and speaking the words that Claudio himself seems unable to say. It is only when his path has thus been cleared for him that he can assume in full his rôle of the lover, and speak the poetic language of love. The moment is pointed up by Beatrice:

> *Leonato* Count, take of me my daughter, and with her my fortunes. His Grace hath made the match, and all grace say amen to it!
>
> *Beatrice* Speak, Count, it is your cue.
>
> *Claudio* Silence is the perfectest herald of joy. I were but little happy if I could say how much. Lady, as you are mine, I am yours. I give myself away for you and dote upon the exchange.
>
> (II, i, ll. 199–306)

Claudio's 'silence' is eloquently expressed: when he finally manages to speak, he does so in 'festival terms', speaking a formal and poetic language of love. Benedick calls it 'orthography . . . a very fantastical banquet' and laments for the old days when Claudio 'was wont to speak plain and to the purpose, like an honest

high-proof melancholy, and would fain have it beaten away. Wilt thou use thy wit?

Benedick It is in my scabbard. Shall I draw it?

Don Pedro Dost thou wear thy wit by thy side?

Claudio Never any did so, though very many have been beside their wit. I will bid thee draw, as we do the minstrels: draw to pleasure us.

Don Pedro As I am an honest man, he looks pale. Art thou sick, or angry?

Claudio What, courage, man! What though care killed a cat, thou hast mettle enough in thee to kill care.

(V, i, ll. 122–33)

The jokes here sound increasingly hollow and forced, not because they are intrinsically any less witty than the earlier banter of the men, but because the context has turned them sour. They need Benedick to join in with their game in order to reassure themselves that things are as they always were: the language of wit is here being used by both men as a shelter behind which to hide. Claudio's resolute lack of response to the news of Hero's 'death' has already made us realize that he will hear only what he wants to hear. Now, as Benedick, charged with the duty to 'kill Claudio', attempts to challenge him to a duel, Claudio and Don Pedro try not to hear the seriousness in his tone. When Benedick not only refuses to humour them, but finally does make his challenge heard, Don Pedro (ironically) puts it down to the corrupting influence of love! But the Prince's exclamation that 'He is in earnest' (V, i, ll. 193) indicates his shocked realization that the camaraderie is at an end; Benedick has dropped his role of jester, and by ceasing to joke he has broken the fellowship.

And yet the language of jokes is reinstated at the very end of the play. Just as Leonato's trick about the 'second Hero' reclaims the practical joke as a benign device, so the jokes which seemed to turn sour in Act V Scene i become light-hearted and celebratory again in the final scene. Whereas most of the characters seem to feel that they must choose either to make jokes or to be in love, Beatrice and Benedick end up by having their cake and eating it. As Benedick says, he and Beatrice are 'too wise to woo peaceably' (V, ii, l. 65); they find, though, that they are able to court each other with banter and jokes – in the very terms, in fact, in which they once abused each other. They reject the language of romantic love in favour of a more everyday language. Benedick, it is true, makes a half-hearted stab at love poetry, but soon gives up:

Benedick . . . Marry, I cannot show it in rhyme. I have tried. I

> can find out no rhyme to 'lady' but 'baby', an innocent rhyme; for 'scorn' 'horn', a hard rhyme; for 'school' 'fool', a babbling rhyme. Very ominous endings. No, I was not born under a rhyming planet. I cannot woo in festival terms.
>
> (V, ii, ll. 34–9)

For Beatrice and Benedick, their jokes become a means to resist the kind of love-match exemplified by Hero and Claudio. By the end of the play they have constructed a loving relationship which is as much of a sparring match as their enmity was.

> *Benedick* Come, I will have thee; but by this light I take thee for pity.
>
> *Beatrice* I would not deny you; but by this good day I yield upon great persuasion, and partly to save your life, for I was told you were in a consumption.
>
> (V, iv, ll. 92–6)

The 'happy end' which sees Hero married off to Claudio is fraught with contradictions, for the conventional relationship founded on romantic love which they exemplify has been severely satirized by Shakespeare. Beatrice and Benedick are offered as an alternative to Hero and Claudio. The festive ending is displaced onto the couple who have managed to deploy their jokes and their bantering not only as a defence against desire, but also as a language of desire. Their relationship – for all its anomalies – is a more equal one than either of them might have expected. In their Messina, unlike in the Padua of *The Taming of the Shrew*, there is no longer any need for the husband to 'win', for him to browbeat the wife into submission as Petruchio does. Beatrice and Benedick end the play more or less even on points, with the promise of frequent friendly re-matches in the future. And if the relationship between the pair is not presented as an ideal, it is nonetheless seen as preferable to the fragility of an idealized romantic love such as Claudio's with all its tendency to collapse into loathing and disgust. And for Beatrice and Benedick to have wrested the language – and the laughter – to their own ends in this way is in itself some cause for celebration.

Notes

1. Louis A. Montrose, 'Sport by Sport O'erthrown: *Love's Labour's Lost* and the politics of play', in Gary Waller, ed., *Shakespeare's Comedies* (Harlow: Longman, 1991) p. 58.
2. Quoted in Brean Hammond, 'Suspicion in Sicily: or, a Hair off the Great Cham's Beard', in Linda Cookson and Bryan Loughrey, eds,

Critical Essays on 'Much Ado About Nothing' (Harlow: Longman, 1989), pp. 63–4.

8 As You Like It

A Midsummer Night's Dream is dominated by the imagery of dreams and the stage. *As You Like It*, with its central disguise-plot, is also concerned with ideas of theatricality, rôle-playing and performance; but it is concerned, too, with an exploration of ideas which derive primarily from contemporary literary rather than theatrical forms. A key image of the play is the one in Act III Scene ii, a scene which in modern productions usually begins the second half of the play. Orlando, exiled in the forest and in love with Rosalind, has written love sonnets to her, which he hangs upon the trees, saying:

> Hang there, my verse, in witness of my love;
> And thou, thrice-crownèd queen of night, survey
> With thy chaste eye, from thy pale sphere above,
> Thy huntress' name that my full life doth sway.
> O Rosalind, these trees shall be my books,
> And in their barks my thoughts I'll character,
> That every eye which in this forest looks
> Shall see thy virtue witnessed everywhere.
> Run, run, Orlando, carve on every tree
> The fair, the chaste, and unexpressive she.
>
> (III, ii, ll. 1–10)

It is a complex stage image: art intertwined with nature. The trees in the Forest of Arden bear poems, not fruit (or 'bad fruit', as Touchstone calls them); their leaves are leaves of paper – derived of course from the wood of trees and now returned to them. Orlando now intends to make the trees his books, substituting them for paper and inscribing his poetry in their living bark. Meanwhile the thoughts which he articulates are themselves not couched in 'natural' language but in the language of poetry. His speech is constructed with a formal rhyme-scheme which resembles that of the Elizabethan sonnet, rhyming ABAB, CDCD, EE; his apostrophe to the moon ('thrice-crownèd queen of night') is purely conventional, a cliché of Elizabethan love poetry.

Just as Orlando decorates (or litters?) the forest with his poetic outpourings, so the play, set in this 'natural' world of the Forest of Arden, is permeated by the various languages of Elizabethan poetry. In this chapter I shall look at ways in which *As You Like It* plays with ideas and meanings derived from the discourses of pastoral, satirical and love poetry, as well as from stage conventions themselves.

'Under the greenwood tree': the pastoral dialectic

In *As You Like It*, as in *A Midsummer Night's Dream*, the opposite of the court is the countryside. Escaping from the cruelty of the real world of Duke Frederick's court, Rosalind, Celia and Orlando enter an impossible forest world, a place of safety outside the usual social order. Like the wood outside Athens, the Forest of Arden is a good example of what Northrop Frye called 'the green world'.[1] However, not all green worlds are the same. The wood to which Rosalind, Celia and Orlando escape is a very different place from that in which the Athenian lovers of the *Dream* find themselves.

The wood of *A Midsummer Night's Dream* was, in the one hand, a leafy deer park only three miles outside Athens, where Duke Theseus rode hunting on his wedding morning, and to which the artisans of the city could conveniently repair for rehearsals of their play. On the other hand it was the perilous domain of Oberon and Titania – an alien place and one ruled by spirits. For the Athenians who strayed there on a midsummer night, it represented a subconscious world, where the realities of everyday awareness were subverted, and the rational mind was acted upon by forces beyond its understanding.

The Forest of Arden is a different matter, both geographically and symbolically. Further from civilization, it also contains sufficient pasture land to sustain herds of sheep and goats, and is farmed by Corin's master until he sells his farm to 'Ganymede' and 'Aliena'. It represents not a psychological subconscious but an arena in which new rôles can be tried out: where lords can play at being foresters and Rosalind can dress up as Ganymede and play courtship games with Orlando. The forest's very name suggests some of its complexity: it is not just an anonymous 'wood outside Athens' but 'The Forest of Arden'. Like so many of the names in the play, the resonances are both English and French (Orlando and Oliver, we remember, are sons of Sir Rowland de Boys – 'Roland of the Woods'). The Oxford Shakespeare's spelling of the name, 'Ardenne', brings out the pun more clearly: it refers both to the Forest of Arden in Warwickshire, and also to the French area of the Ardennes. This makes it simultaneously both mundane and rather exotic: the English forest was an ordinary patch of Midlands landscape, while the French Ardennes was a favourite fictional location for sixteenth-century romance narratives. But the forest's name also has echoes in it of 'Eden', the garden of the golden age before the fall of Adam, to which Elizabethan pastoral literature makes continual implicit reference. The Forest of Arden exists not just somewhere between England and France, but somewhere between the material and the ideal, between reality and illusion.

As the play beings we see that the forest has already achieved a kind of mythic reputation, even among the followers of the usurping Duke Frederick, as a haven, an idyllic place of safety. Charles the Wrestler touches on the pastoral theme of the 'golden world' when he tells Oliver that the banished Duke Senior is

> already in the forest of Ardenne, and a many merry men with him; and there they live like the old Robin Hood of England. They say many young gentlemen flock to him every day, and fleet the time carelessly, as they did in the golden world.
> (I, i, ll. 111–13)

A quasi-biblical golden age lies in the background, but it is glimpsed through the lens of a specifically English folk-version of this idea: 'the old Robin Hood of England' represents a more politically-charged golden age. Kept alive in folk-tales and ballads, in mummers' plays and morris dances, the Robin Hood legends always contained the suggestion of an alternative order, a court in exile 'under the greenwood tree' which would one day challenge the injustice of the actual political order. Robin, it is true, was continually being assimilated and re-assimilated into the English aristocracy as an Earl of Locksley or of Huntingdon, and his outlaw court in Sherwood Forest was never exactly revolutionary. It was always oppositional, though, and was sometimes seen as prefiguring a utopian commonwealth; it represented a version of the green world which was simultaneously politicized and idealized. In *As You Like It* Shakespeare uses this setting to explore some of the issues of pastoral poetry and in doing so both celebrates and questions the values of the 'green world'. Charles's reference to Robin Hood is by no means casual: it has a precise theatrical function in early performances, for when *As You Like It* was first performed, the rival Rose Theatre had been attracting good custom with two Robin Hood plays, in which the old tales had been updated for the commercial theatre: Anthony Munday's *The Downfall of Robert Earl of Huntingdon*, and *The Death of Robert Earl of Huntingdon*.[2] Charles announces that this is Shakespeare's play on a similar theme.

The characters in *As You Like It* who inhabit this 'green world' are very self-conscious about their status in the pastoral landscape. They debate between themselves about the virtues of the simple life and their existence as exiles in the wood. Duke Senior himself paints an idealized picture of life in the forest. His famous first speech is made as he enters with two or three lords 'dressed as foresters'; the visual image reinforces the Robin Hood reference of Charles's comment in Act I Scene i. The Duke picks up the theme by stressing the oppositional nature of his own court in exile.

> Now, my co-mates and brothers in exile,
> Hath not old custom made this life more sweet
> Than that of painted pomp? Are not these woods
> More free from peril than the envious court?
> Here feel we not the penalty of Adam,
> The seasons' difference, as the icy fang
> And churlish chiding of the winter's wind,
> Which when it bites and blows upon my body
> Even till I shrink with cold, I smile and say
> 'This is no flattery. These are counsellors
> That feelingly persuade me what I am.'
> Sweet are the uses of adversity
> Which, like the toad, ugly and venomous,
> Wears yet a precious jewel in his head;
> And this our life, exempt from public haunt,
> Finds tongues in trees, books in the running brooks,
> Sermons in stones, and good in everything.
>
> (II, i, ll. 1–17)

The exiled court is oppositional not in a political sense: it is not preparing to re-take the kingdom from the usurper. Its opposition is in the values to which it subscribes. The idea which the Duke is articulating is a recurrent motif of Renaissance public poetry: the great man's desire for a rural retreat, away from the pressures of court life and in particular away from the court flatterers who lie and deceive. Only in such a retreat – so goes the conventional wisdom – can the public man find his own private identity again. It was an idea which was treated, poetically or in prose, by most of the great writers of the period.

That the wood should be a place of self-knowledge for the Duke is something we are asked to take on trust – we are never given enough psychological insight into him as a character to be able to make a judgement on that score. And there is a danger that the speech may seem a little easy to a modern audience: the ideal of the rural retreat is perhaps rather tarnished nowadays. But the theme of nature's harshness reawakening a ruler to the truth about himself is here dealt with benevolently; in a later play by Shakespeare, *King Lear,* the same idea will be dramatized very differently. *King Lear* bears numerous structural thematic similarities to *As You Like It*, but it is a tale filled with cruelty, and ending in chaos and madness. The comic vision allows for the possibility that self-knowledge can come without self-destruction; the tragic vision declares otherwise.

In Duke Senior's speech the reference to Adam conjures up, once more, images of Eden. They are raised, however, specifically in order to be dispelled. The Duke and his 'co-mates and brothers in exile' live in a forest which *does* experience 'the penalty of Adam/The seasons' difference'. It is made explicit that this is not, after all, an idealized garden of Eden, but a postlapsarian forest in which the winter's wind 'bites and blows'. What prevents it from doing harm, says the Duke, is the exiles' state of mind. They are able to transform adversity into a moral lesson; it is a triumph of mind over matter to find 'Sermons in stones, and good in everything', and it comes about because of their realization of the difference between this life and that of 'painted pomp'. And simultaneously, in true pastoral style, the Duke's enthusiastic idealization of his situation in Arden conjures up its own opposite. In his celebration of the countryside he invokes the real-world corruption of the court.

If the Duke articulates a purely positive view of the pastoral exile in which he finds himself, Jaques represents the negative. When Amiens echoes the Duke's sentiments in song, Jaques is quick to reply. Amiens sings:

Under the greenwood tree
Who loves to lie with me
And turn his merry note
Unto the sweet bird's throat,
Come hither, come hither, come hither
Here shall he see
No enemy
But winter and rough weather . . .

Who doth ambition shun
And loves to live i'th'sun
Seeking the food he eats
And pleased with what he gets,
Come hither, come hither, come hither
Here shall he see
No enemy
But winter and rough weather.

(II, vi, ll. 1–8, 35–42)

And the cynical Jaques responds:

If it do come to pass
That any man turn ass,
Leaving his wealth and ease
A stubborn will to please
Ducdame, ducdame, ducdame
Here shall he see
Gross fools as he
An if he will come to me

(II, vi, ll. 47–54)

In this battle of the realist versus the idealist, the realist wins, and drives home his victory by explaining to the surrounding lord-foresters that 'Ducdame' is 'a Greek invocation to call fools into a circle'.

As You Like It is a pastoral play in which the nature of the pastoral ideal is itself scrutinized. In the song contest between Jaques and Amiens we can hear echoes of another debate about pastoral between two of the key figures of Elizabethan England. The first is Christopher Marlowe, in an uncharacteristically elegiac mood. His famous poem 'The Passionate Shepherd to his Love' offers the possibility of a world of pastoral retreat:

Come live with me and be my love
And we will all the pleasures prove
That valleys, groves, hills and fields,
Woods or steepy mountain yields.

And we will sit upon the rocks,
Seeing the shepherds feed their flocks
By shallow rivers to whose falls
Melodious birds sing madrigals.

And I will make thee beds of roses
And a thousand fragrant posies,
A cap of flowers, and a kirtle
Embroidered all with leaves of myrtle.

A gown made from the finest wool
Which from our pretty lambs we pull;
Fair lined slippers for the cold
With buckles of the purest gold

A belt of straw and ivy buds,
With coral clasps and amber studs;
And if these pleasures may thee move,
Come live with me, and be my love.

The shepherd swains shall dance and sing
For thy delight each May morning
If these delights thy mind may move
Then live with me and be my love.[3]

Here is the perfect example of an idealized Elizabethan pastoral vision. The landscape it creates is similar to that of Amien's song: living and loving amidst woods and birdsong. It lacks Amiens's sense that 'winter and rough weather' *may* constitute an 'enemy'. Ensconced in a perpetual May, the most that this shepherd needs to wear against the cold is a pair of slippers! The shepherd's song also lacks the vestige of political satire contained in Amiens's song – the explicit rejection of courtly ambition. Marlowe's verse, though, is more directly erotic; the pastoral world is not a retreat from the corruption of the court so much as a setting for love. And Marlowe's own art seeks to create a world in which art and nature effortlessly combine. Birds sing madrigals and the shepherd and his love wear garments made of flowers, coral and amber. Populated by idealized shepherds and nymphs, the world offers an image of ease and sensual pleasure.

The poem was not published until about 1599 – about the time that *As You Like It* was written – but there is no doubt that Shakespeare knew it, either in its published or, more likely, in an unpublished form. In *The Merry Wives of Windsor (c.* 1597) the oafish parson Evans sings snatches of it to keep his spirits up while he prepares himself for a duel. The poem was known, too, by other writers besides Shakespeare; it provoked verse responses from both John Donne and Sir Walter Raleigh. Donne plays a variation on the theme, rewriting the poem as an ingenious conceit about sex and fishing. Raleigh, however, answers Marlowe's pastoral more directly.

If all the world and love were young
And truth in every shepherd's tongue,
These pretty pleasures might me move
To live with thee and be thy love.

Time drives the flocks from field to fold,
When rivers rage and rocks grow cold,
And Philomel becometh dumb;
The rest complain of cares to come.

The flowers do fade, and wanton fields
To wayward winter reckoning yields;
A honey tongue, a heart of gall,
Is fancy's spring, but sorrow's fall.

Thy gowns, thy shoes, thy beds of roses
Thy cap, thy kirtle, and thy posies
Soon break, soon wither, soon forgotten
In folly ripe, in reason rotten.

Thy belt of straw and ivy buds,
Thy coral clasps and amber studs,
All these in me no means can move
To come to thee and be thy love.

But could youth last and love still breed,
Had joys no date nor age no need,
Then these delights my mind might move
To live with thee and be thy love.[4]

Raleigh works his way doggedly through Marlowe's poem, answering him point for point, and he makes the same argument in each instance. His rejection of the seductive pastoral world offered by Marlowe's shepherd stems from his own overwhelming awareness of the destructive power of Time. The shepherd's world is one of perpetual summer; Raleigh asks what happens when winter comes. This, too, is the dialectic of pastoral which frames the events of *As You Like It*: the contrast between the idyllic and the real – or, perhaps more precisely, a continual conversation between the two poles of fantasy and reality, between Amien's idyll and Jaques's response. The play moves continually between these modes of knowing, allowing neither of them the last word.

A striking collision of the aesthetic pastoral world and the 'real' world occurs when Rosalind and Celia first meet Corin. The two women have run away to the greenwood, hoping to find a pastoral retreat; they ask Corin for hospitality, but he explains to them that:

I am shepherd to another man,
And do not shear the fleeces that I graze.
My master is of churlish disposition,
And little recks to find the way to heaven
By doing deeds of hospitality.
Besides, his cot, his flocks and bounds of feed
Are now on sale, and at our sheepcote now
By reason of his absence there is nothing
That you will feed on.

(II, iv, ll. 77–85)

Different perspectives on the pastoral world are continually being juxtaposed throughout the play, and here we are given a short but extremely specific glimpse of the social and economic realities which were the real-world equivalents of the fictional Elizabethan courtly pastoral. Corin's world is one of economic necessity, of shepherds employed as hired hands, dependent upon masters and landlords with little interest in charity. A world, too, in which employment is no longer stable. In England between 1580 and 1604 agriculture was in crisis: a combination of high taxes, an alternation of scarcity and abundance in harvests, linked with long-term inflation and overall population expansion meant that Corin's landlord, selling up when he can and leaving his tenants to fend for themselves as best they are able, was by no means an exception. Corin, it should be noted, is himself facing starvation.

Yet this sudden glimpse of reality is not allowed to eclipse the pleasures of the comic-pastoral fiction. *As You Like It* is a comedy, and it calls on the logic of comedy to ensure that things work out for the best. The real world of hardship and scarcity is barely glimpsed; once stated, it is immediately subsumed into the comic narrative. Rosalind has a bag of money and is looking to invest it in the local property market. She is happy enough to become Corin's landlady, and the purchase of the sheepcote gives her the opportunity to obtain a base in Arden where she can be near, but not too near, Orlando and the Duke's court-in-exile.

'A fool i' th' forest': satirical clowning

Arden, like many Elizabethan pastoral landscapes, is a place where court and country can meet. The world of the court intrudes into the rural world of Arden, in fact, on three separate occasions. The first precedes the action of the play, with the arrival of Duke Senior and his exiled court into Arden where they 'usurp' (as Jaques insists) the natural domain much as Duke Frederick had usurped his brother's dukedom. By the time the second wave of outsiders, including Orlando and Rosalind, arrives, Duke Senior and his men have settled themselves into the forest, becoming the courtier-countrymen of some versions of Elizabethan pastoral. At the end of the play, a third generation of courtly intruders appears, as Orlando's brother Oliver and Duke Frederick enter the forest and are immediately magically converted from their evil ways!

The most striking intruder into the pastoral landscape is the figure of the fool, Touchstone. Jaques is quite taken with the incongruity of it; bursting in on the Duke and his forester-lords he exclaims

A fool, a fool! I met a fool i' th' forest,
A motley fool: a miserable world!
As I do live by food, I met a fool,
Who laid him down and bask'd him in the sun,
And rail'd on Lady Fortune in good terms,
In good set terms, and yet a motley fool.

(II, vii, ll. 12–17)

In the meetings between Touchstone and Jaques the play stages a confrontation – or perhaps a conversation – between different versions of the court fool. Both Touchstone and Jaques are exiled members of a court, dependent upon a duke, and both are granted a kind of privileged status because of this dependency. In Touchstone's case his allegiance has switched to his master's daughter and her friend, but the status relationship remains the same: he is the licensed fool, the familiar Shakespearean stock-figure who reappears in *Twelfth Night* as Feste and in *King Lear* as Lear's Fool.

Jaques's case is different. He is, of course, not literally a fool – although he declares at one point that he wishes he were one: 'O that I were a fool!' he cries, 'I am ambitious for a motley coat' (II, vii, ll. 42–3). Shakespeare leaves his status indeterminate, but since the early eighteenth century he has been described in the *dramatis personae* as 'a lord', and actors have usually played him as such. There is no reason to quarrel with this: it certainly seems to fit his bearing and his relationships to the other characters in the play. Yet there is something of the licensed fool about his function. The Duke seeks him out for entertainment, loving, as he says, 'to cope him in these sullen fits, For then he's full of matter' (II, i, ll. 68–9). The exchanges between them have similar tones and structures to the fool-exchanges elsewhere in Shakespeare's plays. (In Act II Scene vii, for example, the way in which the Duke feeds him his straight lines, cues his diatribes, and reproves his scurrility, is particularly reminiscent of the relationship between Olivia and Feste, or between Lear and his Fool.)

Jaques has a different rôle to play, though, from that of the traditional court jester: in his speech to the Duke quoted above he is making clear the distinction between himself and Touchstone, the 'motley' fool he meets in the forest. For Jaques is a much more contemporary figure: he is the epitome of the Elizabethan satirist. Satire was a particularly important literary genre during the 1590s. In some respects it derived from traditions of popular preaching and complaint of the past few centuries, but the expansion of publishing, and the easy availability of printed matter in late-sixteenth-century London, made what had been an ephemeral oral tradition, carried on largely under the auspices of religious organizations, into a secular and – equally importantly – a commercial prospect. As a literary genre it has a natural affinity with pastoral, both genres being essentially unsympathetic to, or critical of, contemporary urban life: while the writer of pastoral may sometimes portray an ideal of simplicity and naturalness, the Elizabethan satirist will often imply it.

Books and pamphlets of social satire, both in verse and in prose, sold and circulated widely in the London of the 1590s. The satirists launched attacks on a range of social abuses (such as drunkenness, flattery, ambition and so on) and on various social groups and professions (such as lawyers, courtiers, churchmen). At one point the writing of religious satires became so heated and abusive that an edict was passed by the Archbishop of Canterbury and the Bishop of London to forbid the publishing of any further satires at all, and various volumes which had already been published were condemned to be burned. The Bishops' Edict of June 1599 suppressed a whole literary genre and forced satire underground. It also forced it into the theatres, since the terms of the prohibition applied only to the printed books of formal satires which had been so popular up until that point. Shakespeare was never himself a writer of formal satires, but in 1599 he anticipated fashion by importing the figure of the satirist into the theatre in the person of Jaques. In doing so, he added a characteristic further twist: the satirist's spleen is directed not only against the follies of the court or the town, but also against the pastoral world which is more usually taken to be their opposite.

The titles of the satiric works of the late sixteenth century are full of images of punishment and purgation. Envisaging themselves as doctors to a sick world, or correctors of an evil one, their works speak the language of chastisement, anatomy or purgation: *The Anatomy of Absurdity*, *The Scourge of Villainy*, *A Medicinable Moral*, and so on. In these works and many others the satirist continually resorts to images of whipping or anatomizing to describe his task – which is to use his verses either to punish a corrupted world or to heal it through purgation or surgery. It is the same language which Jaques speaks when he asks the Duke to

> Invest me in my motley. Give me leave
> To speak my mind, and I will through and through
> Cleanse the foul body of th'infected world,
> If they will patiently receive my medicine.
>
> (II, vii, ll. 58–61)

Significantly, in the same breath as he announces himself as a very contemporary type-character, speaking an up-to-date satirical language, Jaques simultaneously accepts the link with the traditional function of the court fool. 'Invest me in my motley', he says, recognizing the similarity of function between himself and figures like Touchstone, and the extent to which the satirist, too, depends on the 'leave' of his patron in order to be able to 'speak his mind'.

Jaques's function as a satirical spokesman leaves him both central and peripheral to *As You Like It.* He is peripheral to the Duke's court, a continual outsider. When we first hear of him it is because of his absence: not joining in with the Duke and his forester-lords in their praise of the forest life, or in their hunting, but away somewhere else, moralizing the spectacle of the death of a deer into a general, cynical reflection on the ruthlessness of human society. He is frequently by himself, on the outside of the Duke's company of courtiers. He has many of the best lines, yet he contributes little or nothing to the action. His refusal to join in the celebration of the forest lifestyle makes him a kind of comic Hamlet, a perpetual outsider at the wedding feast or coronation. It is no surprise that at the end of the play he refuses, once more, to join in the general merriment of the comic closure. Paradoxically the figure who was so cynical about the Duke's embracing of the life of exile chooses for himself a further exile: that of the religious life. His centrality to the play is of a different kind. It is he who criticizes the unreality of the Duke's pastoral lifestyle, who punctures illusions in a more realistic, down-to-earth voice, which brings him closer to the audience. In a world where dukes and lords are playing pastoral rôles as foresters, he adopts the rôle of urban satirist – the truth-teller who is in direct line of descent from the licensed fool, but who is also a specifically contemporary figure of the London literary scene.

Touchstone belongs to a tradition of performers rather than writers. His is a clown rôle, perhaps *the* clown rôle of the play. Throughout the Folio edition of the play his name is never mentioned in the stage-directions and speech-tags: like Feste in *Twelfth Night* he is simply referred to as 'Clowne'. As we have seen, the word 'clown' itself originally means 'countryman' – yet once more Shakespeare works against the grain, for Touchstone is anything but a countryman! On the contrary when he encounters the working shepherd Corin in Act III, Touchstone assumes the *persona* of the courtier and immediately begins to make fun of the slow-witted rustic.

Just as Jaques and Touchstone represent two types of courtly fool, so Corin and Touchstone stage a meeting between two types of 'clown'. Corin is the clown in the original sense: the unsophisticated countryman. Touchstone's lines belong to the 'clown' in the theatrical and technical sense of the word: the skilled specialist funny man, the member of the acting company whose job it is to play for laughs. Thus the two meanings of the word are brought into confrontation upon the stage in the figures of Touchstone and Corin, as the professional clown makes fun of the rustic one – who has now become, by extension, the straight man in the comic double-act. Corin is made the butt of a comic routine which deliberately inverts the normal values of the pastoral world, and elevates the values of civilized society over those of the rural retreat:

> *Touchstone* . . . Wast ever in court, shepherd?
> *Corin* No, truly.
> *Touchstone* Then thou art damned . . . Why, if thou never wast at court thou never sawest good manners. If thou never sawest good manners, then thy manners must be wicked, and wickedness is sin, and sin is damnation. Thou art in a parlous state, shepherd.
>
> (III, i, ll. 31–3, 39–43)

Touchstone goes on to prove through a series of paradoxes the moral and theological superiority of court over country. Eventually Corin surrenders, crying 'You have too courtly a wit for me' (III, i, l. 68). The argument is not just between Touchstone and Corin, or Touchstone's 'courtliness' and Corin's rusticity. It is a function of an antagonism between two world-views, represented by two stock figures: on the one hand there is that of the theatrical clown (urban, cynical, realistic); on the other that of the somewhat idealized pastoral shepherd (rural, straightforward, honest). It is the old debate between Jaques and Amiens: but now the worldly courtier is a fool in disguise, and the pastoral figure not a forester-lord but a naïve shepherd. Touchstone's specious arguments claim to turn on its head the supposed moral superiority of the idyllic pastoral world over the corruptions of the court; and while they actually do no such thing, they certainly succeed in mocking the slow-wittedness of the countryman.

Nonetheless, for all Touchstone's cleverness, Corin walks away from the encounter with his dignity intact. This stems partly from his eloquent and direct defence of his own lifestyle:

> *Corin* Sir, I am a true labourer. I earn that I eat, get that I wear; owe no man hate, envy no man's happiness; glad of other men's good, content with my harm; and the greatest of my pride is to see my ewes graze and my lambs suck.
>
> (III, ii, ll. 71–5)

Yet this in itself does little more than reinforce a rather common literary stereotype: the sentimental image of the honest and simple shepherd. In fact in this scene there is, effectively, a battle going on between two contrasting literary stereotypes of the countryman: Touchstone is trying hard to cast Corin in the mould of 'clown' – ignorant, slow-witted and a suitable butt for humour. Corin, on the other hand, presents himself as the pastoral ideal of the shepherd, living a simple honest life and happy with his lot. Just as Duke Senior and Jaques argue about the virtues of their rural exile, so Corin and Touchstone here wrangle about the nature of the countryman.

But more important than Corin's idealized pastoral self-image is his earlier response to Touchstone's remarks about court and country manners.

> Those that are good manners at court are as ridiculous in the country as the behaviour of the country is most mockable at the court.
>
> (III, ii, ll. 44–7)

Corin's insight is that 'manners' – the codes of social behaviour – are not theological absolutes, but are culturally relative; they are social inventions, with specific functions according to the society in which they exist. He never manages to convince Touchstone of this; but in any case his aim is not (as Touchstone's is) to impress or to score points, but simply to state what to him seems the truth. In doing so he strikes at the heart of Touchstone's humour, indeed at all humour based on the belief that one sector of society and its code of social behaviour is inherently superior to another. Heard clearly, Corin's reply turns the laughter of the metropolitan audience back on itself.

'No clock in the forest'

The pastoral world was rejected in Raleigh's 'Reply to Marlowe' because of his awareness of the destructive power of Time. In *As You Like It* there are several characters who have the function of bringing Time into the forest to challenge the attractions of the pastoral world. Touchstone is one of these: when Jaques first encounters him he is about to 'moral on the time' (II, vii, l. 29). The audience hear this, his speech about time, as it is recounted by Jaques:

> And then he drew a dial from his poke,
> And looking on it, with lack-lustre eye,

Says, very wisely, 'It is ten o'clock.
Thus we may see' quoth he, 'how the world wags:
'Tis but an hour ago since it was nine,
And after one hour 'twill be eleven;
And so from hour to hour we ripe and ripe,
And then from hour to hour we rot and rot;
And thereby hangs a tale.'

(II, vii, ll. 20–8)

The fact that we hear Touchstone's words through Jaques's reporting makes stronger the link between these two characters. What is more, the last few lines of Touchstone's joke prefigure Jaques's 'Seven Ages' speech, which comes just over a hundred lines later. Indeed Touchstone's 'from hour to hour we ripe and ripe,/And then from hour to hour we rot and rot' effectively cues the more famous speech, stating a theme which Jaques develops into an elaborate satirical set-piece. In the differences betweenthe way the two jokers handle the topic may be seen the larger differences between them. Touchstone offers his observations with self-irony, parodying the manners and affectations of the wise man in order to exaggerate his own seeming foolishness – a foolishness which, according to the usual Shakespearean tradition, nonetheless has wisdom in it. Jaques in his rôle of satirist, claims a more direct authority: the rôle, as he sees it, gives him the right to 'cleanse the foul body of th'infected world'. His social satire is more systematic and less self-mocking than Touchstone's; he takes himself more seriously.

Cued by Touchstone, then, Jaques develops a meditation on Time, the very notion which is most threatening to the peaceful stasis of the pastoral idyll. Jaques's 'Seven Ages' speech seems set, as it starts, to become a conventional Elizabethan disquisition on the theatre as an image for life.

All the world's a stage,
And all the men and women merely players.
They have their exits and their entrances
And one man in his time plays many parts,
His acts being seven ages.

(II, vii, ll. 139–43)

Jaques seems here to be about to tap into yet another familiar Renaissance trope: the world-as-stage metaphor was a cliché by the time Shakespeare used it, and had accrued to itself a set of meanings which would have been familiar to a late-sixteenth-century audience. The metaphor was originally linked with, and drew significance from, the larger medieval trope of *contemptus mundi* ('contempt for the world') – that often-repeated axiom of stoical thought which insisted upon the fleetingness and unimportance of human existence. To say that the world is a stage, in the fifteenth and early sixteenth centuries, was to affirm the transience of the everyday world in contrast with the permanence of life beyond the grave.[5] To link this use of the metaphor with an essentially medieval turn of mind is not to say that it had died out by Shakespeare's day. Once more we can turn to Sir Walter Raleigh for comparison; his poem 'On the Life of Man' was first published in 1612, while he was imprisoned in the Tower of London on charges of treason:

> What is our life? a play of passion,
> Our mirth the music of division;
> Our mother's wombs our tiring-houses be
> Where we are dressed for this short comedy;
> Heaven the judicious sharp spectator is
> That sits and marks still who doth act amiss;
> Our graves that hide us from the searching sun
> Are like drawn curtains when the play is done:
> Thus march we, playing, to our latest rest
> Only we die in earnest, that's no jest.

It is in this direction that Jaques's set-piece seems to be heading: towards a consideration of the vanities of life seen in the context of a heavenly and eternal perspective. But, as the speech develops, its focus changes; rather than a witty development of the similarity between life's vanity and the illusions of the stage, it becomes an increasingly morose catalogue of a man's changing identity through time.

> At first the infant
> Mewling and puking in the nurse's arms
> Then the whining schoolboy with his satchel
> And shining morning face, creeping like snail
> Unwillingly to school . . .
>
> (II, vii, ll. 143–7)

There follow the lover, soldier and justice of the peace; then

> The sixth age shifts
> Into the lean and slippered pantaloon,
> With spectacles on nose and pouch on side,
> His youthful hose, well saved, a world too wide
> For his shrunk shank, and his big, manly voice,
> Turning again toward childish treble, pipes
> And whistles in his sound. Last scene of all,

That ends this strange, eventful history,
Is second childishness and mere oblivion,
Sans teeth, sans eyes, sans taste, sans everything.
(II, vii, ll. 157–66)

At which point, right upon cue, enters Orlando, carrying the near-dead old Adam! Like Raleigh, Jaques posits Time as the reality, in comparison to which the pastoral world of Arden seems insubstantial; it is the destructive force which is also portrayed by Shakespeare in some of his darker sonnets – in *Sonnet 12*, for example:

When I do count the clock that tells the time
And see the brave day sunk in hideous night;
When I behold the violet past prime,
And sable curls all silver'd o'er with white;
When lofty trees I see barren of leaves,
Which erst from heat did canopy the herd,
And summer's green all girded up in sheaves
Borne on the bier with white and bristly beard;
Then of thy beauty do I question make
That thou amongst the wastes of time must go . . .
(*Sonnet 12*, ll. 1–10)

In the sonnets, Time is the problem, to which two main solutions are found: sex and art. Time can be defeated by the power of love – not just the intensity of emotion but the accompanying procreation.

. . . And nothing 'gainst Time's scythe make defence
Save breed, to brave him when he takes thee hence.
(*Sonnet 12*, ll. 13–14)

Having children is one way of defeating Time. Another is by achieving immortality through art. In *Sonnet 19* Shakespeare concludes:

Yet do thy worst, old Time. Despite thy wrong,
My love shall in my verse ever live young.
(*Sonnet 19*, ll. 13–14)

In *As You Like It* the situation is slightly different. A kind of refuge from Time has been found by the Duke and his lords: they have entered this pastoral world of nature (which is paradoxically also a world of art), and they have become figures in a pastoral landscape. Yet at their back, Time's wingèd chariot can be heard blowing his horn. And the world of love is not an alternative to Time, but is intensely engaged with it.

The newcomers to the forest, for all that they have entered the green world, are still acutely aware of Time. Rosalind is particularly concerned with it, especially in her talks with Orlando. This is how they meet: Rosalind opens with one of the corniest lines ever used as an excuse for conversation . . .

Rosalind I pray you, what is't o'clock?
Orlando You should ask me what time o'day. There's no clock in the forest.
Rosalind Then there is no true lover in the forest, else sighing every minute and groaning every hour would detect the lazy foot of time as well as a clock.

(III, ii, ll. 293–8)

Rosalind repeats the old cliché that the lover feels eternity in every second spent out of the loved one's sight. Later on she makes the point again when Orlando is late for an assignation.

Rosalind Why how now, Orlando? Where have you been all this while? You a lover? An you serve me such another trick, never come in my sight more.
Orlando My fair Rosalind, I come within an hour of my promise.
Rosalind Break an hour's promise in love! He that will divide a minute into a thousand parts and break but a part of the thousand part of a minute in the affairs of love . . . I'll warrant him heartwhole.

(IV, i, ll. 37–46)

But the cliché leads Rosalind to a different understanding of the workings of Time from those we have seen so far. Starting from the experience of the lover, she sees Time not as an external and objective force, but as something which operates subjectively and relativistically, affecting everybody differently.

Rosalind . . . Time travels in divers paces with divers persons. I'll tell you whom time ambles withal, who time trots withal, who time gallops withal and who he stand still withal.
Orlando I prithee, who does he trot withal?
Rosalind Marry, he trots hard with a young maid between the contract of her marriage and the day it is solemnized. If the interim be but a se'nnight, time's pace is so hard that it seems the length of seven year.
Orlando Who ambles time withal?
Rosalind With a priest that lacks Latin, and a rich man that hath not the gout . . .

(III, ii, ll. 301–12

And so it continues, detailing different experiences of Time according to different situations. This question-and-answer routine between Rosalind and Orlando is, in its way, as formal a set-piece as Jaques's 'Seven Ages' speech; and perhaps, indeed, it is a reply to it. Jaques sees Time as destructive: it is that which makes the idyllic pastoral existence impossible. For Rosalind the Time of the pastoral world is one experience of Time among many.

'Suit me all points like a man'

Orlando might need to be 'taught' how a lover should experience Time, but he is well aware how a lover should behave in other respects. As we have seen, he turns poet, hangs his verses up around the forest and carves Rosalind's name in the bark of trees. Shakespeare, whose own sequence of love sonnets is among the best-known in the language, takes great delight in parodying the excesses of young men in love – particularly when they turn to poetry! Orlando's poems are just about as accomplished as Peter Quince's playwriting:

> From the east to western Ind
> No jewel is like Rosalind.
> Her worth being mounted on the wind
> Through all the world bears Rosalind . . .
>
> (III, ii, ll. 86–9)

Not even Rosalind can take them terribly seriously: Touchstone's bawdy parody of them (which echoes Jaques's parody of Amien's song) is accurate.

> I'll rhyme you so eight years together, dinners and suppers and sleeping-hours excepted . . . For a taste:
>
> If a hart do lack a hind
> Let him seek out Rosalind.
> If the cat will after kind,
> So, be sure, will Rosalind.
> Wintered garments must be lined
> So must slender Rosalind.
> They that reap must sheaf and bind,
> Then to cart with Rosalind.
> 'Sweetest nut hath sourest rind',
> Such a nut is Rosalind.
> He that sweetest rose will find
> Must find love's prick, and Rosalind.
>
> (III, ii, ll. 94–5, 98–110)

Orlando begins his wooing of Rosalind as a parody of the young lover. He is very much like the caricature drawn by Jaques in the 'Seven Ages' speech: 'the lover, Sighing like a furnace, with a woeful ballad Made to his mistress' eyebrow' (II, vii, ll. 147–9), and only after being educated by 'Ganymede' does he gradually abandon the self-regarding pose which had led Jaques to call him 'Signor Love' (II, ii, l. 285).

But Orlando is not alone: the central narrative which deals with the love-story of him and Rosalind is counterpointed by a series of other parodies of the literary conventions of romantic love. Silvius's lament for Phoebe is the first of these:

> If thou rememberest not the slightest folly
> That ever love did make thee run into,
> Thou hast not loved.
> Or if thou hast not sat as I do now,
> Wearying thy hearer in thy mistress' praise,
> Thou hast not loved.
> Or if thou hast not broke from company
> Abruptly, as my passion now makes me,
> Thou hast not loved.
> O Phoebe, Phoebe, Phoebe!
>
> (*Exit*)
>
> (II, iii, ll. 31–40)

Overheard as he is by Rosalind, Celia and Touchstone – all newly come from the court – the shepherd's solemn explanation to Corin of the role of the courtly lover is undercut both by his own self-consciousness and by the class-conscious humour of the play. That the simple farm-boy should speak the poetic language of courtly love is one of the play's minor jokes.

Touchstone immediately fulfils his usual function of bringing things down to basics; he takes up the theme, and replies with another love-narrative, which juxtaposes the conventions of romantic love and the language of the barnyard.

> I remember when I was in love I broke my sword upon a stone and bid him take that for coming a-night to Jane Smile, and I remember the kissing of her batlet, and the cow's dugs that her pretty chapped hands had milked; and I remember the wooing of a peascod instead of her, from whom I took two cods, and giving her them again, said with weeping tears, 'Wear these for my sake.' We that are true lovers run into strange capers. But as all is mortal in nature, so is all nature in love mortal in folly.
>
> (II, iii, ll. 43–52)

The play continues in this vein. Around the Orlando-Rosalind story are woven other love-stories which in one way or another comment ironically on the conventions of romantic love. The luckless Silvius and his disdainful Phoebe, the knockabout comedy of Touchstone and Audrey, and even the conveniently-matched Celia and Oliver, all set off the central love-story. And, predictably, as the play progresses affections become entangled: Silvius loves Phoebe who loves Ganymede (Rosalind) who loves Orlando who loves Rosalind (Ganymede). This kind of love-knot is a stock device in Shakespearean comedy, of course, and the repeated ease with which affections become misdirected and then reinstated works simultaneously to parody the vagaries and to celebrate the triumphs of romantic love. But in *As You Like It* the situation is further complicated by the cross-dressing plot. The Rosalind that Orlando meets in the forest both is and is not the Rosalind he met in Duke Frederick's castle.

> *Phoebe* Good shepherd, tell this youth what 'tis to love.
> *Silvius* 'Tis to be all made of sighs and tears
> And so am I for Phoebe.
> *Phoebe* And I for Ganymede.
> *Orlando* And I for Rosalind.
> *Rosalind* And I for no woman.
>
> (V, ii, ll. 78–83)

The situation of the woman who disguises herself as a young man is one to which Shakespeare repeatedly returns in his comedies. It is central to *The Two Gentlemen of Verona*, *Twelfth Night* and *The Merchant of Venice* as well as to *As You Like It*, and the device itself has been the subject of much critical debate. Some have seen it as an essentially subversive device: in a culture in which women's rôles were severely limited and proscribed, the cross-dressing allows the heroine a new kind of freedom to act, and (paradoxically) to become herself more fully. The cross-dressing plot can thus be read in a radical and liberating way as a critique of conventional Renaissance gender rôles; at its most extreme it can be seen as an attempt to oppose the structures of domination inherent within patriarchy by destabilizing the very notion of gender.[6] Others have argued the opposite case: that the figure of the cross-dressed woman simply emphasizes the dominant gender relations and stereotypes of the Renaissance; that the temporary 'holiday' in men's clothes is always in the service of the eventual aim of conventional marriage in which the woman will subordinate herself, like Kate, to her husband's domination; and that the situation offers no inherent threat to the established ideology of patriarchy.[7]

Different plays manipulate the same essential situation to different effects, and in *As You Like It*, while there is undoubtedly a trajectory towards a return to 'normal' relationships, with Duke Senior reinstated in his castle and Rosalind in her petticoats, the play's main action dramatizes the extent to which Rosalind is empowered by her disguise. It is as she puts on her male apparel that it becomes clear that she (and not Celia, the Duke's daughter, as an audience might have expected) is to be the central character in the play. As Ganymede, Rosalind takes charge of the plot, improvising and arranging events, from Orlando's supposed 'cure' to the Masque of Hymen which effects the final marrying-off of all the couples concerned – and the audience is encouraged to share her pleasure at her new-found ability to control events.

In the realm of desire, too, traditional gender rôles are destabilized and questioned by the complex play of affections which is enabled by Rosalind's disguise. This can be seen in particular in the rôle-playing scenes, where Rosalind/Ganymede offers to 'cure' Orlando of his love-sickness by a kind of psychodrama in which (s)he plays the part of his lover (i.e. herself).

> *Rosalind* I would cure you if you would but call me Rosalind and come every day to my cot and woo me.
> *Orlando* Now by the faith of my love, I will. Tell me where it is.
> *Rosalind* Go with me to it and I'll show it you. And by the way you shall tell me where in the forest you live. Will you go?
> *Orlando* With all my heart, good youth.
> *Rosalind* Nay, you must call me Rosalind.
>
> (III, ii, ll. 410–18)

Rosalind acts out stereotypes of femininity and courtly love, and by exaggerating these cultural constructions she calls attention to their limitations. Even at the centre of the main love-story, the gender relationships upon which romantic love is predicated are called into question. The joke once again is directed against the conventions of romantic love.

The complications of cross-dressing, however, do not stop there. The original stage conditions which determined the writing of the play pushed the joke even further, for in dressing up as a boy 'Rosalind' is also, in a way, taking off a disguise, and reinstating the original gender of the actor who represents her: the boy actor who on the Elizabethan professional stage invariably played the woman's part, and who, dressed in Ganymede's male clothing, becomes visible once more.

The careers of these boy actors are not well-documented. We know a few names: at the Globe Theatre in 1599, the year of *As You Like It*, there were Samuel Gilburne and Jack Wilson playing women's parts, as well as another boy called Ned – sometimes assumed to be Edmund Shakespeare, William's brother, who would have been eighteen or nineteen at the time. A boy actor in an adult company had an average career span of approximately five or six years, between the ages of about thirteen and nineteen, after which time he might expect to play adult male rôles. Boys at the top end of the age range who, like Francis Flute, might 'have a beard coming' (*Dream*, I, ii, l. 44), may have found themselves playing rôles such as Audrey, whose lack of feminine charms is part of the joke. As for those playing female leads and romantic heroines, it is, of course, impossible to tell how they came across on stage, although this has not prevented theatre historians from attempting to reconstruct what these boys looked like. Most of it boils down to speculation based on scanty evidence from the plays themselves. Remarks about height are available, it is true: Rosalind describes herself as 'more than common tall' (I, iii, l. 118), while Hermia in *A Midsummer Night's Dream* is a 'dwarf . . . [a] minimus' (*Dream*, III, ii, ll. 329–30). But beyond this there is little material evidence that we can bring to bear either on which parts were played by which actors, nor on what the visual effect might have been of the boy dressed as a woman.

It is the nature of this effect which opens up further questions about gender issues in both *As You Like It* and *Twelfth Night*. Until comparatively recently much published Shakespeare criticism seemed to do its best to turn a blind eye to the stage presence of the boy actor in the female rôle. In the last few years, however, this has changed. Recent Renaissance criticism has taken an interest in the body, which has meant that the figure of the boy actor has attracted a good deal of attention. Inevitably, the object of much of this attention has been the figure who complicates and comments on the stage convention of the boy playing a woman's part: figures such as Rosalind and Viola.

At the beginning of *As You Like It* Rosalind, played by a boy actor, is in her own identity: a boy represents a young woman. To escape from the court, she then disguises herself as Ganymede: a boy represents a woman who is playing the part of a boy. Then, in the forest, Rosalind/Ganymede rôle-plays Orlando's 'absent' Rosalind, acting out love scenes with him: a boy represents a young woman playing the part of a boy who represents a young woman. The play does everything it can to foreground and call attention to the very dramatic convention which normally the stage takes trouble to suppress.

The Elizabethan stage operated through a mixture of illusionistic and non-illusionistic theatrical conventions and codes. Some elements of it were highly formalized, with the stage signifiers standing in only the most conventionalized ways for their signifieds. There was, as we know, little or no 'set' on the Elizabethan stage, so that *As You Like It* could move from the courts and houses of dukes and rich men to the sylvan setting of Arden with little or no change to the staging. Other elements, however, were realistically detailed. The costumes owned by an acting company were expensive and often obtained by purchase or gift from the personal wardrobe of a nobleman. A company might pay much more for a good cloak or doublet than it would for a new play. Elizabethan England paid great attention to the language of clothes, to the extent that sumptuary laws existed detailing what kind of material could be worn by which classes of people. These laws were part of the complex language of costume of the Elizabethan stage, a language which could be used to create the illusions of character and rank upon the stage. Thus the difference in status between, for example, Orlando and Oliver in Act I could be clearly signalled through the clothes they wore. Not only character but also space could be established through this language: when the action moves to the Forest of Arden, the forest is brought onto the stage not by scenery but by costume: Duke Senior and his attendant lords are dressed as foresters. Theatrical meaning was created in the interplay between illusory and non-illusory codes of representation.

What is not always recognized is that the convention of the boy playing a woman's part operates in this area too, between the illusory and the non-illusory. We have seen in earlier chapters that clown traditions on the Elizabethan stage involved a certain amount of tension between performance and narrative. The clown might step temporarily out of rôle, suspending the stage illusion in a way which allowed his own *persona* the freedom of the stage. A similar tension between performance and narrative is inherent in the figure of the boy actor playing a female part. At times it is vital that the convention be transparent and unproblematized: that the audience should not be diverted from the fiction that they are watching a woman on the stage. Elsewhere – and this is very much the case with of Rosalind's rôle in *As You Like It* – an essential element of the joke depends upon acknowledging the actor's real gender, and the resultant interplay of meanings between an adolescent male and the part he is playing.

The audience is offered both levels of this interplay: not only the level of the fictional narrative but also the level of the stage performance. If the audience is involved with the story it will be willing to accept whatever dramatic fictions and conventions contribute most to that enjoyment. At the level of narrative involvement it agrees to collaborate in 'seeing' the trees of Arden, the walls of Duke Frederick's castle and Rosalind the female character. The audience is not, however, hypnotized. It also has an everyday awareness of the performance event: it knows that these are just actors, that they are in the theatre, that what is meant to be a tree is actually a pillar, and that the part of Rosalind is being played by an adolescent youth. Part of the pleasure of theatre is the movement between these two knowledges and the resultant participation in the creative process. Frequently this involves a suppression of the latter ('everyday') knowledge in order to allow room for the former to flourish. Occasionally it involves exploiting the paradoxes and contradictions involved in the two different kinds of awareness.

In *As You Like It* the point at which these contradictions are most fully articulated is the play's Epilogue, where the interface between narrative and performance is made explicit. Epilogues in any case are ambiguous and tend to problematize the relationship between actor and rôle. The Epilogue to *As You Like It* has the added gender ambiguity to play with:

> It is not the fashion to see the lady the epilogue; but it is no more unhandsome than to see the lord the prologue . . . My way is to conjure you; and I'll begin with the women. I charge you, O women, for the love you bear to men, to like as much of this play as please you. And I charge you, O men, for the love you bear to women – as I perceive by your simpering that none of you hates them – that between you and the women the play may please. If I were a woman I would kiss as many of you as had beards that pleased me, complexions that like me, and breaths that I defied not. And I am sure, as many as have good beards, or good faces, or sweet breaths will for my kind offer, when I make curtsey, bid me farewell.
>
> (Epilogue, ll. 1–3, 10–21)

And so, just as the play's narrative seemed to have been satisfactorily closed off, with everything about to return to the *status quo* and the conventional social and gender rôles all reinstated, the Epilogue opens it all up again and destabilizes the pattern of things once more. Both Rosalind and the boy actor who portrays her address the spectators, teasing the audience about who is 'really' speaking. It is a question which has no answer, for two voices inhabit the speech. The boy actor's voice acknowledges that they are in a theatre, that the audience has been watching a performance which is almost over, but meanwhile Rosalind's voice continues to characterize him/herself as 'the lady'. She/he 'conjures' the audience, a word which continues the presence of the fictional Rosalind, who claimed to have learned from a magician how to 'do strange things'; and it is Rosalind as well as the boy actor who can lay claim to the gender indeterminacy which allows him/her to flirt with both the women and the men in the audience. Thus the audience is taken back and forth between the two realities, the two kinds of awareness: between the fictional character with whose fortunes it has been engaged, and the actor whose skill in representing that character they are being asked to applaud.

This moment, in which the text plays with an awareness of its own fictionality, is paradigmatic of the whole play, which 'is structured to emphasize the ironic counterpoint between two identities – those of the fictional character Rosalind and the stage persons of the actor playing the rôle'.[8] I introduced the subject of boy actors as part of a more general point that the play not only celebrates but also parodies the conventions of romantic love and the ideologically-inscribed gender rôles on which those conventions depend. The stage convention of the boy actor playing a woman's part is enlisted in this. Ganymede's rôle-playing with Orlando both repeats and also destabilizes the normal modes of stage representation. What Ganymede and Orlando are doing is what the two male actors playing their parts are also doing: acting out the fiction of a heterosexual love-story. But by making visible the normal stage conventions the play also denies them. It offsets the conventional love relationship with a more complex eroticism, staging for the audience a courtship scene laced with all the ambiguities of homoerotic attraction. As if to stress the dangerous nature of this gender-play, the name which is chosen, Ganymede, 'Jove's own page' (I, iii, l. 123), is common Renaissance slang for homosexual. These subtleties, however, are for the benefit of the audience rather than for Orlando. They are part of the performance text rather than the narrative text, and while Ganymede flirts with him Orlando's thoughts are too firmly fastened on the 'absent' (and idealized) Rosalind for him to respond to the ambiguously-gendered figure present before him.

As You Like It stages these ambiguities in a way which is utterly playful. It is a play structured in terms not of one counterpoint but of a whole set of them. Oppositions between art and nature, idealism and realism, optimism and cynicism, time and timelessness, country and court, heterosexual and homosexual, male and female, actor and rôle are interwoven in such a way as to play across and comment upon each other. Central to all of these is the dialectic which the play enacts concerning love and desire. The pastoral world is, after all, an erotic one. The narrative drive towards closure seems to favour a conventional 'happy' ending in which traditional values are reaffirmed. Yet all along the way these values are also being questioned. Just as Corin sees that manners are relative, and as Rosalind sees that Time is relative, so the play works as hard as it can to have it both ways – simultaneously to celebrate and to critique the conventions of pastoral and of romantic love, and to hold both in balance. It is an attempt to affirm a pluralism which is absent from the stage when Shakespeare returns to the cross-dressing plot in *Twelfth Night.*

Notes

1. Northrop Frye, 'The argument of comedy', *English Institute Essays, 1948*, reprinted in D. J. Palmer, *Comedy: Developments in Criticism* (London and Basingstoke: Macmillan, 1984), pp. 74–84.
2. See Anthony Munday, *The Huntingdon Plays*, ed. John C. Meager (New York and London, 1980).
3. Christopher Marlowe, 'The Passionate Shepherd to his Love' (1599–1600), in John Hollander and Frank Kermode, eds, *The Literature of Renaissance England* (Oxford: Oxford University Press, 1973), p. 408.
4. Sir Walter Raleigh, 'Answer to Marlowe' (1600), in Hollander Kermode, *The Literature of Renaissance England*, p. 338.
5. See Jean-Christophe Agnew, *Worlds Apart: The Market and the Theater in Anglo-American Thought 1550–1750* (Cambridge: Cambridge University Press, 1986), for a full discussion of the metaphor.
6. For example, Catherine Belsey, 'Disrupting sexual difference: meaning and gender in the comedies', in John Drakakis, ed, *Alternative Shakespeares* (London: Methuen, 1985).
7. For example, Stephen Greenblatt, *Shakespearean Negotiations: The Circulation of Social Energy in Renaissance England* (Oxford: Clarendon Press, 1988), pp. 86–93.
8. Lesley Anne Soule, 'Subverting Rosalind: Cocky Ros in the Forest of Arden', *New Theatre Quarterly* 7, xxvi, pp. 126–36.

9 Twelfth Night

'Give me excess of it'

Twelfth Night is a play characterized by excess. In the first few lines Orsino calls for an excess of music, and from that moment on the play stages a variety of excesses. On the most mundane level there are the literal excesses of Sir Toby and his drinking partners and their revelries. There are the excessive and obsessive emotional states of Orsino and Olivia; the one overwhelmed by his unrequited love for the other, who is herself trapped in mourning for her dead brother and sworn to wear a veil for seven years. People act and react excessively, too: the trick which Maria and Sir Toby play against Malvolio is funny to begin with, but eventually turns sour. Audiences frequently find the 'mad-house' scene, in which Feste torments the imprisoned steward, uncomfortable, and even Sir Toby thinks that things have been taken too far and says that he 'would we were well rid of this knavery'. The play encompasses an extraordinary range of tones and moods, from melancholy to revelry. There is even an excess of characters in the play: Fabian seems to appear from nowhere and for no apparent reason in Act II Scene v, and then takes over the part which Feste seemed about to play in the early stages of the plot against Malvolio.

As for the plot, Shakespearean comedy is typically complicated in its narrative structure: even so, *Twelfth Night* is unusually ambitious in the number of narratives which it sets going simultaneously, and the complexity with which they need to interrelate. It attempts simultaneously to create both the accelerating fugue-like structure of a good farce, and also a series of characters who are allowed their own space to develop emotionally complex or subtle relationships with each other and with the audience. There are so many narratives going on at the same time that it is easy for an audience to lose track of everything that is happening. Plots of disguise and cross-dressing become interwoven with stories of mistaken identities, separated twins and (again) lost brothers; tricks are played on several characters simultaneously; and there is not one love-story but many.

As in *As You Like It*, all sorts of variations are played upon the theme of love and desire. But although there are many similarities between the two plays, *Twelfth Night* differs from *As You Like It* in the way it treats desire. In *As You Like It* a single kind of love-relationship, romantic love, was parodied in a variety of ways up and down the social classes. But the triangle of desire in which Viola is caught does not involve low-life shepherdesses like Phoebe, patently minor characters who can be relegated at the end of the play to their proper station in the sub-plot: she is adored by the Lady Olivia. Moreover, in *Twelfth Night* love takes on a greater variety of forms. Apart from Orsino's and Olivia's obsessive states there is also Viola's unspoken longing for Orsino; Olivia's impossible desire for Cesario (finally translated into possibility by the appearance of Sebastian); Orsino's fondness for 'Cesario' (which changes quite peremptorily into a willingness to marry Viola); Malvolio's self-interested pursuit of his mistress, which leads to its own kind of excess as he dresses in his ridiculous costume; Sir Andrew's hopes of marriage with Olivia; Antonio's adoration of Sebastian; the fictional sister invented by Viola and her male counterpart, the flamboyant and imaginary lover in the 'willow cabin' at the gate; Sir Toby's marriage to his partner-in-crime Maria; and not least the filial love of Sebastian and Viola, which is as intense as any relationship in the play. *Twelfth Night* is clearly concerned to show how many faces love and desire can have.

Perhaps, too, how many faces comedy can have. It seems at times that there is more material here than can be accommodated in a single play – and this is not entirely surprising, for into *Twelfth Night* Shakespeare crams a whole series of themes, characters, scenes and situations which he has already used in several previous plays.

Twelfth Night re-works, for example, the cross-dressing plot from *As You Like It*, with Viola following Rosalind's lead in donning male attire as protection, and then having to deal with the contradictions which arise from that disguise once people start falling in love with each other. Like another cross-dressed Shakespearean heroine, Julia in *The Two Gentlemen of Verona*, Viola becomes page to the man she loves, and then finds herself in the uncomfortable position of having to plead his cause to another woman. The cross-dressing plot is then interwoven with the 'identical twins' plot which was the central narrative of *The Comedy of Errors*. As in that earlier play, twins are separated by storm and shipwreck; one of them arrives in a strange city to find an unknown woman who lays claim to his love; people are confined in lunatic asylums; misunderstandings arise about ransoms and gifts of gold; and old enmities between cities put at risk the lives of men who are seeking the person they love. From *Much Ado About Nothing* comes the scene in which someone is tricked into believing that someone else is in love with them, while the tricksters look on. From

As You Like It again comes the slightly dissonant ending: just as Jaques in the earlier play refused to join in the celebrations and return to court with the rest of the company, so Malvolio here, much more harshly, rejects the apologies and attempts at reconciliation, storming off-stage with threats of revenge.

Characters reappear, too. The figure of the jester, of course, has been used before, and Feste bears more than a slight resemblance to Touchstone, as Shakespeare and Robert Armin continue to develop the specialized clown rôle as a trademark of the Lord Chamberlain's Men. Several other stock characters, too, probably bear witness to the particular skills or comic routines of other actors: the inept lover Master Slender from *The Merry Wives of Windsor*, for example, reappears as Sir Andrew Aguecheek; the witty female servant Maria has antecedents in Hero's waiting women, Margaret and Ursula in *Much Ado About Nothing*; and Viola, as we have seen, replays Rosalind's breeches part. It has often been pointed out that Sir Toby is an Illyrian equivalent of Falstaff: like the fat knight of the *Henry IV* plays and *The Merry Wives of Windsor*, he is a descendant of the figures of misrule from seasonal entertainments. Like Falstaff, Sir Toby has gathered round him a group of like-minded revellers, with the result that Malvolio accuses him of trying to turn Olivia's house into an 'alehouse' – as if Falstaff's Eastcheap haunts were to be imported into Illyria. Even *Hamlet* finds echoes in *Twelfth Night*, although this is perhaps less surprising than it might seem at first, since the comedy and the tragedy were written very close together in and around 1600–1. At any rate, both of them start with a figure displaying all the signs of mourning: Hamlet's 'inky cloak' is worn in mourning for his father, Olivia's veil is in memory of her brother. In this respect Olivia may also remind readers and audiences of Portia in the early phases of *The Merchant of Venice*, as both are potentially prevented from loving by the influence of a dead relative.

The list could go on. Nor is there anything unusual in itself about the fact that this play contains reworkings of old stories, characters and situations. Throughout his career Shakespeare continually re-uses material, adapting not only other writers' works for the stage (as was common enough in Elizabethan playwriting practice), but reworking his own ideas and narratives, giving new meanings to the stories he tells.[1] What makes *Twelfth Night* special is the relentlessness of these reworkings, the (again) excessiveness of them. It is true that shipwrecks, lost relatives, mistaken identities and love-triangles are standard fare in romantic comedy, but in *Twelfth Night* Shakespeare seems to be attempting – almost desperately – to cram everything in. *Twelfth Night* is a compendium of Shakespearean comedy, and in it it is possible to see Shakespeare taking further, revising and rethinking his attitudes to some of the ideas which comedy had already been a vehicle for expressing.

'At our feast we had a play'

It may seem that this spotting of sources and intertextual relationships is a rather academic exercise: relevant to the classroom, perhaps, but not to the stage. Would Shakespeare have expected his audience to pick up references like these? Would they have noticed, or bothered about, the similarities between one play and another? As it happens we can answer this question with a qualified 'yes'. While we have no way of knowing how Elizabethan audiences in general reacted to the play, or what sort of expectations or understandings they had of it, we do have evidence of the response of one spectator at a performance of *Twelfth Night.*

Twelfth Night, like most of Shakespeare's plays, was written with various possible audiences in mind. It was to be performed at the still-new Globe Theatre, of course, but the Lord Chamberlain's Men would also have hoped, like Bottom and his friends, to be commissioned for performances at court on the occasion of various festivities and celebrations. There is even a tradition that the play was first performed before the Queen on 6 January 1601, on Twelfth Night itself, although there is little or no evidence for such a performance (indeed there is no record of a performance of this play at the court of either Elizabeth or James until 6 April 1618, two years after Shakespeare's death). There was, however, a performance at another prestigious, and possibly better-paying, venue in 1602. A student of law at the Middle Temple, John Manningham, kept a commonplace book in which he noted all sorts of details about his life. This book is known as 'Manningham's Diary', and the first entry for February 1602 reads:

> At our feast we had a play called ['mid' crossed out] *Twelve Night or What You Will,* much like the *Comedy of Errors* or *Menaechmi* in Plautus, but most like and near to that in Italian called *Inganni.* A good practice in it to make the steward believe his Lady widow was in love with him by counterfeiting a letter, as from his Lady in general terms, telling him what she liked best in him and prescribing his gesture in smiling, his apparel etc. And then when he came to practice making him believe they took him to be mad.[2]

This diary entry suggests something of the nature of the audience for which Shakespeare was writing, by showing us something of the mind of one Elizabethan play-goer: not a statistically relevant sample, of course, but useful nonetheless. It is a mind which is extremely well-stocked: Manningham, clearly, is well-read in both contemporary English, recent Italian and classical Latin drama. He not only picks up the resemblance to the *Comedy of Errors*, but is also able to trace both Shakespearean plays back to their common source in Plautus's *Menaechmi*. In addition there is the interesting slip of the pen in Manningham's first line: the word 'mid' is crossed out – as if he might have been about to write '*A Midsummer Night's Dream*', briefly confusing one Shakespearean play with another (which also has a title referring to one specific night of the year). It is unlikely to have been pure coincidence that led Manningham to make the link with the earlier Shakespeare comedies. It would seem that Shakespeare as a writer had made enough of a name for himself by 1602 for an informed play-goer like Manningham to be able to discern an *oeuvre*. Manningham, it seems, was aware not merely of watching a play but of watching a play by a particular writer, William Shakespeare.

Manningham is judicious in his spotting of sources. Having recognized the twins' plot from *The Comedy of Errors* and *Menaechmi*, he goes on to consider the cross-dressing plot, which he correctly traces back to Italian comic traditions. Here, in fact, he may be conflating memories of two plays: the play which he names, *Gl'Inganni (The Deceptions)*, tells the story of a woman who cross-dresses and takes the masculine name of Cesare, just as Viola in *Twelfth Night* becomes Cesario. It is also possible, however, that Manningham is actually thinking of another play, the anonymous *Gl'Ingannati (The Deceived)*, which resembles *Twelfth Night* even more closely. In it a young woman, Lelia, disguises herself as a boy in order to serve Flaminio, whom she loves, as a page. Flaminio employs her as a messenger to Isabella, the woman he loves unrequitedly, and Isabella then falls in love with Lelia. Like Viola, Lelia is saved from these complications by the appearance of her long-lost brother Fabrizio, who falls in love with Isabella, leaving Flaminio and Lelia free to marry each other.

We should not assume that the sophisticated awareness of intertextuality which Manningham shows was typical of play-goers in Shakespeare's London. Clearly, though, Shakespeare was writing for an audience which included a proportion of very well-informed *aficionados* of the theatre, spectators whose experience of one play could be immediately related to memories of others. He might well have been able to expect that the self-referential and intertextual elements of *Twelfth Night* would not have been altogether lost on his audience.

Other things about Manningham's diary entry deserve comment. There is his evidence, for example, that *Twelfth Night* was performed at a feast. This particular play is especially suited to such an occasion: Sir Toby and his fellow-revellers in particular enact a story-line which is in itself 'festive', and the play bears the title of a feast. It would have been nice if Manningham's diary had provided evidence of the play being performed at some Twelfth Night celebrations; however, the feast at which *Twelfth Night* was presented to the Middle Temple seems, from the date of Manningham's diary entry, to have been to celebrate Candlemas rather than Twelfth Night.

The diary entry also gives a sense of what Manningham remembered most vividly from the performance. The romantic plot is mentioned only as it relates to sources, but what seems to have stuck in Manningham's mind is the trick played on Malvolio by Maria, Sir Toby and Feste. What Manningham carries away from the play is precisely the opposite of what the editors of the Arden edition of the play, J. M. Lothian and T. W. Craik, speaking for twentieth-century scholarship, say the modern reader is likely to experience:

> It is probably true to say that a twentieth-century reader, suddenly invited to recall *Twelfth Night*, will think first of Viola's scene with Olivia and Orsino (I. iv and II. iv), and in particular of her 'willow cabin' and 'Patience on a monument' speeches.[3]

They compare this with a typically nineteenth-century perspective on the play, represented by the words of the Victorian scholar F. J. Furnivall, writing in 1877, who saw the below-stairs plot as a rather irritating distraction, behind which the beauties of the romantic plot might be glimpsed:

> The self-conceited Malvolio is brought to the front, the drunkards and the Clown come next; none of these touches any heart; and it's not till we look past them, that we feel the beauty of the characters who stand in half-light behind.[4]

Manningham's memories are different again from this. He is not particularly interested in the shadowy half-light of romantic beauty; for him the 'self-conceited' Malvolio's smiling, his yellow cross-gartered stockings and the tricks played upon him by Sir Toby and his companions are what make the greatest impression:

> A good practice in it to make the steward believe his Lady widow was in love with him by counterfeiting a letter, as from

his Lady in general terms, telling him what she liked best in him and prescribing his gesture in smiling, his apparel etc.. And then when he came to practice making him believe they took him to be mad.[5]

These varying responses provide some useful information about the diversity of ways in which different ages have related to the 'same' play. The changing structures of feeling over the centuries, and the changing expectations both of art and life which people have brought to the text in various ages has meant that different generations have privileged different parts of the story. In addition, though, it is worth noting how the Arden editors resolutely talk about 'the reader' rather than 'the spectator' or 'the audience'. Manningham's response, on the other hand, is to a performance rather than to a text. It may be that the differences in perspective which exist between Manningham and the Arden edition owe something to the difference between reading *Twelfth Night* and watching it.

A play is a paradoxical kind of literary hybrid, one whose 'success' is in part measured by the number of times the text gets staged and re-staged. In the course of this process, of course, the play gets altered from its original appearance. *Twelfth Night*'s history on the English stage between the 1600s and the mid-twentieth century includes such radical transformations as a version played at James I's court in 1623 entitled merely *Malvolio*; a Restoration adaptation by William D'Avenant; an incorporation of sections of it in Charles Burnaby's *Love Betray'd: or the Agreeable Disappointment*; an 1820s musical version by Frederick Reynolds containing 'Songs, Glees and Choruses' from other Shakespeare plays.[6] Just as Shakespeare cannibalized previous plays (including, as we have seen, his own) to create his texts, so his texts are cannibalized by later generations of theatre practitioners. But it is not only a matter of rewritings and adaptations. For each new staging, each new stage, each change of cast or venue means a different experience for the audience. Manningham's diary entry tells us about an early staging of *Twelfth Night*, and reflects accurately an important theatrical dimension of the play which is not always obvious to the reader: the way in which the apparent main plot, the romance involving Viola, Orsino and Olivia, frequently has trouble holding its own in competition with the 'sub-plot', and the below-stairs activities of puritanical stewards and drunken knights threaten continually to take centre stage. As with that 1623 performance at court, *Twelfth Night* can easily metamorphose into *Malvolio*.

'I smell a device'

Let us focus, then, on the below-stairs plot. Act II Scene iii sees the 'low-life' characters of the play, Sir Toby Belch, Sir Andrew Aguecheek, Feste and (after a little persuasion) Maria holding a late-night party. They drink, they sing – and they disturb Malvolio, who bursts into the scene full of righteous indignation:

> *Malvolio* My masters, are you mad? Or what are you? Have you no wit, manners, nor honesty, but to gabble like tinkers at this time of night? Do ye make an alehouse of my lady's house, that ye squeak out your coziers' catches without any mitigation or remorse of voice? Is there no respect of place, persons nor time with you?
>
> (II, iii, ll. 33–9)

His diatribe has little effect on the revellers. Despite Malvolio's attempt to quieten them, they continue with their drinking and singing. Sir Toby retorts, 'Art any more than a steward? Dost thou think because thou art virtuous there shall be no more cakes and ale?' (II, iii, ll. 109–11).

In this below-stairs plot of *Twelfth Night* Shakespeare stages once again the battle between Carnival and Lent. The confrontation between Sir Toby and Malvolio is emblematic: on the one side Malvolio's 'virtuous' mean-spiritedness, on the other Sir Toby, the representative of revelry, with a surname which speaks for itself, and a first name which is pointedly and familiarly English in this alien world of Illyria. As in the famous painting by Bruegel, the personifications of Carnival and Lent confront each other directly.

The title of the play itself draws attention to this confrontation. In Elizabeth's court, as elsewhere in Europe, the Feast of the Epiphany on 6 January, Twelfth Night, was the occasion of the final phase of Christmas-time celebrations, and

> . . . one of the most brilliant and joyful court occasions. Before stepping down, the Lord of Misrule would announce his desire to round off with a kind of apotheosis and a whole succession of spectacular displays of music, dancing and feasting bursting like fireworks one after the other . . . Twelfth Night provided a fine occasion to hand out these titles of king and queen, which appear to have been very popular amongst the rites and traditions of folklore. It was a mimetic ritual of royalty that was probably a survival from the old Saturnalia, giving the king of the evening a chance to masquerade as the monarch, derisively aping his authority . . . Masquerades and fancy-dress mummings are another feature of the lavish amusements of Twelfth

Night . . . Twelfth Night was the festival which brought to an end the long, eventful period of 'Yuletide' revels . . . [7]

The ambiguous nature of these Twelfth Night celebrations is significant. It was a time of revelry, a carnival time at which the world might be turned upside-down, a celebration presided over by the Lord of Misrule and the 'King of the Bean' (a mock king elected by means of a dried bean hidden in the festive cake: whoever found it in his portion was elected 'king'). Yet it also marked the end of revelling: the Christmas holiday was almost over and a return to work and the realities of midwinter imminent. We retain a memory of this in present-day Christmas customs: Twelfth Night is the night the decorations come down. The confrontation between the riotous world of Sir Toby and the sober world of Malvolio could hardly take place in a more fitting context than that of Twelfth Night.

Sir Toby and his drinking companions comprise an carnivalesque underworld, an alternative society to the 'official' world of Olivia and Orsino. This world has all the essential characteristics of Bakhtin's definitions of carnival. The pleasures of the body are paramount; language – especially in Feste's hands – runs riot; and traditional hierarchies and class boundaries have become virtually irrelevant. Knights carouse with servants, fools and other unspecified members of the household. Sir Toby breaks all the rules of Elizabethan decorum by marrying his sister's 'waiting-gentlewoman', thus honouring at one remove Falstaff's promise of marriage to Mistress Quickly. The analogy with Falstaff works theatrically as well as socially. While the social details of the fictional settings are different, the dramatic functions of the two figures are so similar that it is difficult to imagine that the part of Sir Toby was not played by the same actor who created Falstaff.

There are important differences, it is true. Whereas in the history plays Falstaff had to carry the main weight of the plays' foolery, with Pistol, Bardolph, Nym and Mistress Quickly very definitely supporting rôles, *Twelfth Night* spreads the comic burden more evenly. There is a fully-developed fool rôle in the character of Feste, and another excellent comic part in Sir Andrew Aguecheek; Maria, too, is a more interesting and better-established part than Mistress Quickly – indeed she has inherited some of the attributes not only of the witty servant, but also of Shakespeare's witty heroines such as Rosalind and Beatrice. Another important distinction between *Twelfth Night* and the *Henry IV* plays is geographical: in the history plays the world of Bankside was physically as well as socially distant from the court, whereas in Illyria Sir Toby's alternative world exists within the same household as the official one. In *Twelfth Night* the confrontation between the forces of authority and those of licence is played out on a domestic scale. It is not a class conflict, nor is it strictly to do with law and order. There is no opposition between the so-called 'respectable' world and a criminal 'class'. Sir Toby is Olivia's kinsman and the revellers are of her household.

The significance of these similarities and differences between Falstaff and Sir Toby Belch can be seen if we view the confrontation between Sir Toby and Malvolio as a reworking of the confrontation between Falstaff and the Lord Chief Justice in *Henry IV Part 2*. In that play, which was first acted a year or two before *Twelfth Night*, the main narrative concerned the way in which Prince Hal, re-fashioning himself in heroic mode in order to become the warrior-hero Henry V, distanced himself from Falstaff's subversive carnival influence, and aligned himself with the forces of authority, sobriety, law and order, represented in their most extreme form by the Lord Chief Justice. In an early scene in the play the Lord Chief Justice encounters Falstaff and reprimands him, just as Malvolio reprimands Sir Toby. But whereas Malvolio is routed, the Lord Chief Justice is not: Falstaff attempts to answer him, but cannot get the better of him. Eventually, in *Henry IV Part 2* the forces of authority triumph over those of revelry, and Falstaff is banished and imprisoned. *Twelfth Night* replays the same contest but with a different result: here it is the forces of revelry which prevail, and Malvolio who is imprisoned, ridiculed and tormented.

In production it is tempting to represent Malvolio as a stereotyped Puritan figure while Sir Toby becomes the Cavalier of popular imagination: aristocratic and rather dissolute. Such a staging has some historical justification. One of the main social and economic tensions of early-seventeenth-century England involved the shift of real power away from the established but by now fading nobility, whose influence was based on land and tradition, towards the rising middle classes. They were much influenced by Puritan thought, and they were the sector of society which would, on the whole, profit most from the emerging capitalist economy. Thus the confrontation between Carnival and Lent might also be seen as a confrontation between the old order and the new, with Sir Toby representing the traditional values of an already-sentimentalized 'Merrie England' which is being challenged by the likes of the socially ambitious Malvolio. Since, historically, this was a tension which finally erupted in civil war, it gives a sinister power to Malvolio's final line in the play. Humiliated and enraged he exits, vowing 'I'll be revenged on the whole pack of you' (V, i, l. 374). That revenge was forty years brewing and when it came it brought with it Oliver Cromwell.

Caricature Puritans, with names such as Zeal-of-the Land Busy and Tribulation Wholesome, appear on the London stage during this period in Ben Jonson's plays, and Malvolio is a recognizable kinsman to these stereotyped figures: self-righteous, overbearing, a hypocrite and a killjoy. His speech is ostentatiously moralizing and he names 'Jove' frequently and self-importantly, exclaiming piously, for example, that 'Jove, not I, is the doer of this, and he is to be thanked' (III, iv, l. 81). Some scholars, incidentally, suggest that the word 'Jove' is used here, rather than 'God', as a later emendation to the text in accordance with the 1606 Act 'to Restraine Abuses of Players' which outlawed profanity in plays.[8] Yet the word 'God' is used later in the same scene by Andrew Aguecheek, and both the Clown and Viola name 'God' directly in Act I Scene v. It is more likely that this slightly pretentious name for God is simply a feature of Malvolio's idiolect, the function of which is to strengthen the impression of Elizabethan Puritanism: the word contains resonances of the Old Testament 'Jehovah' and the Old Testament was a particular source of inspiration for Puritan preachers and pamphleteers. This kind of stereotyped Puritan was an easy and indeed almost an inevitable target for the Elizabethan playwright: Puritan-led attacks on the stage ensured not only the animosity of most playwrights, but also that of the audience, who by definition were not opposed to the theatre.

Yet it is important not to oversimplify. If Malvolio is, in this loose sense of the word, puritanical, the term 'Puritan' itself is, as historians repeatedly remind us, a notoriously slippery one. It was used at the time to refer to a whole spectrum of Protestant thought and belief (not all of which was ascetically dismissive of worldly pleasure) and a variety of associated political positions ranging from the moderate to the revolutionary. As David Underdown says, 'The term is impossible to define with precision, can mean anything its users want it to mean, and there are modern historians who would like to abandon it altogether'.[9] Nonetheless, the historical movement which we know as Puritanism had certain discernible features. When historians use the word 'Puritan' they generally mean those people who wished

> to emphasize more strongly the Calvinist heritage of the Church of England; to elevate preaching and scripture above sacraments and rituals, the notions of the calling, the elect, the 'saint', the distinctive virtue of the divinely predestined, above the equal worth of all sinful Christians . . . [Puritanism]

> gave its adherents the comforting belief that they were entrusted by God with the special duty of resisting the tide of sin and disorder that surged around them. Through preaching, prayer, the study of scripture, and regular self-examination, it provided a strategy for cultivating the personal qualities necessary to these ends.[10]

Shakespeare goes to some lengths to distance Malvolio from this more precise definition of Puritanism. He expressly states that he does not want simply to label him 'Puritan'. When Toby asks Maria to tell the company something about Malvolio, the following conversation ensues:

> *Maria* Marry, sir, sometimes he is a kind of puritan.
> *Sir Andrew* O, if I thought that I'd beat him like a dog.
> *Sir Toby* What, for being a puritan? Thy exquisite reason, dear knight.
> *Sir Andrew* I have no exquisite reason for't, but I have reason good enough.
> *Maria* The devil a puritan that he is, or anything constantly but a time-pleaser, an affectioned ass that cons state without book and utters it by great swathes; the best persuaded of himself, so crammed, as he thinks, with excellencies, that it is his grounds of faith that all that look on him love him; and on that vice in him will my revenge find notable cause to work.
>
> (II, iii, ll. 135–46)

Maria characterizes Malvolio as 'a time-pleaser', one whose 'Puritanism' has nothing to do with belief or faith. Shakespeare typically draws back from commenting on any specific contemporary theological, philosophical or political position, and contents himself with satirizing the more general and traditional vice of hypocrisy, showing how the trappings of religion are manipulated by the likes of Malvolio in order to further their own ambitions and feed their own vanity. But, as Maria sees, Malvolio's ambition and vanity are the very handles by which the revellers can catch hold of him.

'Are all the people mad?'

John Manningham enjoyed the humour of the prank which the revellers play on Malvolio. A 'good practice', he called it. Yet the plot against Malvolio calls forth a cruel kind of laughter, the laughter of ridicule. Pulled down from his seat of power and imprisoned 'in a dark room and bound', Malvolio is both tortured and humiliated. There is a further psychological torment which Sir Toby and his companions inflict upon Malvolio, however, 'making him believe they took him to be mad', as Manningham puts it.

Acting, as he thinks, on his mistress's instructions, Malvolio adopts uncharacteristic dress and behaviour. He appears to Olivia, yellow-stockinged, cross-gartered, talking unintelligibly and wearing a smile; the Lenten figure has put on, in effect, the garb of Carnival. Acting as he does so far out of his accustomed character, it is small wonder that Olivia is made to think he is deranged.

> *Malvolio* 'Remember who commended thy yellow stockings' –
> *Olivia* 'Thy yellow stockings'?
> *Malvolio,* 'And wished to see thee cross-gartered.'
> *Olivia* 'Cross-gartered'?
> *Malvolio* 'Go to, thou art made, if thou desirest to be so.'
> *Olivia* Am I made?
> *Malvolio* 'If not, let me see thee a servant still.'
> *Olivia* Why, this is very midsummer madness.
>
> (III, iv, ll. 45–54)

In fact the revellers' aim is crueller than this: it is to make Malvolio doubt his own sanity. The techniques which they use on the hapless steward are the classic techniques of brainwashing: sensory deprivation combined with false or contradictory information designed to throw into doubt the subject's usual ways of making sense of the world. In the guise of Sir Topas the priest, Feste visits Malvolio in his dark room:

> *Malvolio* Sir Topas, never was man thus wronged. Good Sir Topas, do not think I am mad. They have laid me here in hideous darkness.
> *Feste* Fie, thou dishonest Satan . . . Say'st thou that house is dark?
> *Malvolio* As hell, Sir Topas.
> *Feste* Why it hath bay windows, transparent as barricadoes, and the clerestories toward the south-north are as lustrous as ebony, and yet complainest thou of obstruction?
> *Malvolio* I am not mad, Sir Topas; I say to you this house is dark.
> *Feste* Madman, thou errest.
>
> (IV, ii, ll. 29–43)

Feste describes a reality to Malvolio which is the opposite of what his senses tell him is the truth. The fact that he does so in nonsensical and contradictory terms ('bay windows, transparent as barricadoes, clerestories toward the south-north . . . lustrous as ebony') only increases the sense of disorientation. Malvolio repeatedly affirms that he is not mad, yet his sanity is under severe attack in this scene.

But it is not only Malvolio who is threatened with madness: a kind of madness seems endemic to Illyria. It is the dominant metaphor of the play. According to Feste, Sir Toby is a 'madman' because of his drink (I, v, l. 126); Orsino thinks Antonio's 'words are madness' (V, i, l. 95) because of his claim to know 'Cesario'; Olivia worries that Viola's unconventionally assertive wooing on behalf of Orsino might amount to madness (I, v, l. 191) and, as we have just seen, is later convinced that the yellow-stockinged Malvolio is suffering from 'midsummer madness' (III, iv, l. 54). Malvolio himself, on the other hand, sees madness in the riotous living of Sir Toby and his friends, and demands of them 'My masters, are you mad?' (II, iii, l. 83). And Sebastian, who finds himself at the centre of the whole network of misunderstandings suspects first of all that in Illyria 'all the people [are] mad' (IV, i, l. 26), and then that the madness might be confined either to Olivia or himself:

> This is the air, that is the glorious sun.
> This pearl she gave me, I do feel't and see't,
> [And] though my soul disputes well with my sense
> That this may be some error but no madness
> Yet doth this accident and flood of fortune
> So far exceed all instance, all discourse,
> That I am ready to distrust mine eyes
> And wrangle with my reason that persuades me
> To any other trust but that I am mad
> Or else the lady's mad.
>
> (IV, iii, ll. 1–2, 9–16)

These repeated references to madness are hardly surprising in a world where people's sensual impressions are often deceiving, and where identities are not always what they appear. Significantly, this speech in which Sebastian tries to make sense of what is happening to him comes immediately after Malvolio's 'madhouse' scene. For, in an odd way, Sebastian and Malvolio are in similar situations. For both of them normal meanings and the evidence of their senses are not operating. Madness is offered as the most rational explanation!

In comedy a little madness can be a liberating thing. The heroes and heroines of Shakespearean comedies typically go through a series of disorienting experiences which eventually act benevolently upon them. The lovers in *A Midsummer Night's Dream* are made 'wood within this wood', and are unable to tell what is real and what is not, but at the end Jack ends up with Jill. In *The Taming of the Shrew* it happens more blatantly and cruelly; yet Petruchio engineers the brainwashing of Kate which has her agreeing that the sun is the moon precisely in order to browbeat her into the supposed 'happiness' of a conventional marriage. The pattern works more subtly in *Twelfth Night*: Viola's traumatic 'loss' of her brother and the disguise she assumes as a result mean that temporarily she loses her own identity and throws other peoples' perceptions of reality out of kilter; yet an equilibrium is reinstated at the end with a joyful reconciliation with Sebastian and eventual marriage to the man she loves. The 'madness' that Sebastian fears is an example of this comedic pattern in which people lose themselves and find themselves once more, often changed for the better by the experience. For Malvolio, however, the pattern does not offer up its traditional rewards.

Like others in the play, he aspires to Olivia's hand. It is one of the signs of Malvolio's ambition that he yearns to rise above his present station in life by marrying Olivia, and much is made (especially by Sir Toby) of his presumption in so aspiring. But Malvolio is by no means the only one whose desire crosses social boundaries: the question of marriage between socially unequal partners is raised several times in the play, from the moment when Sir Toby first tells Sir Andrew that one of Olivia's reasons for rejecting Orsino is that 'She'll not match above her degree, neither in estate, years or wit' (I, v, ll. 105–6). Actually it is not at all clear that Orsino *is* above her in any of these things, yet the marker has been set down. From then on a series of relationships is projected between men and women of unequal status. Malvolio's desire for Olivia is treated comically, as something scandalous, yet Olivia falls in love with Orsino's 'messenger' whom Malvolio can look down on socially. Maria herself marries out of her class when at the end of the play she is wedded to Sir Toby. Nobody makes much of this. But for the steward Malvolio, being in 'love', entering the domain of desire, ends in humiliation and fury. When Viola rejects her customary identity and dresses up in male clothing, it works to her good. When Malvolio rejects his, and dresses up as a lover rather than a steward and disguises himself in smiles, he is made to look ridiculous. The 'madness' Sebastian experiences is a kind of bliss; Malvolio's is a torment, and his spell in the madhouse leads not to a comedic repentance and reconciliation, but to threats of revenge. Malvolio suffers all the disorientations of comedy, but reaps none of the recompense: what acts upon others benevolently acts upon Malvolio . . . malevolently.

That complex latinate pun which is Malvolio's name reads both forwards and backwards. 'Mal' and 'volio' can be put together to suggest 'I want something badly' or (more literally) 'I wish ill' – and both are true of Malvolio. It is also true that he becomes the object of others' malevolence, and that *they* wish *him* ill. But further: just as the names of Viola and Olivia echo and rewrite themselves in each other, so Malvolio's name, too, picks up that same phonetic theme of vowels and consonants: V.L.O.A.I. Malvolio . . . Mal-Olivia . . . Mal-viola . . . Male-viola.[11] He even misreads it himself in his desire to see himself as the object of Olivia's affections:

> 'M.O.A.I. doth sway my life' Nay, but first let me see, let me see, let me see . . . 'M.' Malvolio – 'M' – why, that begins my name . . . But then there is no consonancy in the sequel. That suffers under probation. 'A' should follow, but 'O' does . . . And then 'I' comes behind . . . 'M.O.A.I.' This simulation is not as the former, and yet to crush this a little, it would bow to me, for every one of these letters are in my name.
>
> (II, v, ll. 109–10, 122–3, 126–8, 135–7)

Malvolio's eagerness is self-alienating: it allows him to mistake even his own name.

The relationships between names and people, and between words and meaning, are continually under a strain in *Twelfth Night.* They come under such strain because of ambition, subterfuge, trickery and disguise. They are put under strain most notably by the clown, Feste. In the guise of Sir Topas, Feste creates for Malvolio an illusory world of unreliable meanings. Elsewhere in the play his wit and wordplay are aimed at subverting 'normal' meanings – at proving, for example, that the Lady Olivia, not he himself, is the real fool. In the following exchange with Viola/Cesario, he turns his attention to language itself:

> (*Enter Viola as Cesario and Feste the clown, with [pipe and] tabor*)
> *Viola* Save thee friend, and thy music! Dost thou live by thy tabor?
> *Feste* No, sir, I live by the church.
> *Viola* Art thou a churchman?
> *Feste* No such matter, sir. I do live by the church for I do live at my house, and my house doth stand by the church.
> *Viola* So thou may'st say the king lies by a beggar, if a beggar dwell near him; or the church stands by thy tabor, if thy tabor stand by the church.
> *Feste* You have said, sir. To see this age! A sentence is but a cheveril glove to a good wit – how quickly the wrong side may be turned outward!

Viola Nay, that's certain: they that dally nicely with words may quickly make them wanton.

Feste I would therefore my sister had no name, sir.

Viola Why, man?

Feste Why, sir, her name's a word, and to dally with that word might make my sister wanton. But indeed, words are grown very rascals since bonds disgraced them.

Viola Thy reason, man?

Feste Troth, sir, I can yield you none without words, and words are grown so false, I am loath to prove reason with them.

Viola I warrant thou art a merry fellow and car'st for nothing.

(III, i, ll. 1–26)

It is a verbal duel, of the kind Shakespeare's comedies revel in. Later in the play Viola/Cesario will be tricked into a duel of weapons with Sir Andrew Aguecheek, and will come out of that little better than he/she comes out of this. The followers of carnival in Illyria, it seems, show scant respect for the romantic hero(ine), and insist on challenging and tricking him/her. Here Feste, the clown, outmanoeuvres Viola at every turn and fulfils the fool's traditional function of being able to reduce everything to meaninglessness. It is a paradox of the play that he does so by virtue of his great skill in playing with meanings. Viola's final quoted remark evinces a frustration but also an analysis. Feste's ability to 'dally nicely with words' leads, she is suggesting, not merely to wantonness but to nihilism, to the point where he cares for nothing.

These wordplays about words sound oddly modern. Feste's remarks about the cheveril glove insist on what his own speeches go on to prove, and indeed enact: the slipperiness of language. Signified and signifier do not, in Feste's world, match neatly: it is the truth and also the falsehood of words that allow the anarchic clown to be taken – however briefly – for a churchman. Yet perhaps the 'mistake' is not so outrageous after all, for the function of the fool may be allied in many ways, both straight and parodic, to that of preacher. Certainly, this relation is stressed in *Twelfth Night*: as well as this moment, there is the scene we have already looked at in which Feste takes on the character of a priest in his impersonation of Sir Topas. Earlier, too, Feste has taken on the part of a priest in a rôle-play catechism of Olivia, in which he undertakes to prove that she, not he, is the 'real' fool.

In the exchange with Viola the disguised heroine cannot keep up with Feste, and after a couple of attempts to 'bandy words' with him becomes reduced to the rôle of straight man (or woman?), feeding him the necessary questions to allow him to elaborate upon his paradoxes. The speed at which these paradoxes follow one another demonstrates the truth of Feste's linguistic scepticism; they encompass philosophy, the law and sexuality: the falseness of words is linked (with what now seems a depressing inevitability) to the common Renaissance theme of the falseness of women. This does more than merely imply a link between a world in which language is no longer to be trusted and one in which sexual licence is paramount. For once again, in the person of Viola/Cesario the audience have before them an image of another kind of false woman – doubly so indeed, given the cross-casting of the Elizabethan theatre. What Feste says of his 'sister', that 'her name's a word and to dally with that word might make [her] wanton', has a kind of aptitude to Viola/ Cesario, whose two names themselves denote the duality of her gendered identity.

Feste takes one idea and spins others from it, linking linguistics to economics and changing legal and mercantile practices: 'words are very rascals since bonds disgraced them', says Feste. In the emerging capitalist economy a person's promise is invested not merely in the spoken word but in the legality of a written 'bond'. The legal status of everyday speech is minimal compared to that of the formally drawn-up legal document, and Feste makes the point that truth can no longer be expected to reside in the mere 'word' of a person. Yet we have already seen in the preceding 'letter scene' that the written word is no more to be trusted than the spoken – and as Shylock discovered in *The Merchant of Venice*, legal bonds are also composed of words, whose significance may be open to more than one reading.

And Feste's sceptical inquiry into language is itself a verbal fabric. He concedes as much as he parries Viola's request for 'a reason', and then goes on, typically, to make the point work for him: if words are not to be trusted they cannot be used to prove reason. And thus a central paradox of contemporary linguistics is articulated by a Shakespearean fool: that there is no extra-linguistic standpoint from which to analyse language itself. It is the poststructuralist catchphrase: there is nothing outside the text. And yet, of course, by means of an elegant double-take the analysis *is* after all validated. The rascality of words is proved because Feste's sentence is both self-reflexive and also demonstrative; even as he speaks his words manifest their own slipperiness. When Viola asks 'Thy reason, man?' she is requesting his motive or his justification for a preceding remark. When he replies that 'words are grown so false, I am loath to prove reason with them' he is talking about 'reason' as logic. Thus the sense of the word 'reason' itself hovers uncertainly between the two meanings, and the very inadequacy of language to act as a logical tool proves its own logical point.

Feste's job is to destabilize meanings; he claims as much himself:

> *Viola* Art not thou the Lady Olivia's fool?
> *Feste* No indeed, sir, the Lady Olivia has no folly . . . I am indeed not her fool, but her corrupter of words.
>
> (III, i, ll. 30–1, 34–5)

In the view of this 'corrupter of words', language is – indeed all sign-systems are – deceptive and ambiguous; and he proves the point by exploiting their deceptiveness and ambiguity. Viola understands this element of ambiguity well enough, being herself the epitome of ambiguity, the signifier which belies its signified.

'Like Patience on a monument'

> *Viola* Disguise, I see thou art a wickedness
> Wherein the pregnant enemy does much.
> How easy it is for the proper false
> In women's waxen hearts to set their forms!
> Alas, our frailty is the cause, not we,
> For such as we are made of, such we be.
> How will this fadge? My master loves her dearly,
> And I, poor monster, fond as much on him,
> And she, mistaken, seems to dote on me.
> What will become of this? As I am man,
> My state is desperate for my master's love.
> As I am woman, now, alas the day,
> What thriftless sigh shall poor Olivia breathe!
> O time, thou must untangle this, not I.
> It is too hard a knot for me t' untie.
>
> (II, ii, ll. 27–41)

This speech of Viola's shows the difference in tone between *As You Like It* and *Twelfth Night.* Viola is in a predicament not unlike Rosalind's in the earlier play: disguised as a boy she is in close proximity to the man she loves but remains unknown to him; meanwhile Olivia has fallen in love with her boy-persona, as Phoebe did with Rosalind's. *Twelfth Night* and *As You Like It* share the cross-dressing plot, with its destabilizing of gender identities, but the two plays use the same material in very different ways.

Rosalind enjoys her rôle as Ganymede; it empowers her and allows her to improvise rôle-play games with Orlando. Her response to the love entanglement with Phoebe is to stage the masque which makes all clear: she sorts it out. Viola on the other hand, declares that it is all too hard for her and that she will just leave it to time to sort it all out. And so she does. Eventually her twin brother turns up, they are reunited, Olivia and Orsino recognize the 'true' objects of their affection and the love-relationships sort themselves out accordingly: time, as Viola hoped it would, untangles things, not she.

Viola is the opposite of Rosalind, who enjoyed rôle-playing to the extent of inventing further rôles within the rôles. Rosalind's male disguise allowed her to take the initiative in wooing Orlando; in her love for Orsino Viola behaves as passively as any Renaissance patriarch could wish. Having taken the single active step of disguising herself, she does little more thereafter than wait for him to notice her. The language of love which she has learnt is one of passivity:

> *Viola* My father had a daughter loved a man
> As it might be, perhaps, were I a woman
> I should your lordship.
> *Orsino* And what's her history?
> *Viola* A blank, my lord. She never told her love
> But let concealment, like the worm i' th' bud,
> Feed on her damask cheek. She pined in thought,
> And with a green and yellow melancholy
> She sat like patience on a monument,
> Smiling at grief. Was not this love indeed?
> (II, iv, ll. 107–15)

She is describing herself, of course. Not entirely, but with sufficient accuracy for us to recognize that concealment is working on her, too, 'like the worm i' th' bud'. She can only articulate her love for Orsino in the subjunctive mood.

And so it is not merely that Viola is comparatively passive: she is positively uncomfortable with the disguise she has assumed. While *As You Like It* revelled in the complexities engendered by the cross-dressing plot, *Twelfth Night* continually expresses anxiety about them. Viola considers herself not liberated by her rôle-playing but trapped by it and doubly unfulfilled. 'As I am a man / My state is desperate for my master's love. / As I am a woman now, alas the day . . .' (II, ii, ll. 35–8). And although she later argues with Orsino that women are 'as true of heart as [men]', here her assumed masculine identity gives her a voice in which she articulates misogynistic Renaissance truisms about 'women's waxen hearts' and their 'frailty'. There is little liberation here.

Viola sees herself as a freak and a grotesque; she refers to herself, significantly, as 'poor monster'! The moralizing tone of that self-disparaging comment is revealing: Viola finds herself in agreement with the anti-theatrical propagandists who condemned play-acting as inherently sinful. Disguise, she exclaims, is 'a wickedness / Wherein the pregnant enemy does much'. This is the language of the Elizabethan anti-theatrical pamphleteers, who similarly condemned cross-dressing:

> And so, if any man do put on woman's raiment, he is dishonested and defiled, because he transgresseth the bounds of modesty and comeliness, and weareth that which God's law forbiddeth him to wear, which man's law affirmeth he cannot wear without reproof... [M]en's wearing of women's raiment, though in plays, [is] a heinous crime... Players are abomination that put on women's raiment.[12]

The moralists' usual condemnation was, as it is here, of boy actors dressing up as women. Ironically, Viola's line about disguise being a wickedness is written to be spoken by a boy actor who is *not* dressed up as a woman but who (like the boy actor playing Rosalind in *As You Like It*) has become visible in his own gender once more. Once again, a gap has been created between the line spoken and the actor who speaks it. This gap disturbs any simple acceptance of what Viola says: clearly, on another level, the play does *not* endorse the message that disguise is a wickedness – otherwise there would be no play. Even so, cross-dressing in *Twelfth Night* has the air of a desperate experiment rather than of the playful risk-taking which it had in *As You Like It*. If madness is a central metaphor in this play, then Viola experiences her disguise as something akin to schizophrenia: it alienates her from herself, creating a split personality. She refers to herself in the third person ('My father had a daughter...') and speaks as a divided self ('As I am a man... As I am a woman').

It also gives rise to a set of questions about gender identity which are taken more seriously than they were in *As You Like It*. In *As You Like It* homoerotic attraction tended to be treated quite lightly: Phoebe's crush on Ganymede never amounted to much dramatically, and the complex rôle-playing between Ganymede and Orlando was always counterbalanced by the fact that Orlando's attention was continually fixed on the 'absent' Rosalind of his imagination. In *Twelfth Night*, however, Olivia's desire for 'Cesario' is depicted as something much more uncontrollable, powerful and painful. It is the passion which can break the depressive hold which melancholy has had on her since her brother's death; it is more important to her than her dignity:

> Cesario, by the roses of the spring,
> By maidhood, honour, truth and everything,
> I love thee so that, maugre all thy pride,
> Nor wit nor reason can my passion hide.
> Do not extort thy reasons from this clause,
> For that I woo, thou therefore hast no cause.
>
> (III, i, ll. 147–51)

Another kind of sexual tension exists between Orsino and Viola: charged this time by her desire for him coupled with his response to her ambiguous sexual *persona*. While Orsino, like Orlando in *As You Like It*, remains infatuated with an absent woman, we are left in no doubt that Cesario is present for him in a way that Ganymede never is for Orlando. The language in which he addresses Cesario makes the point:

> *Orsino*
> . . . Diana's lip
> Is not more smooth and rubious; thy small pipe
> Is as the maiden's organ, shrill and sound,
> And all is semblative a woman's part.
>
> (I, iv, ll. 31–4)

Viola and her friend the sea-captain had originally agreed that she would be presented at Orsino's court as a 'eunuch', but there is nothing unsexed about the attraction Orsino feels for 'Cesario'. The physicality of his language is sensuous even without the double-entendres of 'organ' and 'part'. Moreover, the conversation between them is continually *about* sexual desire: ostensibly about Orsino's desire for Olivia, but continually charged by the unspoken actuality of Viola's desire for Orsino.

The gender confusions of *Twelfth Night* are given a context in the portrayal of the relationship between Antonio and Sebastian. In this *Twelfth Night* recognizes, in a way that *As You Like It* does not, a homosexual love-relationship. Antonio's love for Sebastian is couched time and time again in the language of erotic attraction, language drawn from the registers of Elizabethan love poetry: 'I do adore thee so' (II, i, l. 42); 'My desire, / More sharp than filed steel, did spur me forth' (III, iii, ll. 4–5); 'to his image, which methought did promise / Most venerable worth, did I devotion' (III, iv, ll. 354–5). He talks of the 'witchcraft' which led him to follow Sebastian, whom he calls 'this god' (III, iv, l. 357) and to whose physical beauty he continually refers. 'My love without retention or restraint' (another image of excess!) is how he describes his feelings for Sebastian, and his actions in defence of the young man he says he adores bear out his words.[13]

Antonio's adoration of Sebastian gives a depth and a seriousness to the gender confusions of *Twelfth Night*; the stakes here are higher than they were in *As You Like It*. There a fairytale logic was available to make everything fit neatly into conventional patterns, so that cruel brothers repented and became kind, and all the complications of the interwoven love-plots could be sorted out by the stage-managed appearance of Hymen, announcing 'Peace, ho! I bar confusion' (*As You Like It*, V, iv, l. 123). The love-plots of *Twelfth Night* are more urgent and there is a continual sense that things could get out of control.

In both the Viola-Olivia and the Viola-Orsino relationships, then, the text toys with the possibility of same-sex eroticism more intensely than was the case in *As You Like It*. By balancing these two relationships the play does not allow the audience to explain away the gender confusions easily. Some critics have rationalized the attraction Orsino manifests for Cesario by arguing that what he is 'really' responding to is the woman underneath – but if that is so, the same logic leads to the conclusion that Olivia is also 'really' attracted not to Cesario but to Viola. Olivia, faced at the end with the realization that she had fallen in love with a girl, is reassured by Sebastian that her mistake was natural enough:

> So comes it, lady, you have been mistook.
> But nature to her bias drew in that.
> You would have been contracted to a maid,
> Nor are you therein, by my life, deceived.
> You are betrothed both to a maid and man.
>
> (V, i, ll. 257–61)

Sebastian's reassurance, however, does not so much dispel ambiguity as reinforce it: Olivia is betrothed 'both to a maid and man'.

This is typical of the final scene of *Twelfth Night*: like the last scene of so many Shakespeare comedies it both offers and resists closure. Narratives are brought to a climax, yet not everything is resolved: the play leaves a great deal open. The scene contains an immense amount of action: again, it works through excess. It is worth summarizing the scene just to show how much there is going on in it:

> Feste teases Fabian about the contents of Malvolio's letter; Orsino arrives, and Feste goes through a begging routine with him; Antonio is brought on and his story, including back-

ground incidents about his battles against Illyria, is told, ending with his accusation against Viola; Olivia arrives, and Orsino encounters on stage for the first time the woman he has been obsessed with throughout the play; Olivia encounters 'Cesario' and confusion arises – firstly because she now thinks he is Sebastian, and secondly because Orsino begins to suspect that 'Cesario' has been wooing Olivia on his own behalf; his disappointment at Olivia's rejection is expressed in threats of violence against Cesario, who still professes faithfulness to him, and they begin to depart together; Olivia prevents their exit by revealing that she and Sebastian (Cesario, as she thinks) are married, and sends for the priest to prove it; the priest arrives and confirms the marriage; Orsino's anger against Cesario turns to disgust and he rejects him; meanwhile Cesario's protestations of innocence are making Olivia concerned about 'his' love for her.

At this point the action suddenly switches from melodrama to farce: Andrew Aguecheek arrives with a bloodied head (having been fighting with the real Sebastian off-stage); he espies Viola and panics, reprising an earlier encounter between them; then Sir Toby arrives, also with a bloody head, and in a foul temper, rejecting Sir Andrew's offer of help, and going off-stage again almost immediately.

At this point Sebastian finally comes on. Initially he does not notice Viola, although she sees him. He is joyfully reunited with Antonio, and only after that does he see his sister. Carefully, almost tentatively, they begin to come together, testing each other's identity with details of shared memories; Sebastian refers uneasily to the paradox of Olivia's love for Cesario; Viola explains that the sea-captain who saved her life has been imprisoned by Malvolio's request for some unspecified offence.

This reintroduces the Malvolio plot: Feste arrives with the letter and attempts to make a joke of it; Fabian is given the job of reading the letter, which is sober and serious, and Malvolio is sent for; while he is being fetched, attention turns back to the love-plot, with Orsino offering his hand to Viola; Malvolio arrives and he tells his story; Olivia is shown the letter which originally trapped him, and she explains that it is Maria's handwriting; Malvolio is offered recompense; the moment of potential reconciliation is marred by Feste's spiteful interruption as he quotes Malvolio's own words back at him; Malvolio stalks off with threats against the whole company; Orsino sends somebody off to try and persuade him to a peace; addressing Viola, Orsino promises that they will be lovers when she returns to her female attire. At last, the clown steps forward to sing a final song, with the melancholy refrain 'And the rain it raineth every day'.

All this in about three hundred and eighty lines!

It is not only the number of different actions within this one scene which is extraordinary (each paragraph of the above amounts to a small scene or routine in itself), but the variety of them, the speed with which they follow on one from another, and the resulting emotional range of the scene. Its tone continually shifts, moment by moment, between intensity and frivolity, violence and tenderness, melodrama and downright farce, celebration and discord, wonder and harshness, laughter and melancholy. It starts with a couple of (by now familiar) clown routines. Antonio's entry picks up the narrative, laying out his part of the story so far in a way which seems to prepare for a *dénouement* in which all the confusions are unravelled. This is interrupted, though, by the Olivia-Orsino encounter, the climax of another strand of the plot. But far from reaching a resolution, this meeting seems only to complicate things further and threaten the ending with tragedy. These complications are then repeated, but in a different key, as Sir Andrew and Sir Toby pass across the stage. Yet even this tiny scene-within-a-scene contains a sharp tonal shift. It looks as if it is going to be a moment of pure farce; then, without warning, Sir Toby turns to Sir Andrew, insults him, and casts him off with a snarl. The carnivalesqe high spirits of their roistering end in a moment of rejection as bitter as that experienced by Falstaff.

The moment at which things *do* begin to unravel themselves is, of course, the moment when Viola and Sebastian both appear on stage together: from now on, things begin to make sense. Yet some of the surprise value of this moment of revelation was preempted earlier in the play, when Viola first guessed, in Act III Scene iv, that all the confusions were due to her brother's being in Illyria. And then, just as the scene seems set to concentrate on reunions, betrothals and marriages, this, too, is interrupted by the as-yet-unresolved Malvolio plot. The confrontation between Malvolio and his mistress also shifts through a variety of emotional tones, from the comedy of Feste's attempt at 'vox', through the pathos of Malvolio's own account, the offer of reconciliation by Olivia, the interruption of that by Feste, spitefully quoting Malvolio's own words back at him, to the anger of Malvolio's exit. The ending of *Twelfth Night,* in fact, is structured as a series of interruptions. It is this structure which prevents the positive mood of the narrative's romantic-comedy climax from completely dominating the end of the play: the harmony is established and celebrated – but across it can be heard the notes of discord.

Contributing to the same destabilizing effect is the fact that narratives are left unfinished – notably, of course, the Malvolio story itself. Who pursues Malvolio to 'entreat him to a peace'? With what result? What about the power he still holds over Viola's friend the sea-captain, whose story is so strangely re-introduced in these final moments of the play? Most directly, the audience is left with the question of Malvolio's powerful final threat: what sort of revenge is he envisaging? His exit line contains such a blatant promise of the story's continuance, that if Shakespeare were writing for television or the movies we would assume he was setting up the sequel. But it is not only the Malvolio plot which is left unfinished. The reunion of Viola and Sebastian is not fully celebrated; she says to him:

> Do not embrace me till each circumstance
> Of place, time, fortune do cohere and jump
> That I am Viola, which to confirm
> I'll bring you to a captain in this town
> Where lie my maiden weeds.
>
> (V, i, ll. 249–53)

Viola's return to her own female identity is incomplete; unlike Rosalind she never appears on stage again as a woman, and as a result Orsino cannot yet begin to see her as Viola. Even at the very end of the play she is still 'Cesario' to him:

> Cesario come –
> For so you shall be while you are a man;
> But when in other habits you are seen,
> Orsino's mistress and his fancy's queen.
>
> (V, i, ll. 381–4)

Thus Orsino, like Olivia, leaves the stage without having fully resolved the ambiguities about whom he is actually in love with, and the promised love-relationship between him and Viola is deferred until after the play's ending. Feste's final song trips through a nonsense-version of Jaques' Seven Ages speech, set against the gloomy refrain of wind and rain. Its last stanza perfunctorily shrugs away all the problems and uncertainties of the play's ending with an insouciant nonsense of its own:

> A great while ago the world begun
> With hey ho, the wind and the rain,
> But that's all one, our play is done,
> And we'll strive to please you every day.
>
> (V, i, ll. 401–4)

And so Carnival gives way to Lent, and the play named after the final day of revelling is finally done.

Notes

1. An entire book devoted to this subject is Leah Scragg, *Shakespeare's Mouldy Tales: Recurrent Plot Motifs in Shakespearian Drama* (Harlow: Longman, 1992).
2. Quoted in William Shakespeare, *Twelfth Night*, ed. J. M. Lothian and T. W. Craik (London: Methuen, 1975), p. xxvi. My modernization.
3. *Twelfth Night*, ed. Lothian and Craik, p. liii.
4. Quoted in ibid., p. liii.
5. Quoted in ibid., p. xxvi.
6. Ibid., pp. lxxix–lxxxiii.
7. François Laroque, *Shakespeare's Festive World: Elizabethan Seasonal Entertainment and the Professional Stage*, trans. Janet Lloyd (Cambridge: Cambridge University Press, 1991), p. 153.
8. E. K. Chambers, *The Elizabethan Stage* (Oxford: Oxford University Press, 1923), vol. 4, pp. 338–9.
9. David Underdown, *Revel, Riot and Rebellion* (Oxford: Oxford University Press, 1985), p. 41.
10. Underdown, *Revel, Riot and Rebellion*, p. 41.
11. See Matthew H. Wikander, 'As secret as maidenhead: the profession of boy-actress in *Twelfth Night*', *Comparative Drama*, 20, iv, pp. 349–63.
12. Thomas Rainoldes, *The Overthrow of Stage-Plays* (Middleburgh: 1599), p. 16.
13. See Joseph Pequigny, 'The two Antonios and same-sex love in *Twelfth Night* and *The Merchant of Venice*', *English Literary Renaissance* 22, ii, pp. 201–21 for a detailed analysis of Antonio's language.

Part Three
Reference Section

Short biographies

ALLEYN, EDWARD (1566–1626) Edward Alleyn was one of the greatest actors of his time, rivalled only by Richard Burbage. Alleyn was the leader of the Lord Admiral's Men, and the creator of many of the great non-Shakespearean rôles of the Elizabethan theatre, rôles such as Tamburlaine and Doctor Faustus. He was a theatre-owner and theatre-manager as well as being an actor; in partnership with his father-in-law Philip Henslowe he owned shares in various London theatres, such as the Rose and the Fortune. Renowned in particular for his skill as a tragic actor, Alleyn's greatest acting triumphs were in the 1590s. His career did not long survive Elizabeth's reign and he appears to have retired in 1604.

ARMIN, ROBERT (1581–1615) Robert Armin claimed to have served his apprenticeship with Queen Elizabeth's favourite clown, Richard Tarlton. He had also served another kind of apprenticeship in his youth, as a goldsmith, and this may have been reflected in the name of one of the parts written for him by Shakespeare – Touchstone in *As You Like It.* He left Lord Chandos's Men to join the Lord Chamberlain's Men as a sharer in 1599 or 1600. His task was to replace the departed Will Kempe, and his own memoirs refer to him taking over from Kempe in the rôle of Dogberry in *Much Ado About Nothing.* Armin's manner was very different from Kempe's, however, and may have influenced the way in which Shakespeare began to use the clown-figure after 1600. Armin's downbeat, introspective and even melancholy comic style and his fine singing voice were used by Shakespeare as he began to develop the figure of the philosophical fool. Feste in *Twelfth Night* and the Fool in *King Lear* are prime examples of this. Armin himself wrote plays, and other works, including a typology of the clown called *Foole upon Foole or Six Sortes of Sottes.*

ARMSTRONG, ARCHY (d. 1672) Born of Scottish parents, Archy Armstrong probably joined the household of King James VI of Scotland while still a child. When the Scottish monarch also became King James I of England, Archy accompanied him to London. He was James's official court jester – or *joculator domini regis,* as he is referred to in the court account – and was entitled to wear the King's livery. Acerbic in his humour, and rarely tactful, he managed to alienate many members of James's new English court; nonetheless he held a position of influence, accompanying Prince Charles on ambassadorial business to Spain in 1623. When Charles came to the throne, Armstrong kept his position of court fool, but continued to make enemies – his most influential being Archbishop Laud, who in 1637 had him banished from the court. Armstrong had the last laugh, though, celebrating Laud's downfall in 1641 by publishing the satirical *Archy's Dreame.*

BEAUMONT, FRANCIS (1584–1616) Author of several plays, many in collaboration with John Fletcher. Beaumont's most famous work (in which Fletcher probably had a hand) is the comedy *The Knight of the Burning Pestle* (*c.* 1608) a mock-heroic and satirical play which burlesques chivalric romances and the equally popular 'citizen' drama simultaneously. As a team, Beaumont and Fletcher specialized in tragicomedies, the most influential of which was *Philaster* (*c.* 1610). Beaumont stopped writing for the stage in 1612–13.

BURBAGE, JAMES (d. 1597) An actor and theatrical entrepreneur who originally trained as a carpenter, James Burbage had a successful acting career, rising to become the leading member of Lord Leicester's Men. Following the granting of a royal patent to that company in 1574 Burbage moved into theatre management, opening in 1576 what is generally recognized as the first purpose-built theatre in England. Called simply the Theatre, it stood in Shoreditch, north of the city and outside civic jurisdiction. Many of Shakespeare's early plays were performed there.

BURBAGE, RICHARD (*c.* 1567–1619) The son of James Burbage, Richard learnt his trade as an actor with the Admiral's Men, who played mainly at a rival theatre, the Rose. The Admiral's Men were led by Edward Alleyn, the actor who dominated the London stage in the early 1590s, but who was eventually eclipsed by the younger Burbage. When the Lord Chamberlain's Men were formed in 1594 Burbage joined them as an actor and a shareholder, and on the death of his father he and his brother Cuthbert inherited a major shareholding in the company, owning half of it between them. The Burbages' masterminding of the daring theft of the Theatre and the founding of the Globe suggests something about their personal qualities. By all accounts Richard was also a vigorous and dynamic actor, whose presence must have been a vital influence on the way in which Shakespeare went about writing his plays. At least three of the great tragic parts were written for Burbage: we know that he first played the rôles of Hamlet, Othello and Lear as well as Richard III. It is extremely likely that he also played Macbeth. Burbage was a skilled painter as well as one of the most celebrated actors of his age. Of all actors, his name is the one linked with Shakespeare's.

CHETTLE, HENRY (*c.* 1560–1607) Among his contemporaries Henry Chettle seems to have had a high reputation as a comic playwright: in Francis Meres's *Palladis Tamia* (1598) he is referred to as being among 'the best for comedy'. Unfortunately, none of his comedies survives, the only play of his still extant being *The Tragedy of Hoffman.* He was a printer as well as a playwright, and was responsible for editing and publishing Robert Greene's *Groatsworth of Wit* (1592), with its scathing attack on Shakespeare. Clearly embarrassed by his association with that attack, the following year Chettle published a pamphlet of his own, *Kind-heart's Dream,* in which he went out of his way to compliment Shakespeare.

CONDELL, HENRY (d. 1627) An actor with the Lord Chamberlain's Men from its early days, Henry Condell also became a sharer in the company some time after 1603, and thereafter acquired portions of both the Globe and Blackfriars Theatres, as well as valuable properties elsewhere. Condell is known to have played the part of the Cardinal in John Webster's *The Duchess of Malfi,* and it is conjectured that he also played Horatio in *Hamlet,* Cassio in *Othello,* Edgar in *King Lear,* and Malcolm in *Macbeth.* With John Heminges, to whom he may have originally been apprenticed, Condell edited and published the First Folio edition of Shakespeare's plays. Like Heminges, he is mentioned by Shakespeare in his will and appears to have been a close friend.

DEKKER, THOMAS (1572?–1632) A prolific playwright, journalist and pamphleteer, Dekker was responsible for at least forty-four plays, written either alone or in collaboration with other dramatists such as William Rowley, Thomas Middleton and John Ford. His festive comedy *The Shoemaker's Holiday* (1599) was a great success on the London stage; it combines a sentimentalized vision of a mythical merry England with some sharp social satire. Dekker's prose works include the jestbook *Jests to Make You Merry* (1607) and *The Gull's Horn-Book* (1609), which burlesques the style of a conduct-book in its account of a typical day in the life of an affected young man-about-town.

ELIZABETH I (b. 1533. Queen of England 1558–1603) Elizabeth, daughter of Henry VIII and Ann Boleyn, maintained throughout her reign a delicate balance between the various forces which acted upon late-sixteenth-century England. Her claim to the throne was established by an Act of the English Parliament, but she was seen as a usurper and a heretic by most of Catholic Europe. During her reign there were numerous attempts to remove her as head of state, by means both of numerous conspiracies and attempted foreign invasion; however, with the help of a shrewd political mind, a well-disciplined navy and an efficient secret service Elizabeth survived them all and forged the beginnings of a powerful nation state, as well as a considerable personal mythology. This was maintained and propagated by the literary establishment among others, and the Elizabethan court masque was a particularly important form of dramatic propaganda. Elizabeth also took an interest in other forms of drama, and played a part in defending the London theatre against some of its more vehement Puritan opponents: she was the patron of 'Queen Elizabeth's Men', a prestigious acting company formed in 1583 which played at court, in the provinces and in London. Elizabeth, however, was never a generous patron, artistically or politically: her reputation for financial penny-pinching was well-founded, and was a necessary part of her attempt to keep the economy under control. Even this, however, did not prevent the national debt from standing at £400,000 at the time of her death. A major reason was that throughout Elizabeth's reign the national economy had been effectively a war economy; eventually this, combined with a series of bad harvests, led to serious social problems, especially among the increasing numbers of the rural poor. The price of maintaining a strong foreign policy in the face of numerous potential enemies and competitors was that political and social friction increased on the domestic front. The last years of Elizabeth's reign (the period in which Shakespeare began to emerge as the leading playwright of the age) were characterized by crippling inflation, localized famine, bureaucratic inertia and governmental corruption. Elizabeth's death in 1603 was received with ill-concealed relief by many of her subjects.

ESSEX, ROBERT DEVEREUX, SECOND EARL (1566–1601) The Earl of Essex was one of the elderly Queen Elizabeth's favourites, but their relationship was always a stormy one. Essex was a charismatic figure in Elizabethan political life, and one to whom Shakespeare paid homage in *Henry V*, but he was also ambitious, egocentric and unstable. Several times he found himself in trouble with Elizabeth as a result of his defiance of her, and when he finally mismanaged an important military campaign in Ireland he was censured and deprived of office. With bankruptcy staring him in the face, he was foolish enough to attempt to restore his own political power by force: raising a small army, he marched on the court in February 1601. The support he had expected from the City of London failed to materialize and Essex was arrested and executed. Shakespeare's patron, the Earl of Southampton, was implicated in the Earl's downfall.

FIELD, NATHANIEL (1587–?) Field wrote a few plays but is best remembered as an actor, complimented by Jonson for his acting in *Bartholomew Fair.* His career started with the Children of the Chapel, with whom he began to act at about the age of thirteen. By 1613 he was leading the adult company Lady Elizabeth's Men, and he acted with the King's Men between 1613 and 1619, in which year he both parted company with them and fathered the illegitimate child of the Countess of Argyll. Field's father was a Puritan preacher given to aggressive diatribes on the wickedness of the stage.

FLETCHER, JOHN (1579–1625) Fletcher probably succeeded Shakespeare as the King's Men's leading dramatist after 1613. A prolific writer, he seems to have worked best in partnership with other playwrights. In collaboration with Francis Beaumont he produced plays such as *The Knight of the Burning Pestle* (1607) and *Philaster* (*c.* 1610); he wrote several plays with Philip Massinger; and he is thought to have collaborated with Shakespeare in the writing of *The Two Noble Kinsmen* (1613) and *Henry VIII* (1613). His play *The Faithful Shepherdess* (1609) is a pastoral drama which was a failure on the London stage but was successfully revived at the court of Charles I.

GOSSON, STEPHEN (1554–1624) Stephen Gosson was educated at Oxford and after graduating he moved to London, where he attempted to make a career as a playwright. His pastoral plays were praised by Francis Meres in *Palladis Tamia* (1598), but none of them is now extant. His playwriting career did not last long: undergoing a religious conversion to Puritanism, he published *The School of Abuse* in 1579. Dedicated to Sir Philip Sidney, it includes a violent attack on plays, players and poetry. *The School of Abuse* started a small war of words: Thomas Lodge responded with *A Reply to Stephen Gosson Touching Plays* (1579), and Sidney's own *Apology for Poetry* may have been written as a response to Gosson.

GREENE, ROBERT (1558–1592) A dramatist, romance-writer and satirist, Greene seems to have lived mainly from money earned by writing – a rare thing in Elizabethan times. He was, perhaps because he needed to be, immensely prolific. Greene is credited with the first recorded reference to Shakespeare as actor and dramatist, in his satirical work *A Groatsworth of Wit* (1592). It is not a complimentary one: he describes Shakespeare as 'an upstart crow, beautified with our feathers, that with his *tiger's heart wrapped in a player's hide* supposes he is as well able to bombast out a blank verse as the best of you; and . . . is in his own conceit the only Shake-scene in the country'. Greene's implied charge of plagiarism has an ironic aftermath: nearly twenty years later, his prose romance *Pandosto, or The Triumph of Time* (which Greene had published in 1588) supplied Shakespeare with the main plot of *The Winter's Tale* (1610–11).

HATHAWAY, ANNE (*c.* 1556–1623) For some reason, Shakespeare's wife has nearly always been referred to by her maiden name. She was the daughter of a well-off farmer from the village of Shottery, a mile or so from Stratford itself, and the family farmhouse where she grew up has become a national monument, Anne Hathaway's Cottage. Eight years older than her husband, she married him in November 1582; their first child, Susanna, was born in May 1583. Before Shakespeare reached the age of twenty-one he was also the father of two more of Anne's children, the twins Judith and Hamnet; the latter died in 1596. We know very little about Anne Hathaway: this, of course, has not prevented much speculation about her and the details of her married life both with and apart from William Shakespeare.

HEMINGES, JOHN (*c.* 1566–1630) John Heminges acted with Edward Alleyn early in his career, and joined the Lord Chamberlain's Men soon after its formation in 1594. A sharer in both the Globe and later Blackfriars Theatre, he was also a close friend of Shakespeare and was mentioned in his will. It has been suggested that he played Polonius in *Hamlet*, Brabantio in *Othello*, Kent in *King Lear*, and Ross in *Macbeth*, as well as the title rôle in *Julius Caesar*. His fame rests, however, on his involvement in the editing and publishing of the First Folio of Shakespeare's plays in 1623. One of the most respectable members of the Lord Chamberlain's Men, he gave up acting to become the company's financial organizer in 1611; for many years of his life he was a churchwarden in his home parish of St Mary's, and he was granted a coat of arms in 1629, just before his death.

HENSLOWE, PHILIP (*c.* 1550–1616) A businessman and theatrical entrepreneur, Philip Henslowe was the Burbages' biggest commercial rival. He built the Rose Theatre on Bankside, and when that was threatened with competition from Shakespeare's Globe, he opened the Fortune Theatre across the Thames. In 1614 he opened the Hope Theatre, which served the dual purpose of staging plays and animal-baiting spectacles. He was the father-in-law of actor Edward Alleyn and between them they were a formidable business partnership; Henslowe's power over actors and playwrights was legendary. As well as theatres, Henslowe had interests in property (including several brothels), manufacturing and money-lending. The account book which he kept between 1592 and 1603 is known as *Henslowe's Diary*, and is an invaluable source of information about the day-to-day business of the Elizabethan theatre.

HEYWOOD, JOHN (*c.* 1497–*c.* 1578) The nephew-in-law of Sir Thomas More, John Heywood's plays include two farcical interludes, *The Four PP* (*c.* 1521) and *Johan Johan* (1533). Influenced by medieval debate and *fabliau* traditions, and trading heavily on misogynistic folk-humour, these plays are important in the development of English comic traditions because they show the beginnings of the transition between medieval and Elizabethan theatrical styles.

HEYWOOD, THOMAS (1573?-1641) Thomas Heywood was an actor and dramatist whose career is first mentioned in an entry in *Henslowe's Diary* which records a payment to him for a play. Between 1598 and 1600 he was under contract to write exclusively for Henslowe, and he acted with the Admiral's Men as well as with other companies. Both in collaboration and alone he wrote in a great range of styles and was massively prolific: he claimed to have written or contributed to 220 plays in a writing career which spanned nearly fifty years. His defence of the stage, *An Apology for Actors* (1612), is one of the most eloquent replies to the Puritan anti-theatrical pamphlets.

HUNSDON, GEORGE CAREY, SECOND LORD (1547–1603) George Carey, second Lord Hunsdon, was the son of the Lord Chamberlain under whose auspices Shakespeare's theatre company, the Lord Chamberlain's Men, had originally been formed. Upon his father's death in 1596 the new Lord Hunsdon took over as the patron of the company (which became known, for a short period, as Lord Hunsdon's Men); a year later he succeeded to the Lord Chamberlain's office itself. It seems that Hunsdon took no great interest in the acting company which bore his name; indeed, he is known to have supported a petition to ban the opening of a public playhouse in Blackfriars.

JAMES I (b. 1566. King of England 1603–1625) James succeeded Elizabeth in 1603. Towards the end of the reign of Elizabeth I there was uncertainty as to what would happen to the English throne after her death. When James, the son of Mary Queen of Scots and a direct descendant of Henry VII, was named her successor he was generally welcomed; since 1567 he had been King James VI of Scotland, and one of his own dearest political projects was the attempted constitutional union of the kingdoms of England and Scotland. He was unable to achieve this, and as his reign proceeded the early enthusiasm with which he had been greeted began to wane. In his dealings with his own court he earned a reputation for excessive liberality and favouritism, and his court soon came to be seen as a place of corruption. In his dealings with his parliament James was often seen as tactless, and the years of his reign saw growing tensions between king and parliament. Not a stupid man, he seems to have suffered largely from a poor sense of timing and a lack of self-restraint: France's King Henri IV dubbed him 'the wisest fool in Christendom'. He suffered from paranoia about his personal safety, which may have had some bearing on the obsessive interest he began to take in witchcraft shortly before his accession to the English throne. On the whole, however, James's reign saw a consolidation of the national stability which Elizabeth had struggled so hard to establish. It is true that a growing population ensured that the domestic economic problems continued, and inflation was as rampant in James's England as it had been in Elizabeth's, but England enjoyed years of comparative peace, started to make closer links with other European countries, and began to extend her influence into the colonies of the New World. James's influence on the literary and artistic culture of early-seventeenth-century England is now beginning to be recognized. Well-read and cultured, he took an active interest in the arts: he was himself a poet, polemicist and translator, but his most important rôle was as a patron and enabler of other men's genius. Not only did he commission the translation of the Bible which bears his name, he also took under his personal patronage the acting company of which Shakespeare was a key member: in 1603 the Lord Chamberlain's Men became the King's Men, and James himself became the most important single member of Shakespeare's audience.

JONSON, BEN (*c.* 1573–1637) Dramatist, actor, poet and essayist, Jonson studied at Westminster School, worked briefly as a bricklayer, spent time soldiering in Flanders, and began his association with the theatre in the mid-1590s. Shakespeare is known to have acted in some of Jonson's earlier plays, and while the two men were rivals for pre-eminence upon the London stage, Jonson clearly had a high respect for Shakespeare's art. Jonson's influence on later-seventeenth-century drama was considerable – much greater than Shakespeare's own – and the plays of his which have lasted best are comedies such as *Volpone* (1606), *The Alchemist* (1610) and *Bartholomew Fair* (1614). In his chequered career, Jonson was imprisoned both for manslaughter and for over-transparent political satire in his plays; he was also later granted a pension by James I for his part in the creation of a series of brilliant court masques. He subsequently quarrelled with Inigo Jones, his partner in these, and his career declined; under Charles I he fell from favour completely. Jonson's inclusion of plays in his lavishly-produced collected edition of his works marked an important step in the gradual acceptance of dramatic literature as works of art.

KEMPE, WILLIAM (*c.* 1550–*c.* 1607) Will Kempe's influence on the development of the Lord Chamberlain's company was great. His speciality was broad comedy: he played Dogberry in *Much Ado About Nothing*, and in all probability Bottom in *A Midsummer Night's Dream*. He was a great exponent of the jigs and dances which traditionally followed the plays, and not only performed them but also wrote his own jigs, which amounted to small plays in themselves. He was the most popular of the clowns of the 1590s, and was a sharer in the Lord Chamberlain's Men and one of the original Globe syndicate. When the company actually moved to the Globe in 1599, however, Kempe sold up his interest and left. The following year, for a bet, he undertook his famous marathon dance to Norwich, which he recounts in *Kempe's Nine-Day's Wonder* (1600). Kempe's departure must have caused a temporary crisis for the Lord Chamberlain's Men, although his replacement, Robert Armin, with his very different comic style, proved to be a valuable addition to the company. Kempe seems to have had a talent for bawdy and impromptu humour, and an impressive rapport with an audience. Tradition holds that when Hamlet cautions the Player to 'let those that play your clowns speak no more than is set down for them', he is making a reference to Kempe's tendency to improvise wherever possible.

LODGE, THOMAS (1558–1625?) Lodge's *Reply to Stephen Gosson Touching Plays* (1579), a defence of the stage, dates from the early years of his career as a dramatist and pamphleteer. Lodge's early pastoral romances such as *The Delectable History of Forbonius and Priscilla* may have influenced Shakespeare in *Venus and Adonis*. Certainly his *Rosalynde* (1590) is the chief source of *As You Like It*. Lodge gave up writing poetry in 1600 when he converted to Roman Catholicism.

LYLY, JOHN (*c.* 1554–1606) Dramatist and prose-writer John Lyly was one of the so-called 'University Wits' who made a name for themselves in the London of the late Elizabethan period. Much of his fame rests on his proto-novel *Euphues, the Anatomy of Wit* (1578), written while he was still at Oxford. With its highly-wrought prose style and its tale of courtly love, it initiated a sequence of similar writings, and 'Euphuistic' romances by imitators such as Robert Greene were highly popular. As master of the Chapel Royal and St Paul's, Lyly staged his own plays at Blackfriars Theatre with casts of boys. Although they are loosely organized, his comedies, such as *Love's Metamorphosis* (*c.* 1589) and *Endymion, The Man in the Moon* (1588), are witty, polished and sophisticated. He was a shameless sycophant, whose works contain countless idealized references to and portraits of Queen Elizabeth, whose patronage, however, he never received.

MANNINGHAM, JOHN (d. 1622) A law student at the Middle Temple, John Manningham provides us with one of the few eyewitness accounts of contemporary Shakespearean productions. In his commonplace book, now known as *Manningham's Diary*, he provides an erudite description of a performance of *Twelfth Night* which took place at a feast at Middle Temple in the winter of 1601/2.

MARLOWE, CHRISTOPHER (1564–93) Marlowe was Shakespeare's almost exact contemporary, and until his death in suspicious circumstances in a Deptford tavern, he was at least Shakespeare's equal as a writer not only of plays but also of lyric and narrative verse. Like Shakespeare he came from a background of respectable craftsmanship in a small provincial town (his father was a shoemaker in Canterbury), but unlike him Marlowe was University-educated and by 1587 was enjoying the acquaintance of some of the most powerful people in the land, including Sir Walter Raleigh: Marlowe's poem 'The Passionate Shepherd to his Love' evoked a response from the aristocrat in Raleigh's 'Reply to Marlowe'. He seems at one stage of his life to have been associated with Walsingham's secret police, and in all probability spent a period of time abroad, spying on behalf of the English government. He also, however, had the reputation of being a heretic and even an atheist: certainly, in his plays he explores some of the darker sides of Renaissance man: *Doctor Faustus, Tamburlaine the Great,* and *The Jew of Malta* (all written between 1587 and 1593) all depict men obsessed by various kinds of power. Shakespeare's own dramatic writings – in particular his histories and tragedies – are greatly influenced by Marlowe, and it may be more than just coincidence that Shakespeare begins to grow in confidence and stature as a playwright after Marlowe's death. It is not impossible that the young Shakespeare felt a little overshadowed by his brilliant contemporary while Marlowe was still alive.

MARSTON, JOHN (1576?–1634) Marston's early writings were verse satires, and the rôle of the satirist which Jaques adopts in *As You Like It* was based on the sort of speaker created by Marston in *The Metamorphosis of Pygmalion's Image* (1598) and *The Scourge of Villainy* (1598). Marston's were among the satires condemned to be burnt by order of the Archbishop of Canterbury in 1599. Thereafter he began to write regularly for the stage, where the satirical voice was already finding a new form. Marston engaged with Ben Jonson in a long-running literary quarrel, sometimes referred to as the 'war of the theatres', in which the two men repeatedly satirized each other. Marston's literary career ended when he took holy orders, becoming a minister in Hampshire in 1616.

MIDDLETON, THOMAS (1580?–1627) Many of the best citizen comedies of the early seventeenth century were written by Thomas Middleton. Plays such as *A Mad World My Masters* (*c.* 1605) and *A Trick To Catch The Old One* (*c.* 1604) are comedies of manners which were written for the Boys of St Paul's. Middleton's citizen comedies combine realistic urban settings with ingenious plot devices, and (often working in collaboration with William Rowley) he became one of the most successful writers of the early-seventeenth-century theatre. Later works, of which *The Changeling* and *Women Beware Women* are the best-known, tend towards the tragic or the tragicomic.

NASHE, THOMAS (1567–1601) One of the most aggressive of the Elizabethan satirists, Thomas Nashe was educated at St John's College, Cambridge. He announced his arrival on the literary battlefield of Elizabethan England in 1589 with a preface to *Menaphon,* a romance by his friend Robert Greene. In this preface Nashe wrote witheringly about what he saw as the uneducated taste of the English stage – an attack which he continued in his first pamphlet *The Anatomy of Absurdity* (1589). He was engaged as official satirist and propagandist in defence of the Church of England during the so-called Marprelate Controversy, when he wrote a series of tracts in reply to Puritan attacks on the Church of England. Like Shakespeare, Nashe enjoyed the patronage of the Earl of Southampton, to whom he dedicated his most famous work, the prose narrative *The Unfortunate Traveller* (1594).

POPE, THOMAS (d. 1604) Thomas Pope was one of the original shareholders in the Lord Chamberlain's Men in 1594, and is listed in the 1623 Folio as a principal actor with the company. Samuel Rowlands referred to him as 'Pope the clown' and described one of his stock characters: an ignorant yokel. It has been suggested that he might have filled in as the company clown for the Lord Chamberlain's Men after their loss of Will Kempe and before Robert Armin had become fully established with them.

RALEIGH, SIR WALTER (1522?–1618) Raleigh's successful early career as a soldier set him in good stead for his meteoric rise to become one of Queen Elizabeth's court favourites. It has been suggested that *Love's Labour's Lost* contains references to factional in-fighting at court between him and the Earl of Essex. Raleigh was an active proponent of English colonial expansion and spent most of his own fortune funding early attempts to colonize Virginia. An extraordinarily influential man, he was at the very centre of political and cultural life during the 1580s and early 1590s. An accomplished poet himself, he was a friend of Christopher Marlowe, and was thought by many to share Marlowe's atheistic opinions. Raleigh fell from grace during the 1590s, and by the time of James I's accession was thoroughly out of favour. James detested him, and soon had him arrested on trumped-up charges. The death sentence passed upon him at his trial was suspended for thirteen years, during most of which time Raleigh was imprisoned in the Tower, eventually being executed in 1618.

SHAKESPEARE, EDMUND (1580–1607) Edmund, or Ned, Shakespeare was William's brother. Like William, he made the trip from Stratford to London to become an actor, but he did not make a very successful one. It is not known with which company or companies he acted, although there is speculation that he played boys' parts with the Lord Chamberlain's Men during the 1590s.

SHAKESPEARE, WILLIAM (1564–1616) William Shakespeare was born on or around 23 April 1564. He was the son of the Stratford businessman John Shakespeare, and his early education was at the local grammar school. In 1582, when he was eighteen years old, he married Anne Hathaway, and they lived together in Stratford for about two years, but in 1584 or 1585 Shakespeare left Stratford for London. His London career during the years up to 1592 is more or less a mystery, but by 1592 he had a reputation both as an actor and a playwright: the *Henry VI* trilogy comes from this period. During the years 1592–94 the London theatres were frequently closed because of plague, and Shakespeare turned his hand to narrative poetry and sonnet-writing. When the theatres reopened he joined the Lord Chamberlain's Men as a shareholder, so that he was now sharing in the profits of the company as well as receiving payment for his acting and writing. The latter included comedies such as *A Midsummer Night's Dream* and early tragedies such as *Romeo and Juliet.* Clearly Shakespeare did quite well financially out of the next few years, for he was able to buy one of the best houses in Stratford, New Place, in 1597. The Lord Chamberlain's Men's move to the Globe Theatre in 1599 consolidated his fortunes, and their adoption by King James in 1593 improved things even further: the King's Men, as they were now known, gave 177 performances at court between 1603 and 1613. Shakespeare's great tragedies were written between 1601 and 1606, and first performed at the Globe. The romances known as the 'last plays' were all written after the King's Men had expanded to acquire the indoors Blackfriars Theatre in 1608. However, it seems probable that by the time *The Tempest* was first staged in 1611, Shakespeare had already moved back to Stratford. His last play was *Henry VIII*, written in collaboration with John Fletcher. It was an ill-starred work: on the afternoon of its first performance in 1613, a cannon fired in the play caused a fire which destroyed the Globe. Shakespeare's last few years were spent in retirement in Stratford, and he died there on 23 April 1616, aged fifty-two.

SIDNEY, SIR PHILIP (1554–86) As a courtier and career diplomat, Sidney was never particularly successful; Elizabeth seems to have entrusted him with comparatively low-grade tasks and he was only spasmodically in favour at court. This, perhaps, allowed him the time for the literary endeavours which made him famous. He is associated with a circle of writers which also included Edmund Spenser and Fulke Greville, and his most lasting achievements are his two versions of *Arcadia* (wr. 1580–6; pub. 1590–3), in which heroic and epic themes are combined with pastoral;

Astrophel and Stella (wr. 1581–3; pub. 1591), a Petrarchan sonnet sequence composed ten years before Shakespeare's own; and *An Apology for Poetry* (wr. 1581–3; pub. 1595), which was probably written at least partly to confute Stephen Gosson's attack on the stage, and which became the most influential work of literary theory of the English Renaissance. Sidney died from wounds which he received in battle against the Spaniards, fighting in one of the English campaigns in the Netherlands.

SOMERS, WILL (*c.* 1500–1560) Will Somers, or Summers, was a Shropshire man brought to the court of Henry VIII as Henry's household fool. He became a folk-hero whose fame lasted well beyond his own lifetime. Thomas Nashe named a play after him, *Summer's Last Will and Testament* (1592), and William Rowley incorporated him into his play *When You See Me You Know Me* (1604). Robert Armin included many of the traditional anecdotes about him in *Fool Upon Fool* (1600).

SOUTHAMPTON, HENRY WRIOTHESLEY, THIRD EARL (1573–1624) A courtier, a soldier, and a politician, Southampton became Shakespeare's patron in about 1593 or 1594, when Shakespeare, turning his hand to non-dramatic literature, dedicated to him *Venus and Adonis* and *The Rape of Lucrece.* There has been speculation, too, that Southampton was the dedicatee of Shakespeare's sonnets, and the subject of several of them, although nothing has been proved on this score. He patronized other writers apart from Shakespeare, among them Thomas Nashe and John Florio. Southampton himself was a devoted follower of the Earl of Essex, and a supporter of his ill-fated rebellion in 1601. He may have been involved in commissioning the famous performance of *Richard II* which implicated the Lord Chamberlain's Men in Essex's rebellion. For his part in the rebellion Southampton was sentenced to death; the sentence was later commuted by Elizabeth to imprisonment in the Tower, and Southampton was pardoned when James came to the throne. During James's reign Southampton took an active interest in the colonizing of the New World. He was a member of the council of the Virginia Company, set up expressly for that purpose, and his involvement with the Virginia project may have influenced Shakespeare in his writing of *The Tempest* (1611).

TARLTON, RICHARD (d. 1588) Besides being the jester at Queen Elizabeth's court, Richard Tarlton was also a professional player and an innkeeper. Like Will Somers he hailed originally from Shropshire, and was celebrated for his skill as an improviser.

The text of his play *The Seven Deadly Sins* (date unknown) consists largely of cues and episode summaries, suggesting that in this, too, improvisation was a central feature. Tarlton also wrote and performed in jigs at the end of plays. Shakespeare's 'Yorick' in *Hamlet* is traditionally thought to be a reference to Tarlton. A collection of jokes attributed to him and published in the 1590s as *Tarlton's Jests* is almost certainly not his.

Further reading

Texts and textual scholarship

One of the major areas of activity in Shakespeare studies over the past few years has been textual scholarship. Scholars have been exploring once again the possibility that some of the discrepancies between the early printed texts of Shakespeare's plays may be due to Shakespeare's own rewriting of his plays. If this is the case (and disagreements abound as to which, if any, of the plays it might concern) then new insights might be available into the creative process of Shakespeare's playwriting.

Perhaps the most controversial and influential recent work in this field is represented by the collection of essays edited by Gary Taylor and Michael Warren, entitled *The Division of the Kingdoms: Shakespeare's Two Versions of King Lear* (Oxford: Clarendon Press, 1983). Focusing entirely upon *King Lear,* it goes so far as to suggest that the play of that title that we normally read is a muddled amalgam of two separate versions of *King Lear,* both written by Shakespeare and represented by the early published editions of Quarto and Folio. These two versions differ from each other in several respects – so much so, argue the authors, that it may be completely wrong to think of there ever having been a single 'ideal play' of *King Lear,* and that we should instead think in terms of two separate *King Lears.* This kind of reappraisal of long-accepted ideas about Shakespeare's texts have provided a new impetus in Shakespearian textual scholarship.

One of the fruits of this scholarship is the new Oxford Shakespeare series, which has produced the plays both in separate volumes and in editions (both modern and original spelling) of *The Complete Works* (Oxford: Oxford University Press, 1986–87). The General Editors of the series are Stanley Wells and Gary Taylor, and they have included in the series an entire volume, entitled *William Shakespeare: A Textual Companion* (Oxford: Oxford University Press, 1987), which elucidates the ways in which the editors reached their decisions. The principles according to which the Oxford editors have worked have resulted in some radically new versions of texts, and the findings of the new generation of Shakespeare scholars have not always been universally accepted. However, they have certainly provided new stimulus for thought about the plays. It is the Oxford *Complete Works* which has been referred to throughout this volume.

Facsimile versions both of quartos and of the 1623 Folio are available and are useful aids to further textual study. *The Norton Facsimile: The First Folio of Shakespeare* (New York: Norton, 1968) is edited by Charlton Hinman, while Michael J. B. Allen and Kenneth Muir have co-edited a collection of *Shakespeare's Plays in Quarto: A Facsimile Edition of Copies Primarily from the Henry E. Huntington Library* (Berkeley: University of California Press, 1981).

Biography

For many years the best biographical study of Shakespeare was E. K. Chambers's *William Shakespeare: A Study of Facts and Problems* (Oxford: Clarendon Press, 1930). This has now been replaced as the standard work of biographical reference by Samuel Schoenbaum's *William Shakespeare: A Documentary Life* (Oxford: Oxford University Press, 1975; revised and re-issued in a compact edition as *William Shakespeare: A Compact Documentary Life*, 1977). Scrupulous in its scholarship, Schoenbaum's book makes few claims that are not backed up by hard evidence, and surveys with admirable thoroughness alternative interpretations of the available documents. Schoenbaum has also written a fascinating critical survey of other people's biographies of Shakespeare, entitled *Shakespeare's Lives* (Oxford: Oxford University Press, 1970), which throws much light on the way in which the Shakespeare legend grew up. Recent accessible biographies have been published by Peter Levi, *The Life and Times of William Shakespeare* (London: Macmillan, 1988), and S. H. Burton, *Shakespeare's Life and Stage* (Edinburgh, Chambers, 1989). Peter Thomson's *Shakespeare's Professional Career* (Cambridge: Cambridge University Press, 1992) is 'not a book about Shakespeare but about Shakespeare's job' (p. xv), and places his life and career in a detailed theatrical and historical context.

History

Historians divide up the world, and divide up time, in different ways from literary scholars; the 'age of Shakespeare' is not a recognizable entity to historians, and we have to look for information about his world in the context of studies of wider social, political and economic issues which concern the England of the sixteenth and seventeenth centuries. Traditionally, at least, historians have often thought in terms of reigning monarchs, and Shakespeare's career spanned the reign of two monarchs: generally speaking, books which concentrate on the reign of Elizabeth are more useful to the Shakespeare student than those focusing upon James and the Stuarts. This is particularly true for the middle and early comedies: the plays examined in this volume are all Elizabethan rather than Jacobean texts. Even so, some knowledge of the early years of James's reign is essential to understand the plays in their full historical context: history is about where things are going as well as about where they've been.

Of the various writings by historians on the Elizabethan and Jacobean periods which are easily accessible to the non-specialist reader, the following have been found particularly useful. A thoroughly-researched social and economic history of the England of Elizabeth is to be found in D. M. Palliser's *The Age of Elizabeth: England under the later Tudors, 1547–1603* (Harlow: Longman, 1983), which is particularly illuminating on the economic trends of the period. Barry Coward's *The Stuart Age* (Harlow: Longman, 1980) deals with the period 1603 to 1714, but its early chapters provide a useful analysis of political, economic and intellectual movements in the early seventeenth century. S. J. Houston's small book simply entitled *James I* (Harlow: Longman, 1973) contains both essays on key aspects of James's reign and a section of documents. Keith Wrightson's *English Society 1590–1680* (London: Hutchinson, 1982) is an eminently readable account of the changes which were taking place in English society in the seventeenth century. It both synthesizes much of the new wave of thinking about English social history of the period, and advances some stimulating personal interpretations of the nature and development of English society at this time. The approach taken by Alan G. R. Smith in *The Emergence of a Nation State: The Commonwealth of England 1529–1660* (Harlow: Longman, 1984) is to relate social and economic issues to the emergence of England as, first, a disparate political unit, and then a major world power.

The primary theme of Shakespeare's comedies is love and marriage: Lawrence Stone's *The Family, Sex and Marriage in England, 1500–1800* (London: Weidenfeld and Nicolson, 1977) has made a great, and sometimes controversial, contribution to knowledge of family structures in Shakespeare's age, and has provoked much rethinking of the ways in which family relationships are portrayed in the plays. An accompanying volume, *The Road to Divorce: England 1530–1987* (Oxford: Oxford University Press, 1990) may well prove equally influential. A useful documentary source-book for material about family life is *English Family Life 1576–1716: An Anthology from Diaries*, edited by Ralph Houlbrooke (Oxford: Basil Blackwell, 1988).

The New Mermaid 'background' book entitled simply (if a little misleadingly) *Elizabethan-Jacobean Drama* (London: A & C

Black, 1987) and edited by G. Blakemore Evans, performs a similar function within a more limited time-span and with material chosen in a way which is particularly useful for those interested in the relationships between theatre and society in Shakespeare's England. This collection includes a large range of contemporary Elizabethan and Jacobean texts, culled from both printed and manuscript sources, which relate to the theatre and to everyday life in the period.

Language

There are several general books about the development of the English language which contain sections on Elizabethan English. The most easily available to the English reader is C. L. Barber's *The Story of Language* (London: Pan Books, 1964), a lively general study of the topic, but one which is disappointingly thin on material about Shakespearean English. Less easy to get hold of, but more instructive, are the relevant chapters in Albert C. Baugh and Thomas Cable's *A History of the English Language*, 3rd edn (London: Routledge, 1957, re-issued 1978).

Two books which take a detailed look at the problems of Shakespeare's plays from a linguist's point of view are *Shakespeare's Language: An Introduction* (London and Basingstoke: Macmillan, 1983) by N. F. Blake and *The Language of Shakespeare* (London: Andre Deutsch, 1976) by G. L. Brook. Both deal with issues of Shakespearean grammar and vocabulary: the former is more accessible to the general reader, the latter is more usefully regarded as a reference book. A much more free-wheeling and polemical work than either is Terence Hawkes's *Shakespeare's Talking Animals: Language and Drama in Society* (London: Edward Arnold, 1973), which takes as its starting point the problematic relationship between the spoken and the written word in Shakespeare's age, and goes on to offer a series of thought-provoking essays about the language of Shakespeare's plays.

Laughter and society

There is a valuable article by Keith Thomas in the *Times Literary Supplement* (21 January 1977, pp. 77–81), entitled 'The place of laughter in Tudor and Stuart England', which raises several issues about the social function of laughter. David Underdown has published several articles in academic journals about seventeenth-century popular culture, and has written extensively about charivari, rough riding and other popular protests and social rituals: his book on this subject, *Revel, Riot and Rebellion: Popular Politics and Culture in England 1603–1660* (Oxford: Oxford University Press, 1987), takes its material primarily from the period just after the writing of the comedies, but its analysis of the cultural and political tensions and struggles within English society says much which is relevant to the late years of Elizabeth's reign. Gail Kern Paster's *The Body Embarrassed: Drama and the Disciplines of Shame in Early Modern England* (Ithaca, NY: Cornell University Press, 1992) deals with some of the implications these ideas have for the drama. François Laroque's *Shakespeare's Festive World: Elizabethan Seasonal Entertainment and the Professional Stage,* translated by Janet Lloyd (Cambridge: Cambridge University Press, 1991), makes a detailed study of Elizabethan festivities and considers their relationship to the emerging professional theatre; while Michael Bristol's *Carnival and Theater: Plebeian Culture and the Structure of Authority in Renaissance England* (London: Methuen, 1985) explores Bakhtinian notions of carnival in relation to the theatre of the period.

Fools, clowns and jesters

The classic work on the fool is Enid Welsford's marvellous *The Fool: His Social and Literary History* (London: Faber and Faber, 1935). This set the agenda for all future work on the topic, tackling the history of the European court fool, both in reality and in the imagination, from the Middle Ages to the nineteenth century. Sandra Billington's *A Social History of the Fool* (Brighton: Harvester, 1984) updates some of Welsford's arguments in the light of more recent historical investigations, and Paul V. A. Williams's *The Fool and the Trickster* (Cambridge and Ipswich: D. S. Brewer and Rowman and Littlefield, 1979) is a collection of essays on the subject from literary and folkloric perspectives. In *The Fool and his Sceptre* (London: Edward Arnold, 1969) William Willeford provides a psychotherapist's viewpoint on the history and function of the fool, while Joel Schechter's *Durov's Pig: Clowns, Politics and the Theater* (New York: Theater Communications Group, 1985) looks at more recent clown traditions. One of the best recent books on the Elizabethan theatre also focuses specifically on clowns: David Wiles's *Shakespeare's Clown: Actor and Text in the Elizabethan Playhouse* (Cambridge: Cambridge University Press, 1987) is a fascinating exploration of the function of the clown in the Elizabethan playhouse company, which looks in detail at the careers of Tarlton, Kempe and Armin. For a good collection of early jest-book material, see John Wardroper, ed., *Jest Upon Jest: A Selection from the Jestbooks and Collections of Merry*

Tales Published from the Reign of Richard III to George III (London: Routledge and Kegan Paul, 1970).

Elizabethan and Jacobean theatre

Among the more general works on the theatre of the period the standard work of reference is now J. Leeds Barroll's *The Revels History of Drama in English, vol. III* (London: Methuen, 1975). However, two classic early-twentieth-century studies of theatre practice in Elizabethan times are E. K. Chambers's *The Elizabethan Stage* (Oxford: Clarendon Press, 1923) and T. W. Baldwin's *The Organization and Personnel of the Shakespearean Company* (Princeton: Princeton University Press, 1927; re-issued New York: Russell and Russell, 1961). Both are still worth reading, Chambers's book for his wide-ranging erudition about the Elizabethan theatre in general, Baldwin's for his (occasionally speculative but always informative) focus on the details of organization in Shakespeare's company of players. More recent works which tackle the same area, but with the benefit of more recent research, include Andrew Gurr's *The Shakespearean Stage* (Cambridge: Cambridge University Press, 1970) and Michael Hattaway's *Elizabethan Popular Theatre: Plays in Performance* (London: Routledge and Kegan Paul, 1982). Hattaway's book analyses several Elizabethan plays in terms of their relationship with popular dramatic forms. In the same series, Peter Thomson's *Shakespeare's Theatre* (London: Routledge and Kegan Paul, 1983) examines pragmatically some of the issues relating to the staging of plays in Shakespeare's Globe Theatre, as well as giving a readable and fascinating interpretation of the known facts about the Globe Theatre. An earlier work which remains informative about the Globe is *Shakespeare at the Globe* (London: Macmillan, 1962) by Bernard Beckermann. Recent archaeological finds concerning Elizabethan theatres are detailed in Christine Eccles's *The Rose Theatre* (London: Nick Hern Books, 1990), and the architectural debates surrounding the Globe are most fully set out in *Rebuilding Shakespeare's Globe* (London: Weidenfeld and Nicholson, 1989) by Andrew Gurr and John Orrell. A short factual account of the London theatres of the sixteenth and early seventeenth centuries is published by The Bear Gardens Museum; it is edited by C. Edwards and is entitled *A London Theatre Guide, 1576–1642*. Steven Mullaney's *The Place of the Stage: License, Play and Power in Renaissance England* (Chicago: University of Chicago Press, 1988) combines theatre history and new historical/cultural materialist analyses in order to discuss the cultural position of the stage in the period.

Audiences

Audiences in Shakespeare's theatre have been much discussed; Alfred Harbage's *Shakespeare's Audience* (New York, 1941) offered a picture of a homogeneous audience spanning all classes of society, a picture firmly rejected by Ann Jennalie Cook in her book, *The Privileged Playgoers of Shakespeare's London, 1576–1642* (Princeton: Princeton University Press, 1982). Andrew Gurr's *Playgoing in Shakespeare's London* (Cambridge: Cambridge University Press, 1987) treads a judicious middle ground between two extremes, and as well as offering a convincing and detailed argument about changing play-going patterns in Elizabethan and Jacobean London, he reprints a large amount of the relevant contemporary material. Various articles deal with more detailed questions of Elizabethan play-going; one which deals with female spectatorship is Richard Levin's 'Women in the Renaissance theatre audience' *Shakespeare Quarterly*, 40, pp. 163–174. Susan Bennett's *Theatre Audiences: A Theory of Production and Reception* (London: Routledge, 1990), on the other hand, is not specifically about the Elizabethan theatre at all, but is worth reading for the general questions it raises about the topic.

Shakespeare reference books

So much has been written about Shakespeare that it is often difficult to know where to start looking for secondary material. To aid the task, there are in existence various bibliographical studies of Shakespeare, and they range in their scope from the exhaustive to the selective. Most useful for our purposes is Stanley Wells's *Shakespeare: A Bibliographical Guide* (Oxford: Clarendon Press, 1990).

For a student of Shakespeare's language it is invaluable to have access to a concordance, which tabulates where and how various words are used. Marvin Spevack's *Harvard Concordance to Shakespeare* (Cambridge, MA: Harvard University Press, 1968–80) was compiled from a computer database, and it records, analyses and cross-references Shakespeare's vocabulary and the contexts of word-usage in the plays. It effectively supercedes John Bartlett's *New and Complete Concordance or Verbal Index to the Words, Phrases and Passages in the Dramatic Works of Shakespeare with a Supplementary Concordance to the Poems* (London: Macmillan, 1894), which had been the standard work since the end of the last century. The Bartlett concordance, however, is still a useful reference tool, and may be more easily available, since Spevack's updated concordance has not yet found its way into all libraries.

Shakespeare was notoriously an adapter of other writers' stories and a good deal of work has gone into tracking down the original sources of his plays. Two complementary studies of Shakespeare's source material deserve particular mention. The definitive work is now Geoffrey Bullough's massive eight-volume study entitled *Narrative and Dramatic Sources of Shakespeare* (London: Routledge and Kegan Paul, 1957–75). Each play is dealt with by means of an introductory essay surveying the field and tracing various influences, direct sources and analogous material. All relevant material is then printed in as full detail as necessary, so that readers can make comparisons for themselves between Shakespeare's sources and his own plays. Bullough's study is indispensable for any serious study of the literary background to the plays, and it has prompted many new insights into the plays themselves. Less detailed but more affordable is Kenneth Muir's *The Sources of Shakespeare's Plays* (London: Methuen, 1977) which effectively operates as a digest of information about the plays. Muir surveys a similar range of material to Bullough, but does not attempt, in his single-volume study, to reproduce the documentation.

A useful general collection of essays which provides fairly up-to-date material about recent developments in many areas of Shakespeare criticism and scholarship is *The Cambridge Companion to Shakespeare Studies* (Cambridge: Cambridge University Press, 1986) edited by Stanley Wells. This supercedes Kenneth Muir and S. Schoenbaum's *New Companion to Shakespeare Studies* (Cambridge: Cambridge University Press, 1971), which in turn replaced the original *Companion to Shakespeare Studies* (Cambridge: Cambridge University Press, 1934), and it contains essays which place Shakespeare in the context of the thought of his age, as well as accounts of twentieth-century approaches, both critical and theatrical.

The two most influential periodicals in the field of Shakespeare studies are *Shakespeare Survey* and *Shakespeare Quarterly*. The former is published by Cambridge University Press and it appears annually. Subtitled 'An Annual Survey of Shakespearian Study and Production' it contains reviews of British, European and American productions of Shakespeare as well as reports of recent work in Shakespeare studies and individual monographs on particular topics – often thematically related volume by volume. *Shakespeare Quarterly* is produced by the Folger Shakespeare Library in Washington D.C. and it appears, as its name suggests, four times a year. While it, too, contains articles on recent academic and theatrical developments, its monographs tend not to be linked thematically.

Shakespeare: general criticism

General studies of Shakespeare are too numerous to count, and each age, predictably, produces its own. The ones mentioned here are comparatively recent; some of them had a specific influence on the writing of this book, others simply offer a particular approach which readers might find useful.

Two books about the way in which literary and dramatic material gets re-used and transformed, but which look at very different aspects of the question, are Leah Scragg's *Shakespeare's Mouldy Tales: Recurrent Plot Motifs in Shakespearian Drama* (Harlow: Longman, 1992) and Gary Taylor's *Reinventing Shakespeare: A Cultural History from the Restoration to the Present* (London: Hogarth Press, 1990). The former explores Shakespeare's use of his sources, and also the ways in which he adapts and exploits similar narrative material in different plays; the latter is a history of the ways in which Shakespeare's own plays have been read, staged, and understood in different generations.

In the last few years several 'overviews' of Shakespeare's plays have been published, and two in particular are worth listing here since, while similar in format, they exemplify very different approaches. Neither of them deals with any one play at any length, but both offer comments on a wide range of plays. Philip Edwards's *Shakespeare: a Writer's Progress* (Oxford: Oxford University Press, 1986) looks at the plays in more or less chronological order, in an attempt to chart the development of the writer. Edwards describes the book as a personal view of the plays, but it also embodies many of the main tendencies of liberal Shakespeare criticism of the past few decades. Terry Eagleton, on the other hand, provides a swashbuckling radicalism with his *William Shakespeare* (Oxford: Basil Blackwell, 1986), a reappraisal of the plays in the context of recent developments in Marxist, feminist, semiotic and post-structuralist criticism. Deliberately provocative and aggressively readable, it challenges many assumptions of Shakespeare teaching.

Some other collections of essays which share with Eagleton's work the desire to disrupt conventional assumptions about the significance of Shakespeare's plays are *Alternative Shakespeares* (London: Methuen, 1985) edited by John Drakakis, and *Political Shakespeare* (Manchester: Manchester University Press, 1985) edited by Jonathan Dollimore and Alan Sinfield. Ivo Kamps's edition, *Shakespeare Left and Right* (London: Routledge, 1991), contains essays drawn primarily from American academic debate between radical and conservative approaches to the plays; *Shakespeare and the Changing Curriculum* (London: Routledge, 1991) edited by Lesley Aers and Nigel Wheale focuses more on the pedagogic dimensions of Shakespeare studies: how, why, with what expected results should we teach Shakespeare in schools and colleges today? A collection, not of essays but of debates, is John Elsom's *Is Shakespeare Still Our Contemporary?* (London: Routledge, 1989), the record of a public symposium held at the Young Vic Theatre, London to mark the twenty-fifth anniversary of the publication of Jan Kott's ground-breaking study *Shakespeare Our Contemporary* (London: Methuen, 1965). All these collections draw attention to the political dimensions of Shakespearean drama, both in its own time and as a force in contemporary culture.

Feminist criticism has been one of the main forces behind rethinking Shakespeare studies in the last quarter-century, and some of its starting-points can be found in the collection of essays entitled *The Woman's Part: Feminist Criticism of Shakespeare* (Urbana: University of Illinois Press, 1980) edited by Carolyn Lenz, Gayle Green and Carol Thomas Neely. Juliet Dusinberre's *Shakespeare and the Nature of Women* (London: Macmillan, 1975) was an early attempt to claim Shakespeare for feminism, as a writer whose basic attitude to women was sympathetic. This agenda also informs, in a very different way, Marilyn French's *Shakespeare's Division of Experience* (London: Jonathan Cape, 1982), which uses a particular version of essentialist feminist theory as an analytical tool: starting from the premise that 'the basic distinction in human social order since the beginning of recorded history has been gender' (p. 11), French looks at the plays as dramatizations of shifting relationships between the two gender principles, the masculine and the feminine. A very different line is taken by Lisa Jardine in her historically-based *Still Harping on Daughters: Women and Drama in the Age of Shakespeare* (Brighton: Harvester, 1983), which deals with attitudes towards women in Shakespeare's age, attitudes which, it is argued, Shakespeare necessarily shared, so that his very maleness 'makes it inevitable that his female characters are warped and distorted' (p. 3). Influenced by new trends in psychoanalytically-based literary theory, recent criticism, such as Valerie Traub's *Desire and Anxiety: Circulations of Sexuality in Shakespearian Drama* (London: Routledge, 1992), extends the agenda to deal with a variety of issues relating to gender politics.

Stage-centred criticism of Shakespeare's plays has involved, on the one hand, description and performance analysis of twentieth-century productions, and on the other attempts to explore the relationship between texts and performance on the Elizabethan and Jacobean stage. The Macmillan series entitled 'Text and Performance' (General Editor, Michael Scott) and the Manchester University Press series 'Shakespeare in Performance' have taken the former route, documenting various ways in which the plays have been interpreted on stage. Ann Pasternak Slater's *Shakespeare the Director* (Brighton: Harvester, 1982) tries, not always successfully, to integrate a study of Shakespeare's language with a study of his stagecraft. Emrys Jones, in *Scenic Form in Shakespeare* (Oxford: Clarendon Press, 1971), explores the ways in which an understanding of some of the principles of Shakespeare's dramatic construction enriches our enjoyment of the plays. Questions of performance have been closely studied by critics interested in gender issues in the plays: in particular the phenomenon of the boy actor playing a woman's part has raised heated arguments in articles and books. Jean Howard's 1988 article 'Crossdressing, the theater, and gender struggle in early modern England', *Shakespeare Quarterly* 39, pp. 418–41, is one of the most important articles on this subject.

A very different kind of approach to the study of the plays by way of theatrical practice can be seen in John Barton's *Playing Shakespeare* (London: Methuen, 1984), based on his series of masterclass programmes on Channel 4, and in Peter Reynolds's *Practical Approaches to Teaching Shakespeare* (Oxford: Oxford University Press, 1991), which derives from the 'Shakespeare and Schools' project originated by the Cambridge Institute of Education.

Shakespeare: comedy and comedies

Among the more general books about comedy as a literary form Moelwyn Merchant's small volume in the Critical Idiom series, *Comedy* (London: Methuen, 1972), is still worth reading. T. G. A. Nelson's *Comedy: The Theory of Comedy in Literature, Drama and Cinema* (Oxford: Oxford University Press, 1990) is more accessible than its subtitle may make it sound: it covers the topic thematically, drawing examples from a variety of literary, dramatic and cinematic sources. Wylie Sypher's much-cited *Comedy* (Garden City, NY: Doubleday, 1956) is actually an edition of the writings of George Meredith and Henri Bergson on laughter and comedy, with an introduction and appendix by Sypher himself. Another volume which brings together some famous names' writings on comedy is D. J. Palmer, ed., *Comedy: Developments in Criticism* (London and Basingstoke: Macmillan, 1984); this casebook contains short extracts from Aristotle to Bergson, and some longer pieces by twentieth-century critics.

The work of C. L. Barber and Northrop Frye has been discussed elsewhere in the book, so at this point I shall only say that the two major books on Shakespearean comedy by these writers are

C. L. Barber, *Shakespeare's Festive Comedy* (Princeton, NJ: Princeton University Press, 1959) and Northrop Frye, *A Natural Perspective: the Development of Shakespearean Comedy and Romance* (New York: Columbia University Press, 1965). Two other major works which were influential in their time, although perhaps less so now, are H. B. Charlton's *Shakespearian Comedy* (London: Methuen, 1939) and M. C. Bradbrook's *The Growth and Structure of Elizabethan Comedy* (London: Chatto and Windus, 1955). Bradbrook's work traced relationships between Shakespearean and other Elizabethan comedy, and earlier English, continental and classical traditions. A more detailed book on the same theme, which in many respects updates Bradbrook's work, is Leo Salingar's *Shakespeare and the Traditions of Comedy* (Cambridge: Cambridge University Press, 1974). Edward Berry, on the other hand, in *Shakespeare's Comic Rites* (Cambridge: Cambridge University Press, 1984) works from a perspective which owes a great deal, initially to Barber, but also to recent anthropological theory; he looks at the plays in terms of social and psychological meanings analogous to those of rites of passage. In *Staging the Gaze: Poststructuralism, Psychoanalysis and Shakespearean Comedy* (Ithaca, NY and London: Cornell University Press, 1991) Barbara Freedman uses post-Lacanian psychoanalytic theory and some theoretical positions drawn from film theory to interrogate the comedies. Readers interested in understanding some of the most important recent trends in literary criticism as they have been applied to Shakespeare studies should consult the excellent collection of essays and extracts edited by Gary Waller, *Shakespeare's Comedies* (Harlow: Longman, 1991); this contains a representative variety of recent criticism from a variety of standpoints.

Early comedies

There has been a renewal of interest in some of the early plays – in all of them, that is, except *The Two Gentlemen of Verona*, which remains comparatively neglected. Of those articles which have concentrated on the play Inga-Stina Ewbank's article ' "Were man but constant, he were perfect"; constancy and consistency in *The Two Gentlemen of Verona*', in M. Bradbury and D. J. Palmer, eds, *Shakespearian Comedy* (London: Stratford-on-Avon Studies 14, 1972) is one of the best-known.

The Taming of the Shrew is another matter. Karen Newman's 'Renaissance family politics and Shakespeare's *The Taming of the Shrew*', *English Literary Renaissance*, 16 (1986), pp. 86–100, is a good example of the recent interest which feminist critics have shown in the play; it is reprinted in Gary Waller, ed., *Shakespeare's*

Comedies (Harlow: Longman, 1991). The ideology of the play in performance is analysed by Graham Holderness in his volume in the 'Text and Performance' series, *The Taming of the Shrew* (Manchester: Manchester University Press, 1989), which documents four major productions of the play. Similarly, Geraldine Cousin's article 'The Touring of the Shrew', *New Theatre Quarterly* 2, vii (1986), pp. 275–81, documents two 1985 touring productions of the play. Textual questions about the play are debated by Leah Marcus in 'The Shakespearean editor as Shrew-Tamer', *English Literary Renaissance* 22, ii (1992), pp. 177–200, and an edition of the anonymous *The Taming of A Shrew* (Brighton: Harvester Wheatsheaf, 1992) has been produced by Graham Holderness and Bryan Loughrey.

Frances Yates's *A Study of 'Love's Labour's Lost'* (Cambridge: Cambridge University Press, 1936) is an exception to the rule stated earlier, in that it is an entire book on a single play. It concentrates on the topical allusions which it sees as comprising the play's essential meaning. An essay which looks in detail at the language of the play is Terence Hawkes's '*Love's Labour's Lost*: rhyme against reason', in *Shakespeare's Talking Animals* (London: Edward Arnold, 1973). Mark Breitenberg explores the play from the perspective of gender issues in 'The anatomy of masculine desire in *Love's Labour's Lost*', *Shakespeare Quarterly* 43, iv (1992), pp. 430–49.

A Midsummer Night's Dream

Harold Bloom's edition of collected critical essays on *William Shakespeare: 'A Midsummer Night's Dream'* (New York: Chelsea House, 1987) is a good starting-point. A classic essay, which argues that the humour of *A Midsummer Night's Dream* is essentially cruel, is Jan Kott's 'Titania and the ass's head', in *Shakespeare Our Contemporary* (London: Methuen, 1965). More recently there have been fruitful discussions of the play in terms of festive theory. Thomas Healey uses it as an example of this in the chapter entitled 'The drama's place' in *New Latitudes. Theory and English* (London: Edward Arnold, 1992). A more detailed treatment of the play in these terms is Annabel Patterson's excellent chapter, 'Bottom's up: festive theory', in *Shakespeare and the Popular Voice* (Oxford and Cambridge, MA: Basil Blackwell, 1989). This relates festive theory to the concerns of new historicism, such as the forms of power. This is also the subject of an essay by Louis A. Montrose, '*A Midsummer Night's Dream* and the shaping fantasies of Elizabethan culture: gender, power, form', in Margaret W. Ferguson, Maureen Quilligan and Nancy J. Vickers, eds, *Rewriting the Renaissance:*

The Discourses of Sexual Difference in Early Modern Europe (Chicago: University of Chicago Press, 1986). Some recent viewpoints are gathered together in Linda Cookson and Bryan Loughrey, eds, *A Midsummer Night's Dream* (London: Longman Critical Essays, 1991).

Much Ado About Nothing

Linda Cookson and Bryan Loughrey have also edited a collection entitled *Critical Essays on 'Much Ado About Nothing'* (London: Longman, 1991); like its companion volume, it is aimed at literature students. John Russell Brown's '*Much Ado About Nothing' and 'As You Like It': A Casebook* (London: Macmillan, 1979) reprints some useful essays on both plays. *Much Ado* has a chapter to itself in Marilyn French's *Shakespeare's Division of Experience* (London: Jonathan Cape, 1982), in which the play is read emblematically. Barbara Everett looks at the play in terms of its opposed worlds, the masculine and the feminine, in an essay on *Much Ado About Nothing* in *Critical Quarterly* 3 (1961), pp. 320–32. The problems of closure in the play are discussed in Ejner J. Jensen's 'The Career of . . . humour: comedy's triumph in *Much Ado About Nothing*', in *Shakespeare and the Ends of Comedy* (Bloomington and Indianapolis: Indiana University Press, 1991). Carol Neely's book on the theme of *Broken Nuptials in Shakespeare* (New Haven, CN: Yale University Press, 1985) contains a chapter on the play, which is reprinted in Gary Waller, ed., *Shakespeare's Comedies* (Harlow: Longman, 1991).

As You Like It

The issues surrounding cross-dressing and the convention of the boy actor have attracted much attention in discussions of *As You Like It.* A pair of papers offering contrasting views on the subject are Jan Kott's 'The gender of Rosalind', which links the play with other explorations of androgyny, and Lesley Anne Soule's 'Subverting Rosalind: Cocky Ros in the Forest of Arden', which relates the portrayal of Rosalind with traditions of popular theatre. Both essays appear in *New Theatre Quarterly* 7 (1991), pp. 113–36. A chapter in Valerie Traub's *Desire and Anxiety: Circulations of Sexuality in Shakespearean Drama* (London: Routledge, 1992), entitled 'The homoerotics of Shakespearean comedy', argues that in *As You Like It* the theatrical convention works as a basis upon which homoeroticism can be safely explored. The pedagogic implications of this reading are argued by Elaine Hobby in 'My affection hath an unknown bottom: homosexuality and the teaching of *As You Like It*', in Lesley Aers and Nigel Wheale, eds, *Shakespeare and the Changing Curriculum* (London: Routledge, 1991). A more conventional approach is taken by Marjorie Garber, 'The education of Orlando', in A. R. Braunmuller and J. C. Bulman, eds, *Comedy from Shakespeare to Sheridan: Change and Continuity in the English and European Dramatic Tradition: Essays in Honour of Eugene M. Waith* (Newark, NJ: University of Delaware Press, 1986), which concentrates on the play as an educative process for Orlando. In *Shakespeare: Out of Court: Dramatizations of Court Society* (London and Basingstoke: Macmillan, 1990), Graham Holderness, Nick Potter and John Turner devote two chapters to the portrayal of the outlaw court in *As You Like It.*

Twelfth Night

There are several essays and chapters which compare *Twelfth Night* and *As You Like It*: one famous example is Jan Kott's 'Shakespeare's Bitter Arcadia', in *Shakespeare Our Contemporary* (London: Methuen, 1965). Joseph Pequigny, on the other hand, relates *Twelfth Night* to a different play in 'The Two Antonios and same-sex love in *Twelfth Night* and *The Merchant of Venice*', *English Literary Renaissance*, 22, ii (1992), pp. 201–21. Some influential ideas concerning the earliest stagings of *Twelfth Night*, and some the play's contemporary cultural meanings, were put forward in Leslie Hotson's *The First Night of Twelfth Night* (London: Hart-Davis, 1954). A more recent stage-centred approach is exemplified by Peter Thomson's chapter on '*Twelfth Night* and playhouse practice', in *Shakespeare's Theatre* (London: Routledge and Kegan Paul, 1983), which asks questions about theatrical effects such as music, hand-props, costume and stage space in order to throw light on the play's meaning. Another essay which concentrates on the play's theatrical dimension, although to rather different effect, is Ralph Berry's '*Twelfth Night*: the experience of the audience', in *Shakespeare and the Awareness of the Audience* (London and Basingstoke: Macmillan, 1985). There is a collection of critical essays edited by D. J. Palmer, *Shakespeare, 'Twelfth Night': a Casebook* (London: Macmillan, 1972).

Appendix: The theatres of Shakespeare's London

THEATRE	DATES	PRINCIPAL OWNER
The Theatre (near Holywell Lane)	1576–98	James Burbage Richard Burbage
The Curtain (near Holywell Lane, opposite the Theatre)	1577–*c.* 1627	Henry Laneman
The Rose (Rose Alley, Liberty of the Clink, Bankside)	*c.* 1587–*c.* 1605	Philip Henslowe
The Swan (Paris Garden, Bankside)	1595–*c.* 1637)	Francis Langley Hugh Browker
The Globe (Maiden Lane, Bankside)	1599–1613. Rebuilt 1614	Richard Burbage *et al.*
The Fortune (near Cripplegate, Finsbury)	1600–1621	Philip Henslowe Edward Alleyn

COMPANIES, PLAYWRIGHTS AND AUDIENCES

Most of the major companies used 'the Theatre' at one time or another, and it must have seen performances of many of the best Elizabethan plays of the early period. Probably all of Shakespeare's plays before 1598 were performed here, at some point.

Again, used by most major companies, especially before 1587. Lord Chamberlain's Company seem to have made it their base in 1598, just before the opening of the Globe. It was also famous for displays of jigs and combats, and its audience had the reputation of being unruly.

The Lord Admiral's Men, with Edward Alleyn as their leading actor, dominated the London stage during the early years of the Rose's existence. Marlowe's works were staged here, as were plays by Chapman, Dekker, Greene, Kyd and others. Other companies also used the Rose occasionally (Shakespeare's *Titus Andronicus* was performed here in 1594).

Earl of Pembroke's Company, until 1597, when the satirical play *The Isle of Dogs* incurred the censor's wrath. The Swan thereafter fared poorly as a playhouse, staging a mixture of entertainments including both plays and prize-fights.

Took over from the Rose as the most important London Playhouse in the early years of the seventeenth century. Home of Shakespeare's company, the Lord Chamberlain's Men, called the ng's Men after 1603. Among the plays performed here were akespeare's works from 1599 to 1608, revivals of some earlier ys and probably most of the post-1608 plays as well. In dition, plays by Jonson, Dekker, Marston, and Tourneur are own to have been staged here.

nslowe and Alleyn's attempt to challenge the increasing premacy of the Globe was based here. Many revivals of old ourites from the Rose were staged here, since Henslowe and eyn owned many of these scripts. These included plays by arlowe, Jonson, Dekker and Kyd. New writers who were com-

THEATRE	DATES	PRINCIPAL OWNER
The Hope (Hopton Street, East of Bankside)	1614–1656	Philip Henslowe Edward Alleyn
Blackfriars (1) (The Blackfriars' Monastery)	1576–1584	Richard Farrant
Blackfriars (2) (The Blackfriars' Monastery)	1596–1655	James Burbage Richard Burbage